THE LAST LINE

PACKIE BONNER

THE LAST LINE

MY AUTOBIOGRAPHY

With Gerard McDade

EBURY
PRESS

1 3 5 7 9 10 8 6 4 2

Ebury Press, an imprint of Ebury Publishing,
20 Vauxhall Bridge Road,
London SW1V 2SA

Ebury Press is part of the Penguin Random House group of companies
whose addresses can be found at global.penguinrandomhouse.com

Penguin
Random House
UK

First published in the United Kingdom by Ebury Press in 2015

www.eburypublishing.co.uk

A CIP catalogue record for this book is available from
the British Library

Hardback ISBN: 9781785031847
Trade Paperback ISBN: 9781785031854

796.334092

BON

Printed and bound by Clays Ltd, St Ives PLC

MIX
Paper from
responsible sources
FSC
www.fsc.org   FSC® C018179

Penguin Random House is committed to a
sustainable future for our business, our readers
and our planet. This book is made from Forest
Stewardship Council® certified paper.

This book is dedicated to the memory of
Grace Bonner 1924–2014
Jess Kerr 1935–2015

CONTENTS

'THE MOMENT'

I HAD SPENT THE NIGHT IN LETTERKENNY, CATCHING UP WITH my brother Denis and our cousin, Connell Boyle, and in the morning I realised that the best way to get to Dungloe was to cadge a lift, which I did.

From there, I knew there was only one way to get back to Cloughglass, to get back home, and that was to take the school bus.

And so I sat, as I had so many, many times before, in the single-decker, alongside the children of various ages. The difference was that I was gripped with the excitement and the emotion of going home for the first time.

I knew virtually all of the children and they, of course, knew that I was no outsider and, yet, strange it was to squeeze my frame into the battered seats and look out of the window, remembering those countless occasions when I had done so in the past.

Staring through the glass and daydreaming of what the future could hold for me.

By now, it was dusk, a grey dusk that painted itself across the sky and all I could really see was my reflection but the memory was as clear as sunlight.

When we got to the bus stop, I disembarked at the road end along with my fellow passengers and as they scurried off to their various houses I knew that I still had a mile-long walk before I would be at Castleport House. The last leg of a journey that had started the day before in the Gorbals district of Glasgow where the welcome sight of Doherty's Coaches had greeted me from its traditional starting point as it prepared to ferry us back across the Irish Sea.

As always, that last leg gave me a chance to think – to think about the changes this last year.

A year when I had set my stall out to complete my Leaving Certificate and then go away to college and start working towards a career as a PE teacher.

The trial period that I had spent at Leicester City, working with the men who had honed the skills of Gordon Banks and Peter Shilton, that had come to nothing, but I was too young to be disillusioned and so I worked hard at school, as my parents had always insisted upon, and closed in on the required grades – yet, football was always a disruptive influence.

I was close to home now but at the top of the hill I stopped to take in a view that I could never and *would* never tire of – off to the right was the clearly visible Owey Island; to my left, I could make out the shadow of Arranmore Island in the diminishing light and right in front of them was the roar of the Atlantic Ocean that separated both parcels of land from each other.

The rush of the water was a well-kent tune in my ear and I knew full well every rock and crevice in this rugged coastline for a three-mile radius. Beyond that lay America.

I had not applied to college because another Irishman, a great man, a *Sligo* man named Sean Fallon whose accent had never left the county even if he had many years before, had contacted me first and told me that I was wanted in Glasgow, wanted to learn my apprenticeship at one of the biggest names in world football.

Castleport House had been constructed as a bed and breakfast and I could now see its two storeys partially lit and what looked like a Christmas tree in the front room. There was the gable end of the house that had felt the thump-thump of a football on it a million times over without complaint when I was a child and it an open goal at Highbury, White Hart Lane or even Celtic Park in my vivid imagination.

I made my way down the road and around the corner. Down below the house and yet, in close proximity, was the garage, door open, despite the cold, lights on, and within was my father – the ol' fella – working with his hands, as usual.

There was no manual task that was beyond Andrew Bonner and his devotion to a job well done was absolute but now he was peering out into the gloom at the tall figure ambling around the hill. Against the backdrop of the evening, it could only be a silhouette to him and yet, quietly, he laid down his tools and started out towards me.

I hadn't told my parents that I would be coming home that Christmas but, at eighteen, I was third-choice goalkeeper and I had been allowed back home to Ireland for the festive period.

The ol' fella reached me and we embraced warmly before he led me back up to the house.

It was a moment, a very *special* moment, and I will assuredly take it with me to the grave.

I was Packie Bonner of the Celtic and I had come home, home to Donegal, in December 1978 for Christmas.

*

Memories like that are important.

Important in the sense that they remind you of your roots.

There is nowhere you can travel in this world without knowing that you can return home and the crystal-clear memory of that Christmas always takes me home.

Back to where I started.

Back to where I was reared.

And back to where I was hewn into the man that I could and would become.

But it's a private memory – personal – shared only with the few who were there and not open to public scrutiny.

Other memories can be far more public and such memories, by their very nature, have to be shared and each of us can take a moment, an event, and remember where we were, what we were doing and how it affected us in the fulfilment of that memory.

Eleven and a half years on from that Christmas of 1978 and I'm now walking around the centre circle of a football pitch.

Around me are the players and coaching staff of the very first Republic of Ireland side to go to a World Cup tournament.

A hundred and twenty minutes of football in a gasping heat had remained goal-less and it was now down to Ireland and Romania to take penalty kicks to decide who would progress to the quarter-final stage of Italia '90 for the very first time in either country's history.

All around the Luigi Ferraris Stadium in Genoa there is a vast throng of green, white and gold supporters who have grasped the history of the moment.

I can see Jack Charlton, our manager, trying to organise the penalty-takers. Jack's philosophy was not to pick these men before the match as those plans could go awry with substitutions, injuries or a player being sent off. Equally, he is offering words of encouragement, asking for that final push.

If I am to be entirely honest, up until this match it had been a tournament in which I felt I hadn't quite found my feet.

I had put in solid yet unspectacular performances against England, Holland and Egypt in the group stages.

The English were always hard to beat and perhaps the occasion, the fact that we both knew each other's strengths and weaknesses so well and a rain-saturated Sardinian pitch combined to produce a 1–1 draw with Gary Lineker, a man whom I had defied two years previously in Stuttgart at Euro '88, grabbing the opener before Kevin Sheedy pulled us level.

Ah, but we should have beaten the Egyptians instead of a 0–0 draw and the fact that they had drawn with Holland put a bit more pressure on ourselves and the Dutch in the final group match.

Holland, as always, were highly quoted to win the World Cup but this time there was a difference, a justification to the betting.

The Dutch were European champions from two years before and had actually eliminated us from that tournament en route to the final. So, when Ruud Gullit picked up the ball in the tenth minute, played a one-two on the edge of the box before racing into the penalty area and drilling a low shot across me into the net to put them ahead, many would have foreseen an Irish exit from the tournament.

Yet we rallied. Spirit was never in short supply among that group of players and, with twenty minutes to play, Niall Quinn grabbed an equaliser to close the game out at 1–1. England topped the group as we tied with Holland in joint second spot.

We drew lots with the Dutch for our respective venues which, significantly, sent us to Genoa to face Romania while Gullit and co. headed for Milan and a bad-tempered exit at the feet of Germany.

There are days in all sports when you feel particularly *in the zone* and throughout the ninety minutes plus extra-time I felt I had finally made my contribution to the cause.

Against Romania, a decent side but one we felt we could beat, my eye was in.

Gheorghe Hagi was the danger man.

Elusive, strong-willed and a gifted footballer, he always seemed to find space and was the eager out-ball from defence. Romanian midfielder Ioan Lupescu, now a key member of the UEFA Coach Education Department, was on the pitch that day and later told me that Hagi was given licence to play as he wished but, crucially, when he was on the ball, he *had* to perform! He had made a fine art out of playing just on the edge of the opponents' defence and had been pinging shots in at me from all angles that day – but I was equal to the task.

The game started to slow towards the end of extra-time and I can honestly say those were the first moments when my thoughts started to wander to the prospect of a penalty shoot-out.

The freshest thing in my mind was the recent Scottish Cup Final between Celtic and Aberdeen.

It too had finished goal-less after extra-time and for the first time ever in the story of the competition the trophy would be decided from twelve yards out.

The stakes were high. Aberdeen had finished second to Rangers in the title race and were guaranteed, at least, a UEFA Cup spot, but we were in a very unfamiliar position for a Celtic team. Our fifth-place finish in the table meant that, unless we could prevail in the Scottish Cup Final, we would not be contesting European football the following season for the first time in twelve years.

As such, it had been a very dissatisfying season but the Hampden showpiece offered some kind of redemption – something to lift the pervasion of gloom around the club.

The history books will record a 9–8 victory for the Dons and tell you that Brian Irvine scored the vital kick after a miss from Anton Rogan.

What it won't tell you is that, for *every single one* of the Aberdeen kicks bar one, I had gone the wrong way.

I had guessed right for Jim Bett's spot-kick but had only got my fingertips to it and certainly not enough to stop a ball hit with such direction and pace going into the net.

After the Cup Final and before heading off to Italy with the Irish squad, I had retreated home, as I so often did, looking for solace and the opportunity to recharge my energy levels.

My introvert nature has always been a complex thing, vying

as it does with my ability to perform in front of 60,000 people and in the full glare of a television audience.

In later years, I would bring myself willingly to public speaking, focused mainly on motivation, but I have always felt that such events, along with the demands of a professional football career, sap the energy and drain my life force and therefore a return to my homeland and the opportunity to have my own space as well as catch up with trusted friends and family have been essential to my stability.

Once I had recharged my batteries I headed off to Dublin to meet up with the Irish squad and in particular to consult with Gerry Peyton.

Gerry was at that time between the posts for Bournemouth after a distinguished career at Fulham.

I had replaced him in the Irish set-up but he was never a man to bear a grudge and, in actual fact, despite his being only four years older than myself, I regarded him as a mentor. He remains a trusted friend and confidant to this day.

He too had watched the Scottish Cup Final, fully understood the immense pressure of the occasion and had noted my inability to guess correctly at the penalty stages.

The camaraderie between goalkeepers is a tight one.

By its nature it's a singular position, a solitary outpost, and the men who are entrusted with its custody understand far better than anyone else out on the pitch the consequences of errors and mistakes.

Gerry and I came up with a plan, a template if you like.

We decided that if a player placed the ball down on the penalty spot and paced back directly facing it, then he would be inclined to shoot straighter, opting for power rather than placement.

Should a player place the ball down and then move out to an acute angle, say right or left of the ball he is addressing, then chances are he will be shooting to the side that he stands on.

So, we had a plan.

The big question was – would it work?

We were about to find out.

Football is an inexact science and who knows what goes through the head of a professional player as he races up towards the kick? But the human mind can be more than occasionally predictable.

As if to confirm this, I wandered over to where Kevin Sheedy, an experienced international and title-winning Everton player, was sitting and asked him if he was taking a kick.

His reply was short and to the point.

'I am. It will be the first and I'm going to hit it straight down the middle.'

It would be ten minutes before Sheeds could take that kick but he was clearly focused.

I trotted off to the side and started doing some stretches, only to notice a bizarre little incident that was so utterly FIFA.

As grown men were contemplating the most important kick of their lives, as they debated whether or not to step up to the plate and take the chance of going down in history with *success* or *fail* stamped on them, the Brazilian referee, the oddly named José Ramiz Wright, and his assistants were scurrying around the centre circle telling everyone to pull their socks up, presumably for the television audience!

As diktats go, it was beyond bizarre.

Years later, people would always ask me how I felt in the lead-up to the shoot-out. What was going through my mind?

As a motivational speaker, I have used my experiences from that day to, I hope, inspire and certainly focus individuals on attaining goals.

I knew I had to concentrate. I had to get my body physically right for the task ahead and I had to calm down my thought process, keeping my emotions in check to fully address the situation.

Looking up into the crowd beyond the goal I could feel the inspiration of what seemed like a million of my countrymen willing me on.

I went the right way for *all* the spot-kicks.

The plan that Gerry and I had formulated was ringing true and, for one, I even got a fingertip to the ball, but just not enough to stop it going in.

And that's the secret of the penalty shoot-out – stop the ball.

You don't have to worry about the striker following up so that you must parry to safety or even hold the ball – You. Just. Have. To. Stop. It.

I always return to this moment in my mind.

Gheorghe Hagi is first up.

I'd defied him throughout the 120 minutes of open play but, even as I go to the right side for his kick, it has too much power and height for me to stop it.

Next, it's Sheeds and just as he laid out to me moments ago, he goes straight down the middle.

I'm disappointed in myself with Dănuț Lupu's kick. He'd come on as a substitute and I don't read him properly as he strolls up to the spot and places the ball low to my left. My movement is too slow. I need to adjust my feet more quickly.

I think about that as Ray Houghton tucks away our second and drops to his knees in delight.

Now, I'm back on my line, focusing ... blessing and reblessing myself.

Iosif Rotariu moves back to an acute angle and I know he's going to change direction for this one, unlike the first two Romanian kicks. He does so and I spring to my right but, once again, it's a precise penalty and it whooshes into the net behind me.

Andy Townsend draws us level again with a confident kick and just before I go back to my line I shoot a quick look once again, back into the crowd.

From out of nowhere, I suddenly recognise Jim Boyle.

Jim Boyle of Dungloe!

I'd been to school with his brother, Frank.

I knew his mother, 'Aggie', who worked for years in Sweeney's Hotel in the centre of town!

Jim is here, in Genoa, and out of a million faces I can pick him out – a friend from back home in Donegal.

It has never happened in my career before, it never will again.

Big Jim is here, willing us on to the quarter-final, hugging strangers when we score and no doubt clenching his hands as each successive Romanian steps up to the spot, praying for a save, a slip, a miss – *anything* to create history for Ireland.

I can feel the passion and it boosts my adrenalin.

Then it's Ioan Lupescu.

This is the one.

I can feel it.

I know where he's going to put it – up and to my right.

This time I move fast.

It's powerful with a high trajectory but I have that split second when I feel my fingertips connect with the ball and … and …

I hit the grass in disgust.

I've guessed right for every kick, even got the very edge of my fingers to one but Romania are 4–3 ahead.

My disgust is mirrored by my opposite number seconds later as Tony Cascarino hits the weakest kick so far, just under Silviu Lung's body with the divot of turf passing the Romanian captain by as he dives low to his right and almost defies Cas.

It's now the final kick of the opening five for both teams and from a distance I can see Daniel Timofte of Steaua Bucharest making his way down from the centre circle.

The game had kicked off two hours and forty-two minutes ago and we're still all out on the pitch waiting for the outcome.

I remember Timofte's been brought on as a substitute in extra-time and I wonder now if that was because he would be a safe bet should it come to penalties.

If that's the case then why is he so nervous – *really* nervous?

He looks so ill at ease placing the ball down on the spot and when he steps back with every stride betraying his tension and moves to an acute angle to the right of me, I *know* where he's going with the kick …

… but I have another trick up my sleeve.

I can move slightly in one direction, hopefully to fool Timofte, before I shift my feet quickly then spring in the opposite direction.

There's an art to this.

Don't go too early and, at all times, keep your eye on the ball.

So, here now, I have a plan – I have a technique – my confidence is high from getting so close to the other kicks and I sincerely feel it – *this* is the moment!

I look into Timofte's eyes – bless myself – look down at the placed ball – rebless myself!

Daniel Timofte of Romania addresses the ball and begins his run-up.

Here it comes.

Here it comes.

As soon as he hits it, I just *know* I am going to get to it.

Certainly, it's true that, in these decisive moments in life, everything appears to be in slow motion.

In truth, it isn't the greatest penalty, close to the post but only a metre off the ground and, crucially, without much pace to it.

I spring to my right, feeling this huge gulp in my throat and then the immense satisfaction of the ball thudding off my gloves and away to safety.

What follows is a moment of pure, unadulterated, raw emotion.

A physical rush of blood to the head and the heart thumping within my chest so hard that I can feel it in my larynx.

I've done it.

Daniel Timofte has his hands on his head, pulling away at his hair in despair.

I feel the vibrations of the entire country back in Ireland as they jump for joy!

I leap higher in the air than I have ever done in my entire life and suddenly I'm joined by Andy Townsend and Tony Cascarino who start hugging me.

But they shouldn't be *there*!

The referee has made it clear that no one was to leave the centre circle without his permission and, for one horrible moment, I think *he'll order a retake for this*!

Thank God he doesn't although, technically, it is only half-time.

The save would come to nothing if Ireland don't convert their fifth penalty.

So engrossed in my thoughts and preparations have I been that I hadn't really noticed who had been selected to take the kicks and now David O'Leary was making his way towards the penalty area.

David O'Leary of the Arsenal.

A player who had clashed with Jack Charlton on many an occasion but had worked hard to get himself back into Big Jack's plans after an opening period in the manager's debut days when David had pulled out of a tournament in Iceland after a long season.

Jack Charlton did not forget that incident but, typical of the big man that he was, refused to let it cloud his judgement when he had to make decisions about his players.

And now, just four short years later, David O'Leary has the opportunity to justify his manager's faith and propel the

Republic of Ireland into unknown territory as well as trigger a gigantic wave of celebrations throughout our homeland.

Anyone with any football knowledge will tell you that David is a centre-half and a good one but had he ever taken such a high-pressure kick in his life?

I only know two things.

David O'Leary is a 'big moment' person.

Comfortable in the spotlight, confident about his ability and at his best when under the most intense scrutiny.

Secondly, Niall Quinn had been running a book for three weeks at the training camp. The big fella would stick on my gloves, go into goal and challenge the rest of the squad to put penalties past his six-foot, five-inch frame.

If you scored all three, he owed you a fiver but if he saved just one you had to cough up your *own* fiver.

David O'Leary was Niall's room-mate and they'd been at it for weeks.

The Arsenal centre-half with fifty-two caps to his name had been banging the penalties in since we'd arrived in Italy.

Perhaps now, like me, David felt it was his turn to make a contribution.

He strides up confidently to the ball, sends Romanian goal-keeper Silviu Lung the wrong way, the only penalty in the entire shoot-out to do so, and then sinks to his knees as every single member of the Italia '90 Republic of Ireland squad descends on him bursting with joy.

Even wee Charlie O'Leary (no relation to Dave), Charlie the kitman, all five-foot-one of him, is jumping up and down trying to join in the huddle but his diminutive frame keeps bouncing off the stramash of celebrating players taller than him by far!

And there is Gerry Peyton.

He smiles broadly at me and we embrace.

No words are necessary – we both know what each other is thinking.

It is the emotion of a united group of individuals, but, more than that, a camaraderie. A camaraderie that, in what today seems a more simple time even though it was barely a quarter of a century ago, involved supporters and press and media alike.

In time I would come to realise its true significance.

I would return to Ireland with the squad and fly over half a million people who thronged the route from Dublin Airport all the way into the city.

I would hear countless stories of where you were and what you were doing when Ireland made it to the quarter-finals of the 1990 World Cup.

I would be present at my mother's house when people from all over the world would take in that view of the islands of Owey and Arranmore and the tumult of the Atlantic before following the road around the hill as I had done on that cold, winter night of 1978 and then asking my mother if this was the house where 'that Irish goalkeeper had lived'.

And I would contemplate the story of John Healy, the grizzled political correspondent of the *Irish Times*, a man in his early seventies, well-respected by his peers and opponents alike who had seen it all and written about most of it, who, on that day, excused himself from the EU Summit in Dublin to watch the shoot-out only to sob uncontrollably as we cavorted around the pitch in Genoa.

He knew what had been achieved.

But, right now, the overriding feeling was to live in the moment. The time for true reflection would be later on but *now*, in the heat of an Italian stadium, with thousands of my own people waving down from the terracing and rejoicing, it was time for me to enjoy myself.

It was also time to remember.

To remember that thin line between success and failure.

To understand that, in the midst of the plaudits coming for myself and David, there should also be the recognition for Sheeds, Ray, Andy and Cas as the men who had the guts to step into that eighteen-yard box and set up this glorious moment for their team-mates.

Inevitably, there were tears. They stung my eyes and ran down my cheeks in a messy fashion as I ambled around the pitch but I cared very little.

This wasn't just a professional achievement – this was a personal moment with all the emotion and pride that flowed naturally through me as a man who loves his country and is privileged enough to experience an episode of national joy as a humble participant.

This was why I had become a footballer.

This was why I had worked hard at my craft.

And *this* was why I had always believed in my dream to play the game as a professional and represent my country.

There would be moments throughout the next few years when I would feel a range of other emotions about what came to be known simply as 'the save'.

Strangely enough, for a period, embarrassment was one of them.

It's not the Donegal way to bask in glory. That can be a self-aggrandising act and I sometimes found it difficult to deal with the number of people who, in the oddest of situations and the most inappropriate times, would come up to me just to relive an occasion that meant a very great deal to them.

I had been brought up with four pillars of support from my parents that have guided me throughout my life.

Hard work.

Respect.

Humility.

Resilience.

Not that those qualities were preached to us as a family.

One of my weaknesses was that I always tended to be quite judgemental. I made an instant assessment of a person when I met them and I suppose my default position was always to be wary until someone won my trust.

I still get wrapped up in the emotions of things, which isn't always good, and yet I am, by nature, a very cautious person.

However, as I've got older, gained more experience, I find that I am able to deal with things a little more objectively.

Your actions on the field of play or, for that matter, in life, would never allow you to become big-headed and there was always someone, particularly in your own family, who would put you in your place.

Putting in the effort could be its own reward.

Respecting others from all the highways and byways of life in turn earns respect.

Retain a humility in all that you achieve. Believe me, sometimes the margins are so very tight in the pages that define 'success' and 'failure' especially when you earn your corn as a goalkeeper and the next mistake could be just around the corner.

Above all, maintain a resilience that can take you through your life and all the inevitable highs, lows, triumphs and setbacks that come on down the road to meet you.

And so, I brought all of those principles to the table.

The events of 25 June 1990 in the Luigi Ferraris Stadium certainly required them.

I didn't realise at the time that those events could and would shape the rest of my life both personally and professionally.

As I say, the trick was to take in the moment and reflect on how a raw Donegal boy, reared on the north-west coast of Ireland and only truly comfortable within the roots of family and home, could have made a journey that crossed on to the international stage and, in the most public of acts, played *his* part in a truly unique moment for Irish sport and, as many would comment later, perhaps Irish culture as well.

DONEGAL ROOTS

THE DRAMA OF A WORLD CUP WITH A CAPTIVE GLOBAL AUDIENCE and the searing heat of Genoa were, metaphorically, a million miles away from where I was born.

County Donegal lies to the north-west of the Republic of Ireland. It is a location with some of the best beaches in the world, some of the roughest landscape in the country and, for the first eighteen years of my life, comprised my entire world.

My parents, Andrew and Grace, were also born and reared in this part of Ireland. The ol' fella came from Cloughglass which, in Irish, means 'green stone'. An apt description as the area was lush with grass and shrubbery yet had an almighty volume of boulders as well. Although, in truth and perhaps oddly, the stones were something that I little noticed until one day when I returned to Donegal as an adult and, for some inexplicable reason, was suddenly very aware that the land was strewn with rocks. It's funny how you can live beside something all your life but are never really aware of it.

Castleport House was, quite literally, the family home, built as it was by my father and my grandfather, Denis, to provide alternative accommodation for Andrew's brother and sisters from the little thatched cottage that lay on the land nearby to the new property.

My mother hailed from Mullaghduff which lies some ten miles away from Cloughglass, not a major distance even in an age when most travelling was done on foot, by bus or even bicycle and I suspect that both of my parents would have been aware of each other through the various social dances that sprung up in the area.

As Grace grew up, she worked briefly in service in the local town of Burtonport. This was in an imposing house later to be owned by a man known as Master Murray, so-called because he was brought back from England to run the local comprehensive school in Dungloe.

The house itself would go down in local folklore in the 1970s when it became occupied by a commune known as the 'screamers' who seemed to be in search of the lost world of Atlantis! Not an everyday occurrence in Burtonport, I grant you, but I suppose if that's your thing then the obvious starting point would be as close to the Atlantic Ocean as you can get.

I am fairly certain they never found the lost city as I'm sure we would have known about it but I did meet one their former members one day not so long ago in the south of Ireland where he is now a lecturer. I didn't have the heart to ask!

Back in the day then, there was a poverty of employment throughout the county and, indeed, the country and so, like many of her compatriots including her older sisters, Grace crossed the Irish Sea looking to earn a living.

For a while, she worked in various hotels around Scotland including a period in North Berwick where the Americans used to come to relax and play some golf. Years later, she would put me right on my back swing. 'Only go to "ten o'clock",' she would say and justify it as something she had picked up from the US golfers at Gullane.

Not long after she left, Andrew followed the same route. He made his way over to Scotland and worked in the fishing industry with groups of other Irishmen.

In saying that, there may have been another reason for my father's move away from Cloughglass as a catastrophic series of tragedies hit Castleport House. Within the space of a very few short years, he lost his father, two sisters and a brother to illness. Theresa died in 1944 at the young age of sixteen, then his father Denis passed away the following year aged sixty-six. Mamie was twenty-nine when she died in 1946 and five years later, on 15 September 1951, Packie Joe, after whom I would be named, succumbed to tuberculosis, a very common illness at the time.

It was an era when mortality rates were high but, even so, half his family were wiped out as well as his father and it's difficult to imagine how Dad coped with all of it other than by remaining stoic – a quality he never lost.

And so, it may have taken tragedy for Andrew to leave the house but I also suspect it was to follow my mother.

Grace was still working in Edinburgh with her sisters when my father met up with her again and, after a short courtship, they were married in the capital, at St Francis's Church, with a small wedding party as guests and witnesses. It was February 1952, just a few months after Packie Joe's death.

For a while, they returned to Ireland where my mother gave birth to Margaret and then Mamie.

However, it wasn't uncommon at that time for people to move back and forth across the Irish Sea and so there was also a spell when they settled back in Glasgow. To be precise, in the Copland Road area of Govan which, as any Glaswegian could tell you, football-oriented or not, is where the East Stand of Ibrox Park, home of Glasgow Rangers, is situated.

It is one of those peculiarities in my life that there would be many a time when I would be asked to guard the Copland Road goal, packed with Rangers supporters in the stand behind me, during the tumult of yet another Glasgow derby. Throughout the ninety minutes they would have been 'reminding' me of exactly where I was in the world. They needn't have bothered. I already had a fair idea, thanks to the Bonner family history.

But that was for another day.

When he was in Glasgow, Andrew once again worked at various jobs, even as a conductor on the trams that crossed the city.

He used to tell the story that it was common practice to get rid of your change throughout the day so as not to be encumbered by the weight of the coins but the ol' fella thought, 'To Hell with that idea,' and held on to every single penny.

He only did it the once though as, by the end of the day, he could barely get up and down the steps of the tram. Every pocket he had, including the ones on his shirt, were so weighted down with the coppers!

The west coast of Scotland offered employment and a certain amount of security but the pull of Ireland, the fishing boats of Burtonport, the rugged Atlantic coastline and the wide open spaces of Donegal were in stark contrast to claustrophobic Glasgow and so my parents returned home.

They moved into Castleport House with my gran, Maggie, and over the next few years my mother gave birth to Anne and then Cathy.

By the time I came along, on 24 May 1960, I'd imagine that the family would have been hoping for a boy.

What they got was two of them!

Twin brothers, Denis, after my late grandfather, and myself, Patrick Joseph, in tribute, as I mentioned earlier, to my father's brother.

Denis and I shared the tag as youngest until Bridget Mary, known as Bea, arrived a year or so down the road to complete the family.

I always admired my mother for her willingness to up sticks and come back to a house that was not her own and to share that house with a mother-in-law whom she could barely have known. Her ability to engage with others and let her personality shine through were forever traits of her character.

Castleport House had once been a bed and breakfast establishment and my parents reinstated it as one although the ol' fella continued to work outside as my mother kept a house that offered full board with breakfast, lunch and evening meal.

In fact, in her autobiography singer Susan Boyle spoke about the time that she was a guest in the house courtesy of a friendly Irish family who brought her to stay there once when she was a child. She would have been one of many who passed through Castleport House.

When I look back at it now it's hard to believe the amount of work that my mother would have put in tending to the food and cleanliness of the B & B in addition to all the other tasks both inside and outside the house, *plus* those years when they started to build a family of seven children.

Including my grandmother, therefore, it was a combined number of ten who occupied Castleport House throughout the 1960s and 1970s.

At the time, the house was a unique property given that most of the houses nearby or thereabouts the area would all be cottages or bungalows whereas our home was a fairly modern two-storey detached dwelling that backed on to the Atlantic.

In those early days, the ol' fella turned his hand to taxiing.

Many a person he ferried all the way to the 'Derry Boat' before swapping the smell of diesel for the salty whiff of the ocean and the fishing in that rugged, unforgiving Atlantic on one of the new ninety-foot wooden trawlers, *Ard Dalain*, that was to arrive in Burtonport.

However, he always maintained that the industry, lifeblood of the local economy that it was, never really agreed with him and so he now turned his methodical skills into house-building.

And when I say 'build', I mean build *everything*.

Andrew Bonner had a talent for block-laying, plumbing, joinery, electrics, roofing and more that was truly hands-on. In addition, his keen eye and analytical mind enabled him to draw up the plans for the houses he was about to build.

I can still wander through the country roads on my frequent visits back home and point out any number of houses that the ol' fella built brick by brick. As Denis and I grew older and stronger, we were fortunate enough to lend a hand over the summer holidays to my father's endeavours.

Of course, most have been renovated as is the modern way, but still they stand bearing the mark of my father.

He was a very deliberate man who would spend hours assessing a problem, debating with himself how best to come up with a solution, which he would inevitably find, and then taking the correct course of action.

One of our neighbours brought in a clock for him one day to see if he could fix it. I remember watching him undo the timepiece when the main spring burst out from the housing and all the little cogs and pieces scattered wide and far around the room. It seemed to be beyond repair but the ol' fella went out and bought a replica clock, studied it for months before slowly deconstructing it and then, painstakingly with his fine eye for the most minute detail, fixed the original clock back to perfection.

I like to think that some of his eye for detail and forensic thought process has rubbed off on me as it's within my nature to look at a problem out on the field of play or even off the pitch and deliberate on it until I have the answer.

One area where I do not share his talent, though, is in the art of story-telling.

The ol' fella was a master at holding an audience in the grip of his stories and I don't just mean us kids although there were endless occasions when we would sit around and listen to his tales.

Some were relative to his life, where he had been and worked, whereas others were just stories that he had picked up throughout his life.

He had a wonderful gift for recounting a tale that would have you glued to his every word even though you may have heard it a dozen times before and on each occasion it grew more and more exaggerated.

People used to come to the house – family, friends and, of course, paying guests – just to hear some of these great tales being told by a man who knew how to yarn away without ever making it a chore either to listen to or tell.

My sister Cathy has that gift and when I hear her now recount her stories of holidays and work etc. etc. I am instantly reminded of the ol' fella and transported back to those happy times when we liked nothing better than to hear him hold court at Castleport House.

However, whatever he was my father was not a rich man, far from it in the material sense, and there was very little to go around when I was growing up.

My aunt bought us our first television set in 1970 and even though the ol' fella once had a taxi, there was no family car to speak of until I was into my teens.

Even the very first football boots that Denis and I owned were bought by my dad's cousin Toney Ownie Manus Gallagher and his friend Ray Ham.

What a Christmas that was!

You never forget who bought you your first boots or what they looked like, how they smelt and what they felt like the very first time you wore them out on to the pitch.

Ours were 'Blackthorns' – solid studs to grip the turf, sleek black leather that glistened like coal when they were polished and the obligatory for the time steel toecaps!

When Denis and I put them on, we felt like *real* footballers.

My late uncle, Packie Joe, played football, not a commonplace thing in his time, and for many years a pair of battered old hobnailed boots were hung by their laces over a peg in the downstairs closet along with so many other relics. They *had* to be his! When I was around eight years old and beginning to develop my interest in the game, I became fascinated by the boots and the thought that a man to whom I owed my name, and one whom I would never know other than by the stories of others, shared my passion for the game.

Inevitably, I sneaked away with the boots one day to try them on and see how it would have felt to play the game back in the day. Suffice to say, given their age and condition, they started to cut up badly when they hit the soft, wet grass. The boots lasted barely half an hour on my feet before they completely disintegrated!

I never, ever told anyone that I had taken the boots for their short-lived kick about but, then again, I was never asked!

Our family had the existence of a traditional Irish croft and a self-sufficiency that was based on a small area of land with a few head of cattle, some chickens, potatoes, vegetables and hay.

As a boy I came to know the seasons by the work that we all undertook.

Autumn and winter were all about looking after the livestock; making sure that the cows were fed as well as the chickens and that there was plenty of hay for warmth.

Springtime could be the toughest of all as, in addition to setting the spuds in the ground, there was the turf-cutting to undertake.

When we were young, this was tended to by my dad and a few local men who would reciprocate each other in turn, but, as we grew older, everyone in the family mucked in to cut it, turn it, foot it, then lump it together and eventually take it home to provide a fire for the winter.

Many's the time when Denis and I went straight from school out to 'the bog', as it was known, to cut the turf. It was absolutely freezing! The kind of cold that creeps inside your bones and you feel as if even your hair is icing over. Hard, manual labour it was but, I tell you, it didn't hurt. In fact, if anything, it gave you something. A resilience. A toughness, if you like, that you take with you into adulthood.

Summer almost felt like a break although, even then, there was the opportunity to go pulling dulce which, as a family, was hugely enjoyable, in particular for my mother. If she wasn't sitting back in the twenty-foot punt that we had out on the ocean watching as we leapt from rock to rock along the coast picking up the shells that contained the seaweed, she was mucking in with all her children as the ol' fella steadied the boat.

Perhaps it was in this environment that I first learned about teamwork and honed my speed and agility, for the rocks could be quite slippery, as the ol' fella found out to his cost one time.

The weather was calm so he moored the boat to a rock. Ultra-cautious as ever, he made sure that we were all safe in our tasks before his eye caught a beautiful flag of dulce stretched out on a forebidding rock.

He couldn't resist it so he edged his way across to it and we were all pulling away on other rocks when we heard this almighty *splash* and turned to see my father up to his neck in a pool of water.

We waited for a moment to see how my mother would react but, before she did, the ol' fella threw back his head and roared out a huge laugh. It was the cue for everybody to join in although he spent the rest of the day stripped to his long johns as his satu-rated clothes were splayed out on a rock to dry in the sun.

Ah, those were wonderful days.

People laugh at me now and my wife Ann rolls her eyes every time I say that I don't remember the rain.

My summer upbringings in Donegal always seemed to be laced with beautiful sunshine.

Anyway, once we had collected enough dulce, it was brought to shore and laid out on flagstones at the house. My grandmother would help to ensure the seaweed stayed dry until we could place it in the barn to let it mature. Once it had reached that point, we bagged it, weighed it and the ol' fella took off around County Donegal selling it to shopkeepers.

As always, the proceeds were fed back into the house and although there was no such thing as pocket money, ends were met and occasions provided for, when required.

It was, I have to say, a unique upbringing and one that I look back at fondly with great joy and pleasure.

Even my schooling was different from what passes as the norm nowadays.

Denis and I started out at Keadue Primary in 1964. The first three days were spent in the company of an elderly lady teacher who thought nothing of smashing her ruler down on to the desks until they shuddered and we cried but, miraculously, she retired and in her place came a saint of a woman, Bridget Dougan.

She had a calming nature and a good way with children which was vital as her influence would be upon us from infancy through to Primary 3.

From there, we were placed in charge of the master, Naul McCole, who would educate us all up until we turned twelve.

In total, there were roughly a hundred children dispersed between seven classes, yet housed in only two rooms and completely educated by two teachers!

As unusual as this may sound now, at the time it was fairly normal not just in Cloughglass but in most of County Donegal. Rural areas, rural communities and therefore small school rolls but fuelled by dedicated staff.

By the time we were ready for higher education, the choice was Loch an Iúir Tech or Dungloe Comprehensive.

The former was viewed as a school that prepared you for the working life whereas the Comp saw itself as being more academic: a privately run establishment that catered for pupils with, shall I say, 'higher expectations' that were, of course, shared by their parents.

We all went to Loch an Iúir without complaint.

If we weren't chomping down on the cheese sandwiches at lunchtime that my mother had prepared for us in the early morning then we were heading for 'Cassie's Shop' on those odd days when we had a penny or two to spend. Cassie was a cousin of my mother and she was always delighted when any of the family dropped in. She ran a particular sideline that was well popular and that was her capacity for selling single cigarettes to some of the schoolchildren.

There's many a boy *and* girl from down that way who got his or her first draw on a filtered Gold Bond courtesy of Cassie!

And, of course, there was always the football.

Burtonport was once a small coastguard town, protected by a group of islands, with Arranmore being the most populated. Many of the locals moved over and back from Scotland and had brought football to this part of the world even though the game was still in its infancy.

Nowadays, and perhaps not surprisingly given the success Donegal had under coach Jim McGuinness, Gaelic football, or GAA, has probably become more popular in the county but throughout the 1960s, 1970s and into the 1980s, (Association) football was the game keenly played by a lot of my contemporaries.

Naturally, as a lover of sport, I played GAA and even represented the county at all levels in a single year. I enjoyed the game but played outfield as I found the restrictions on a GAA goalkeeper hard to comprehend. For a start, in those days you had to stay glued to your goal-line in case an opponent punched the ball over your head with his hand. Well, that wasn't any good to me!

In addition, my GAA team, Rosses Rovers, played close to Rosses Bakery at times and it was common practice to take the spent cinders from the huge kilns and scatter them around the goal area to fill in some of the holes that inevitably formed through overuse.

One dive for a goalkeeper into that lot and you came up choking with dust in your throat as well as being coated in black ash from head to toe! Of course, this wasn't unlike the red blaes pitches that I was to encounter later on in Glasgow.

So, midfield it was and my goalie training came in handy for rising above a ruck of players and 'fielding the ball' as they call it. I could catch, I could pass and I had a reasonable pace but I needed the quick players around me to become effective.

Denis, on the other hand, was a tough-tackling, uncompromising player with a no-nonsense approach to the game and, therefore, slotted in well as a right half-back.

In our time with the Senior county team we would join local players such as Noel McCole, Jim Brennan, Eugene Sharkey and play alongside great GAA colleagues like Martin Carney, Seamus Bonner, Brendan Dunleavy and the formidable Martin Griffen.

I remember a particular Championship game against Cavan, when the then manager, Sean O'Donnell, put Denis and I in the Minor team to protect us as we travelled up with the Seniors to the match.

We were all billeted overnight at a top hotel and as we all assembled for dinner the word came around that we should eat as much as we wanted as the County Board were *picking up the tab*.

What riches for a horde of hungry young lads from Donegal!

There were prawn cocktails, sirloins, T-bone steaks, you name it.

Few of us, including Denis and myself, had ever *heard* of T-bone steak let alone eaten one but what the hell – we gave it a go!

We got stuck into the grub like men who hadn't had a square meal in a decade, stomachs groaning as we all waddled off to bed. I think a few of the Senior players might even have sneaked a couple of pints of Guinness as well to wash it all down.

Not surprisingly both ourselves and the Seniors were destroyed the following day out on the field of play.

It would be fair to say that Jim McGuinness would not have approved of our preparations the night before!

I loved GAA but I enjoyed my Association football better especially as I was honing my skills between the sticks and making progress.

Like most goalies, I didn't start out that way but I found when I was playing in either midfield, defence or attack that I would get a pain in my side. In later life, I would link this to a hernia condition but, at the time, I just reverted to going in goal and found, to my delight, that I loved the position.

The fact that we had a television in the house and in a location that not only picked up the local channel RTÉ but UTV and the BBC as well meant that I was getting to see *Match of the Day* on a Saturday followed by *The Big Match*, hosted by Brian Moore, on a Sunday.

I guess everybody's favourite player would be Georgie Best, and what a phenomenal talent he was, but my heroes were the last lines of defence. Men like Peter Shilton, Ray Clemence and, of course, the Irish legend Pat Jennings. It seemed to me that the English First Division had some of the finest goalkeepers in the world. A fact that was underlined when the ol' fella sat with myself and Denis in 1970 to watch the Mexico World Cup. England v. Brazil and somehow Gordon Banks managed to get down low and quickly to scoop the ball off the line and over the bar from a Pelé header that had goal stamped all over it!

Recently, I attended a goalkeeping conference in St George's Park, Burton upon Trent, England, where the great man would tell us, with a smile, that his first reaction to that magnificent stop, as he lay stretched out on the ground and looking up at

Pelé›s goal-bound header looping over the bar thanks to his agility, was … 'You lucky twat, Gordon!'

See what I mean about the margins between success and failure?!

Mexico 1970 was also when Denis and I got to see a Czechoslovakian player bless himself after scoring a goal – we'd never seen anything like that before – and, of course, we marvelled at the genius of the Brazilians, as did everyone.

I absolutely loved the game and would play football any place and any time.

You have to understand that back in those days, in Donegal certainly, there really was no organised schoolboy football as such. Leagues, divisions, relegation, titles, trophies – these were all things of the future.

Basically, we organised games among ourselves.

A typical routine for me was to race home from school, have my dinner, get stuck into my chores and, once all that was done, Denis and I would get to the football. Our pitch was an area we called the 'block yard'. This was a piece of land, extremely basic but perfect for us, that was owned by Anthony Boyle. The Boyles were all great football people in both codes and Anthony's boy, Tony, would go on to win the All-Ireland with Donegal.

Anthony's brother Manus later settled in Boyd Street, Glasgow, and it's no exaggeration to say that along with his wife, Mary, and family, their house became a home from home for me when I was trying to settle in at Celtic. Our friendship still endures.

The block yard was our 'home ground' and, like everything else I attended to back in the day, it was within running distance of my house. I seemed to spend all my childhood running places! Still, it helps to make you an athlete.

To be honest, the nearest we got to organised matches when I was at primary school was when Father Con Cunningham took a hand in such matters.

Father Con was from a neighbouring parish and knew my mother well. It wasn't unusual for him to land at the house with a crowd of boys and say to me and Denis: 'Right, get your side together and we'll get a game going down at Keadue!'

That was the cue for myself and Denis to run (inevitably) around all the houses in the area recruiting a 'team'. We never were short of a squad.

Strips, however, were another thing.

A strip for a football club is an identity and at Keadue Primary we were desperate to look the part but there was nowhere local that sold football kit and so *Shoot!* magazine came to the rescue.

Shoot! was our contact with the modern football world featuring star columnists like England captain Bobby Moore and sifting through all the leagues and divisions awash with up-to-date information on the game. They also had a classified section that sold everything from ciné film of FA Cup Finals through to books, T-shirts *and* complete football strips for an entire team.

And so we saved up our money and sent off to the magazine and in return were delighted when, a couple of weeks later, a full set of Arsenal football strips arrived.

Don't ask me why we picked the Arsenal, possibly because the club colours of Keadue Rovers were similar, but the red shirt with white sleeves was a distinctive design and, once we had ironed the club crest on, we actually felt like a proper football team!

It's difficult from this point in time to look back to a period only forty-plus years ago and realise how basic it all was just to get some football under your belt but, in that era and especially in rural Donegal, that was how we went about our business.

I reflect on this today when I see my seven-year-old grandson Alan play the game. Even at his tender age, there is a structure in place and co-ordination to his football with coaches, leagues and development. They deal with the fundamentals of the game, teaching skills and allowing for plenty of competition with other teams.

Having said that, it strikes me that there is one aspect of his experience where I think I had the advantage.

When I was his age, there were always loads of guys around to play football and we played the game all the time. I'm not so sure Alan or any children of his age have that freedom just to run down to waste ground, throw their jackets to the ground and get stuck into a ten-half-time, twenty-the-winner the way we did and that is a shame.

Of course, I had Denis.

I would say my brother loved football as much as I did although, when I look back, I reckon it was always me who pushed for him to get outside and kick a ball around.

He was a fair man for the old blackmail as well, I can tell you, and many's the time when I would have to polish his boots, fix his laces or undertake some other task before he would agree to play.

Yet, once he did, we would set up goals at either end of the beautiful green grass that grew in front of Castleport House and then spend hours just playing shoot-in, practising our skills, honing our craft.

There is such a thing as 'falling in love with practice'.

The former table-tennis player Matthew Syed refers to this constantly in his excellent book *Bounce: The Myth of Talent and the Power of Practice*. He is an advocate of practising as much as you can, and not just in sport, and I knew when I read his book that I had found a kindred spirit.

Equally, the Williams sisters, Venus and Serena, had a not dissimilar background to mine in terms of breaking into sport. Their father, Richard, encouraged them to practise tennis as often as they could and they, too, never got to play competitively until they were sixteen. Look at how they have developed!

However, it still seems incredible to me that I went from a set-up with no truly organised facilities right up until I was sixteen and then, barely two years later, had signed for one of the biggest professional football clubs in the world at Celtic.

The nearest I ever came to a coach was our next-door neighbour, Dom O'Donnell, who would nip over to the green grass and watch Denis and I banging shots away at each other as well as joining in and then he would impart some wisdom to us. Little insights on how to improve our game.

Dom was about fifteen years our senior and had played a bit for local outfit Keadue Rovers. In addition to being my godfather, he was a huge Celtic man and a frequent visitor on match day to the East End of Glasgow when he worked in Scotland.

There was a massive picture of the 1967 Lisbon Lions hanging in his house and, although there was absolutely no Scottish football available to us on the television then, I knew full well the names of the men who had conquered Europe by beating Inter Milan and was able to recite them like a mantra.

Certainly Dom was an influence on me and I was always eager to learn new skills and improve my development as a goalkeeper, no matter how obscure the source.

I had a cousin who was married to a fellow called Josie Kyles. Josie was a big man for the judo and the karate and so on. Martial arts were very much a thing in the 1970s and I remember once watching him give a demonstration at our local festival in Burtonport. I couldn't help but notice that he spent a great deal of his time falling on to the ground, which looked sore, so I asked him how he didn't hurt himself.

I felt like the fictional 'grasshopper' as he explained to me – 'Look carefully at *how* I fall. The first thing that always hits the ground is my forearm. It breaks the fall, prevents injuries. It's the most important thing in the art.'

I was always a quick learner and so I used that piece of advice, going on to perfect it in my teenage years, and it was a technique that I continued to utilise throughout my career.

Diving was never anything that I feared thanks to Josie and his black belt. As a result of my hours and hours of practice I played, pretty much, at all levels right through primary school all the way to my years at Loch an Iúir.

Around that time, I caught the eye of a remarkable character called Manus McCole. Manus ran Keadue Rovers and he started an Under-16s and 18s side as well. He was a local legend whose love for the game and the chance to compete with other sides was in no way hampered by the fact that he was confined to a wheelchair.

We were about fifteen when we first started playing under the watchful eye of Manus McCole and he it was who introduced Denis and I to our first real stab at competitive football.

The ol' fella started to follow us around when we were with Keadue. Dad loved his sport but not as a participant, which is ironic since one of his biggest yarns was that he played for Sligo Rovers when he was younger. I think he even convinced himself of that notion. Interestingly enough, Denis *did* go on to star for the Rovers in his League of Ireland career as a centre-back!

One of my earliest memories is of the ol' fella sitting in a chair at home, glued to the radio and RTÉ as it brought the prize fights of the then Cassius Clay across the airwaves. His enthusiasm was as an active supporter and he always encouraged Denis and I to play sport to the best of our ability and remember to enjoy it as well. Once we were at Keadue he, and another parent of two of the other players, old John Andy Boner, became a common sight on the team bus as we travelled around the county.

Again, there were no facilities to speak of at Keadue or, indeed, any of the places we visited and so it was nothing to arrive at a ground, slip off somewhere as discreet as possible to get changed – *all of us* – and then after the game travel back home on the bus still bedecked in our strips. This routine didn't change even in the foulest of weather which would be a frequent caller on the windswept coasts of Donegal.

Keadue Rovers were a useful side and we won the Donegal Youth League. The next year, most of that team were elevated to the Senior team and we went on to win the League and Cup double. Not bad for a bunch of young fellas who, barely a year before, had little experience of competitive football. A number of us, myself included, were picked to represent Ulster in an Inter-Provincial tournament under the guidance of Richie Kelly, later of BBC Northern Ireland, and Pat McColgan. The tournament was being held at the Butlin's holiday camp in Dublin.

Along with Ulster, there were the other three provinces, Munster, Connacht and Leinster.

The first game was against Munster and it ended badly for our first-choice goalkeeper, Declan McIntyre, when he came off worse in a clash that saw him break a couple of ribs.

Declan was from Donegal Town and in later years was a huge influence on the remarkable number of young goalkeepers who came out of the county and into the Scottish and English games.

Young goalkeepers like Conrad Logan, Lee Boyle, Gavin Carling, James Gallagher and Joe Coll, who went on to take their chances in the professional game, owe much to Declan's teaching methods and I was delighted to work with him when I was at the FAI.

It's a generational thing, I guess.

When I played for the international team, much was made of my Donegal background as it was with Shay Given after me. Perhaps that was why there was almost a cottage industry of goalkeepers who came from Donegal and all the keepers who worked with Declan went on to represent their country at youth level.

However, that was in the future and Declan McIntyre's broken ribs were my first experience of that anomaly for a goalkeeper that the direct result of an injury to a fellow member of the union plunges him into the first team at their expense.

This time we were up against Leinster.

They were the big shots from Dublin, hand-picked from the likes of useful schoolboy sides like Cherry Orchard, Stella Maris, Home Farm, St Kevin's, St Joseph's and more.

And I reckon, like most big-city outfits, they had a fair conceit of themselves.

We lost the match but I had acquitted myself well and up against top opposition, but it was still a surprise to find out that the selectors of the Irish Youth team were there and that I was being asked to join the squad.

If you made it to this side then you had a fair inkling that you had to be half decent.

I had been working away at my goalkeeping for a few years, developing techniques and enjoying more than the odd exchange with my defence for constantly talking and shouting, but that's how I saw the game and I wanted to stay involved.

The Irish Youth set-up was a grand experience and you were always aware that you might be getting watched by some of the top scouts from all over Britain.

Tony Finucane was a great lad and the product of a fine football family from Limerick. For my first year with the Irish Youth, I was number two to him but, in my second year, I was promoted to become the first-choice goalkeeper.

I had my first excursion abroad in my inaugural year to St-Malo in France for an international youth tournament in a squad that included a young fella called John Devine. John would go on to play in the Arsenal first team, a side full of great Irish internationals, and I would have the pleasure of picking his brains many years later when both of us worked for the FAI.

In my second year, the squad was managed by a lovely man called Bob Dillon (yes, really!) and Padraig Coyle, another

Donegal boy from just up the road in Gweedore, was also there. He enjoyed a career with Blackpool until injury forced him eventually to return to Ireland where he played for Sligo Rovers.

There was John Anderson of Newcastle United and Gary Waddock, who would have a productive career with Queens Park Rangers in that squad also, along with a lad who I would play with for Celtic, Pierce O'Leary, and then Kevin Sheedy.

Sheeds and I could little have guessed the roles we would go on to play in that fateful shoot-out in Italy a decade and a half later.

That would be a future date with destiny, of course, while, for the moment, we would just be concentrating on what we could bring to the youth set-up.

It certainly was a mixed bunch for, as well as those Irish players who mainly hailed from the likes of Dublin, Limerick and Cork, there were English-based players who added a bit of swagger to the squad.

I do not deny that I have always considered myself a bit of an introvert, at ease in my own company and around my own people, so it was a tough learning curve to overcome a certain inferiority complex that I naturally felt when mixing with this group of individuals.

There has always been a feeling in Donegal that we are the forgotten county of the Republic. This is partly because of our geography, being furthest away from the seat of power in Dublin, the political machinations of the capital, big business and all of that sort of stuff, but also because of our culture.

That feeling gives you a certain chip on your shoulder, a sense that you always have to look after yourself. An independence, if you like, and a favourite staple of Donegal is *adaptability*.

We adapt as a people and therefore I adapted to my new sur-roundings and the diverse influences interacting all around me at that time, especially when Leicester City came calling.

The Midlands club had a scout across the border called Jim O'Hea and it was he who invited me to a trial out at a local sports centre in Derry. I must have impressed as, before I knew it, I was off to Leicester.

The plan was that I would make my way over to England after school on a Friday. This was a bit more complicated than it sounds as it would involve my parents driving into Derry with me, dropping me off with Jim, who would, in turn, travel with me to Belfast whereupon I would board a plane for Leicester, on the other side, where I would be met.

I stayed with the club throughout their run in the Youth Cup.

Once again, I experienced that little bit of swagger that the English game can give to a young man, even a reserve player at Leicester City.

A few of their lads, like Steve Sims, Scots boy Peter Welch and Derry native John O'Neill would play with the second team on a Saturday before heading into town for a slice of the nightlife. They would get back to the dormitory we shared in the small hours whereupon they would stick a little music on the record player, enjoy a wee drink and a bit of craic through the night. It was all a new experience for a sixteen-year-old Irish fella who would lie under the sheets marvelling at their maturity!

Leicester at the time were a First Division club and suddenly I was in the company, on the training ground, of Foxes legends like Keith Weller, Alan Birchenall and Frank Worthington.

Big Frank was everything that I had been led to believe.

A fantastic character right out of a comic book, with superb ability and who seriously thought he was Elvis Presley, he would show up at the ground wearing a Stetson, eye-wateringly tight jeans and a T-shirt with the King of Rock 'n' Roll on it.

One day I was paired off with him and so, this England international, a man who exuded the word 'star' and who would have been the leader of the pack even in today's generation of football celebrities, had a sixteen-year-old schoolboy from Donegal holding his leg as he stretched his muscles

Mark Wallington was the first-team goalkeeper at a club that enjoyed a rich heritage of supplying top-flight keepers such as Gordon Banks and Peter Shilton, who, at the time, was playing for Stoke City.

Mark wore the original green cotton goalkeeping gloves and I have to admit that I whipped a few discarded pairs of *those* from the boot room, but I had a nylon pair with a sort of plastic table tennis bat texture for the palms. They were extremely popular in the mid-seventies. I washed them one night back at the dormitory and laid them over a radiator to dry and the plastic melted but, I'll tell you this, the melted grip was a revelation as the ball seemed to stick to my hands regardless of the weather.

To be honest, it would be a few years before I had a real professional set of gloves and they came courtesy of a fellow who played in goal professionally and ran a sports shop in Girvan. His name was Peter McCloy and he was a legend at Glasgow Rangers.

I often wondered, on those occasions when I had a decent game against Celtic's biggest rivals, if the Rangers supporters knew that my good performance was enhanced by the equipment given to me by one of their own heroes!

I was keen to learn from the experience at Leicester but when my trial period was up at the end of the season, I left for home and no contract was offered to me.

As I mentioned earlier, that was disappointing but I was young, confident in my ability and by now had a dream that I could play in the professional game.

I needed to hang on to that dream because my education undoubtedly stuttered a fair bit while I was heading over to

Leicester every weekend and the immediate worry was that I wouldn't get the required grades to get into Thomond and study to become a PE teacher.

Of course, in my dream that was only Plan B.

THE ROAD TO GLASGOW

CUP FINALS ARE ALWAYS SPECIAL EVENTS FULL OF PAGEANTRY, colour and expectation and in today's world that has been greatly increased by the big bucks of satellite television. But it's not that long ago, relatively speaking, that in order to watch the gala match that concluded the domestic season in both Scotland and England, you had to go to the game.

If I remember correctly, the 1977 Scottish Cup Final was the first one to have been televised live for twenty years and it was made all the more special because it was Celtic against Rangers.

For all my interest in the football, for all my understanding of the link between Ireland and Celtic and for all the Dom O'Donnells of the world, I had only ever seen Celtic live once.

They had come over to play Finn Harps in a charity match in July 1975. The Harps were the local team, managed by the unpredictable Patsy McGowan. It had become a ritual for myself and Denis to get a lift up to Ballybofey with Harps supporter and close neighbour, Owen Bonner.

To Denis and I, who dreamed of playing the game to a successful level, Finn Park was where our hopes were ignited and the players of Finn Harps were our heroes: men like Brendan Bradley, who would score two goals in the Harps's most famous match, the FAI Cup Final of 1974, when they beat St Patrick's Athletic 3–1 against all the accepted odds. Or Charlie Ferry, dead-ball specialist, who opened the scoring that day with a superb free-kick. Jim Sheridan, immortalised as the only Harps captain to date to lift the famous trophy; and, of course, the pick of the bunch, Tony O'Doherty, a sweeper of superb ability who was rumoured to have turned down a substantial offer from Aberdeen. He had been outstanding against the Dons in a UEFA Cup tie but Tony loved living in Derry and didn't want to leave the city. These players plus their team-mates epitomised the excitement of playing football to a level where trophies could be won with all the attendant glamour of success.

Sean Fallon took charge of Celtic that day as he would go on to do so for the season with the legendary Jock Stein recuperating from a car crash that almost claimed his life barely weeks before.

Years later, Tommy Burns, who had made the trip as a raw sixteen-year-old, told me that Sean had waxed lyrical about the view of the Atlantic from Rosses Point and, for sure, nothing would do but for him to take the entire Celtic party out to the point to marvel at the vista.

Back in the seventies that was a bit of a trek but Sean insisted upon it and so they set out on the trip to see one of the most magnificent views unique to the Irish coastline. Only trouble was, when they reached Rosses Point there was a mist thick enough for Victorian London and the Celts could barely see *themselves*, never mind the Atlantic! To Sean, though, that didn't matter one bit.

He had brought his beloved Celtic there and could not have been more proud – a feeling, I might add, with which I can totally empathise.

I can't remember the score from that charity game but the allure of the Celtic name was enough to make me tune in two years later, at home in Donegal, to watch them play out the Scottish Cup Final against their fiercest rivals.

The atmosphere was electric and I freely admit I was fascinated by those green and white hoops.

Over on UTV, Liverpool were playing Manchester United in the FA Cup Final and trying to become only the fifth team in England, at the time, to be double winners of both League and Cup, but, for me, there was only one ticket in town and that was watching Celtic play Rangers.

As it turned out, Andy Lynch scored the only goal of the game from the penalty spot as Jock Stein picked up what would prove to be the last significant trophy of his Celtic managerial career.

If you had told me then that, within little over a year, I would be in the same Celtic squad as Andy Lynch and be Jock Stein's final signing for the club as well as go on to play in a whole host of Glasgow derbies in a seventeen-year career ... I would not, *could* not, have believed you. That's the great thing about life: the twists, turns and unexpected developments.

My own personal development that year was, first and foremost, to knuckle down to the school work that I had to do in order to go to Thomond College and then concentrate on my football.

The second one was easy and, by chance, as the pre-season kicked off, I was invited by Finn Harps to guest in a friendly at Finn Park.

I leapt at the opportunity, especially when I found out the opposition were Stoke City complete with Garth Crooks, Denis Smith, Terry Conroy, Mike Pejic and, of course, the one, the only, Peter Shilton.

The game itself was a typical stretch of the legs for the English outfit but, once again, I felt I played well in a narrow defeat.

At the end, I shook hands with Peter, but there was no master/ apprentice-type conversation between us which was satisfying in a way. It was like one professional to another.

That year would be a significant one for Peter Shilton as he signed for Brian Clough at Nottingham Forest, picked up his only ever League-winners' medal before going on to win the European Cup twice in the coming seasons.

It was no less significant for Packie Bonner in his own small way.

I was seventeen and had to make choices.

PE teaching seemed a good fit for me and, equally, moving to Limerick where Thomond was situated, leaving the family home at eighteen, would offer new challenges.

And then Finn Harps offered me a six-month contract.

I loved the Harps but didn't want to tie myself down … just in case.

The fellow who handled the deal was the club's manager, Eunan 'Busty' Blake. Busty was a well-known figure who always acted with the best intentions for Harps and, although I could be considered to be a bit naive at that stage of my life, I knew that I had to make sure that any agreement was flexible.

To my surprise, Busty agreed that if anyone came in for me during that period then he would personally tear up my contract.

He knew all about Leicester, of course, but I often wondered if he had ever seriously thought that I would get to sign for a top professional club.

One evening, in the late autumn, Manus McCole landed out at the house from Keadue Rovers. That wasn't particularly unusual but this time Manus was on a mission. He came to inform me that, in a gesture typical of the man, Sean Fallon had contacted him and asked if it would be possible for me to come over to Glasgow for a trial at Celtic?

Sean Fallon!

Many times later, down through the years, I would hear people say to me with a wink and a smile: 'Ah now; I mentioned to Sean that he should take a look at you for the Celtic.'

To be completely honest, I'm not sure what the truth is relating to remarks like that but if there is a backbone to them then all I can say is one almighty *Thank You!*

I do remember meeting Sean, once in Dublin, albeit briefly, out on the pitch after training with the Irish Youth. He shook my hand, as was his way, and spoke to me but I would be lying if I could tell you right now the exact conversation.

Yes, this was exciting news but, as I had found from my time in the Midlands with Leicester, it was best not to get too carried away with this sort of thing. It was only a trial and I think the best news for my parents, and I guess myself as well, was that it would be in Scotland.

We had family in Glasgow which meant I wouldn't have to stay in digs. Uncle John and Aunt Bridget Mary lived in Muirend and they would be more than happy to put a roof over my head. Domestic contentment was, quite rightly, at the forefront of my parents' thinking.

Celtic were the number one team in Donegal.

Times were hard for a lot of people and that limited the number of supporters who could actually make the journey to Glasgow every fortnight but there was no mistaking the sentiment for the Bhoys in this part of the world.

Truthfully, though, I didn't know that much about their current set-up even though I had watched them win the Cup on television about six months before.

Strangely enough, given future events, cousin Connell had once given me the autobiography of the man who was considered to be Celtic's greatest goalkeeper, Ronnie Simpson of the Lisbon Lions.

Perhaps he knew something!

Anyway, as I mentioned, Sean Fallon had been the facilitator for the trial and he it was who greeted my parents and myself when we landed in Glasgow.

His first task was to take me out to Celtic Park.

I remember smelling the malted hops from a local brewery and the sight of the red sandstone buildings surrounding Parkhead as clearly as I remember that Sean drove a dark purple Ford Granada – just like something right out of that television series *The Sweeney*.

You didn't get to see many of *them* in Cloughglass.

What is there to say about Sean Fallon?

Only that, when he took your grip in friendship and you felt the power of that handshake, you knew instantly that you were in safe hands.

Here was a man you could trust.

A figure of integrity who addressed my parents with respect and yet had managed to maintain a humility as to his part in the greatest chapters of the Celtic story.

With that slow Sligo burr of his, possibly a by-product of his fondness for a cigarette or two, Sean told me that I would be playing in a bounce match with a local amateur side so that I could be assessed.

Before all that, though, he took me straight into the first-team dressing room to get the feel for the club.

This was the sanctuary where the Lisbon Lions had prepared for their home matches. Where Jock Stein had delivered his pre-match sermons and was wont to open the window so that his men could hear the footsteps of the people who had come along in great numbers, handed their money over at the turnstiles and paid to, as he put it, 'be entertained'.

There was another reason that Sean wanted me to get into that changing room and there they were – the current Celtic first team returned from training.

Alfie Conn, Paul Wilson, Pat Stanton, Johnny Doyle and others in addition to two players who would go on to be my team-mates as well as close friends, Roy Aitken and Tommy Burns.

Finally, there was the legendary Danny McGrain, barely twenty-six yet already established as one of the best full-backs in the world and club captain since the departure of Kenny Dalglish to Liverpool the previous summer.

Sean took it in turn to go around all the players and introduce me. I must have looked about twelve to them, standing there in my duffel coat and feeling a lot out of my depth, but Sean took the time to tell them that I was over on trial from Ireland and they, in their turn, shook my hand. I didn't know if this was a typical welcome to Celtic Park but it left an impression on me.

My playing introduction to Scottish football would be at a tight little ground with a surprisingly large crowd that pressed hard in on you from all angles as I lined up for Coltness United against East Kilbride Thistle.

I loved that kind of environment.

Red-hot atmosphere, an audience so close you could hear them breathe and every player giving it his all.

This was the first time I met a tremendous man who would influence my career greatly – Frank Connor.

Frank worked with the then Celtic assistant manager, Dave McParland, and both of them reported back to Jock Stein on individual performances as well as collective duties. Most important to me was that Dave was a former pro goalkeeper who had once been on Celtic's books as well as playing for Derry City at the Brandywell and Ballymena.

In time, he would be instrumental as the first true goalie coach that I ever worked with, but, for now, he was in the Hoops's backroom set-up and would be assessing my progress throughout my trial period.

The Coltness game had gone well and I enjoyed the whole trial but, once again, I wondered if the chance had passed me by when I returned to Ireland and it looked for all the world that I would be heading to Thomond and the course as a PE instructor.

Then came Easter 1978 when I was asked to return to Celtic Park and was immediately sent out to an Under-18s' tournament in Roubaix, France.

This was the real deal.

Club blazers and ties were issued, pennants were ordered for the games and in the middle of all this preparation I was given the most severe instructions by Frank Connor.

'Get yer hair cut, son!'

And so it was, with my infant Celtic career hanging in the balance because of my long locks, that Uncle John traipsed me through a number of city hairdressers and barbers for me to have my wavy thatch tamed.

Eventually, we alighted on an establishment in Clarkston that had not progressed beyond the Clark Gable look and he lopped off my hair before adding a 'tonic' as a styling tool.

I emerged with a slicked-down style looking like a cross between Stanley Matthews and Oor Wullie going to piano lessons! It wasn't exactly John Travolta but it assured me that I had done as Mr Connor had demanded and that I would be going to France.

I can recall two things about the Roubaix tournament.

The first was that I got picked for the opening game against a local side and on emerging from the tunnel at the top corner of the pitch we lined up to exchange pennants.

Once we'd done that, I turned around and headed towards the away goal.

I had a ritual that I liked to do before every game and that was to have a ball that I could bounce a couple of times, kick it into the goal on my approach before tossing my bag of gloves, Elastoplast and rosary beads etc. into the net and then, finally, jumping up and touching the crossbar for luck.

Unfortunately, it was only once I had slapped the woodwork and come down to earth that I turned around and realised that both teams were still lined up on the halfway line and listening to the British national anthem!

Ach, Jesus, how was an Irishman to know the words to 'God Save the Queen'?!

The second was that I lost a bad goal.

The worst type of goal for a keeper to lose – through the legs and nestling in the back of the net.

And that was it.

I was certain that I had blown it and that, whatever my destination, wherever the path of life was to take me, it would not be G40 3RE, Glasgow, home of the Celtic – Paradise.

Then it happened.

No sooner was I back in Ireland when I had a call to Castleport House to tell me that Celtic wanted to sign me on a professional contract and that Jock Stein would be flying to Ireland personally to conduct the arrangements.

The venue was the Ballyraine Hotel in Letterkenny, now the Mount Errigal, and that was where I showed up with my parents on 14 May 1978.

Looking back, it was like a scene from a movie.

When we arrived, I could see Manus McCole and the Keadue Rovers committee and, although we joined them, it never seemed as if we were part of the same party.

We bided our time, exchanging pleasantries but it was all a bit surreal.

And then Jock Stein arrived.

The Jock Stein.

I had seen him on a few occasions when I had been on trial. To be honest, I hadn't really kept up with events in Scottish football so I wasn't to know that Celtic had endured their worst season since Mr Stein had arrived in 1965 and that a fifth-place finish and no trophies were as good as it got.

One day at Celtic Park, during my trial period, I was heading down the trackside when I saw Mr Stein pacing around the centre circle out on the pitch ... alone.

Apparently he did this after a defeat, almost taking it personally.

If he wasn't feeling quite himself when he entered the Ballyraine, it wasn't apparent. He was larger than life with a presence to match.

I remember noticing that Fran Fields, chairman of Finn Harps, accompanied him but, at the time, I thought no further than that they were good friends and perhaps Mr Stein was staying overnight at Fran's house.

A few years down the road, I would find out *exactly* why Fran was there.

Mr Stein immediately cut to the chase.

I was to be offered a starting wage of £70 a week when I reported for duty, a not inconsiderable sum in 1978, and a signing-on fee of £1000.

That was huge.

I hadn't expected such largesse and was inwardly quite pleased although, let's be honest, I wasn't even thinking about terms and conditions.

And then Jock Stein, the Jock Stein of Lisbon, nine-in-a-row, countless trophies and more, took my hand in a similar fashion to Sean Fallon and issued these words to me, more as a command than a request – 'Make sure you look after your parents with that.'

It was official.

I was now Packie Bonner of the Celtic.

There was still a little bit of business to be taken care of and to that matter I entrusted my sister, Mamie, to go up to Busty Blake's house in Letterkenny and remind him of our deal. When she did so, Busty took her into the living room of his house, lifted my Harps contract out of the drawer and, true to his word, tore up the document in front of her eyes without so much as a by your leave.

It was a fantastic gesture because, to be honest, if Fran Fields had known about our arrangement, then I am 100 per cent certain he would not have done the same as Busty. At best, he would have wanted recompense from Celtic; at worst, he could have scuppered my professional career before it really got started.

The whole thing could have got messy and there might never have been a Packie Bonner of Celtic and Republic of Ireland.

It is a gesture from Busty Blake that I have never forgotten and I am eternally grateful to a man who was as good as his word and, believe me, that's not as common an occurrence as you might think in the world of football.

Of course, technically I was also still at school and I have to admit that it was strange, even at that stage, to suddenly have £25 arrive, *in cash*, through the post now that I was on Celtic's books.

It had all happened very quickly and the early summer months shot by equally as fast as I prepared to leave home for Glasgow. I did manage, however, to finish my Leaving Cert Exams, something that I would be extremely grateful for in later life.

In saying that, nothing ever really prepares you for that eventuality.

I guess they would call it psychosomatic but the day before I was due to leave for Scotland I was very ill. So sick, in fact, that I took to my bed and didn't get up for the rest of the day.

It was nerves, naturally, but such was my condition that I couldn't even rouse myself to greet friends, even from just up the road, like Anne Patricia McGonagle, who dropped in, asked after me and left a St Christopher medal for my journey.

We weren't an overly emotional family but the day that they all took me down to catch the bus for the trip across the Irish Sea was a hard one. And yet, there we all were, with our best smiles and stiff upper lips, but I knew that, in particular, my parents were feeling the break as much as I was – neither of us was going to show it, though!

As Doherty's Coaches pulled away from the stop I sat with my duffel coat wrapped around me and held on to my bag for dear life, trying not to look back.

Doherty's made one stop along the route before joining the ferries at Larne. That was just at the border, in Lifford, and as we pulled up I could see a young girl, perhaps of my age, and her family who were all out to wave her off on the bus.

And they weren't holding their emotions in check in any shape or form – any of them!

The girl slumped down in a seat a few rows in front of me and I swear that she continued to sob uncontrollably until way after we'd left her family behind.

It didn't exactly help *my* mood and then, just as it looked as if my companion was reaching a point of dry eyes and getting her act together, the bus driver, Anthony Doherty, dealt a deadly blow from his eight-track stereo system.

Out of the archaic speakers above our head came the voice of Margo O'Donnell, the queen of Irish country music and one of her many songs full of 'the leaving of Ireland for distant lands never to return, the loss of family and the regret and the hurt and the fear and on and on and on ...'

I'm afraid it was back to the tears after that for our girl there and I wasn't more than a half-yard behind her thanks to the travelling entertainment of Doherty's Coaches. She cried all the way to the boat!

As I mentioned earlier, I signed for Celtic on 14 May and the fortnight after that proved to be a significant milestone in my life and career; on the 24th, I turned eighteen (officially an adult!) and on the 28th of the month Jock Stein stepped down as the manager of Celtic Football Club after thirteen years and outstanding, unprecedented success.

His career in Glasgow was the template for any other Celtic boss to follow and in the days leading up to him clearing his desk he had made me his very last professional signing for the club.

I can't be sure what was going on in his mind although, looking back, it would appear that he had made the decision to leave months before and even gone to the bother of talking his former captain, Billy McNeill, into replacing him. Billy had enjoyed a decent season in charge of Aberdeen and was seen as the natural choice.

With all that going on it still amazes me that he took the time to come over to Donegal and personally conduct my transfer. He clearly was a total professional right down to the last detail.

It also meant that, when I landed in Glasgow, both he and, more alarmingly, Sean Fallon, were no longer at the club.

Again, at the time, this made the whole adventure for me a bit daunting.

I was very impressed with Sean and felt that, with his Irish background and his ability to nurture young talent, he would help me to adapt to the 360-degree change to my life.

On reflection, though, perhaps the departures of both of these Celtic legends was a blessing to me.

It meant that when Billy McNeill and his assistant, John Clark, sat down with a full squad list they would just see the name *Patrick Bonner* listed alongside all the other players. I would be judged as an equal rather than some daft big Irish boy in a duffel coat who'd just landed at the club from Donegal. I'm not saying that Jock Stein would necessarily have viewed the situation that way, although he did have a reputation for not being too keen on goalkeepers, but my position wasn't too dissimilar from Big Billy's. He, too, was making his Celtic debut, as the club's manager, and for both of us it was a clean slate.

Celtic had three goalkeepers on their books. Myself, Peter Latchford and Roy Baines. Two Englishmen and an Irishman – that must have been a fairly unique situation for a Scottish club at that time.

Peter was the number-one choice with Roy as his back-up and, although Celtic had endured a fairly miserable last season under Jock Stein, Peter Latchford had been named as the club's Player of the Year by the Celtic Supporters' Association.

I hoped that I was equal to the challenge and got my first taste of life as a professional goalkeeper at a top club when I got out to the Barrowfield training pitch.

After a warm-up session, I went into goal for some shooting and heading practice.

Celtic had Roddie MacDonald from the Highlands and Icelandic international Johánnes 'Shuggy' Eđvaldsson in their ranks; two burly six-footers with superb heading ability and for half an hour crosses were lobbed towards them and from the edge of the eighteen-yard box they would bullet their headers towards me in goal. I'd never seen the ball being struck so forcibly with the head and with such accuracy, and if I had needed any reassurance that this was a step-up to the big time in football, then this was it.

Even the shots were struck with ferocity and accuracy and with the old Mitre '6' ball as well. This was a ball that had a plastic coating on it and, at the end of the session, I had lumps of skin torn from both my hands.

It was a long way from Keadue, I can tell you!

The conclusion to training would be the games between the first team and the reserves. They didn't so much need a referee as a United Nations Secretary General.

These matches were about fifteen-a-side, no quarter given, with even Billy McNeill and John Clark playing in them.

We used to call them 'Mad Mentals'.

There must have been a period when Big Billy and John Clark felt that I needed toughening up a bit. They would deliberately set up camp with the big lads in the First XI like Roddie, Shuggy, Roy Aitken, Tom McAdam and Billy himself, then take it in turns to pile on top of me for any cross ball that came into the area.

My job was to clear my lines with a punch or, if I was feeling optimistic, catch the ball before looking for the nearest defender to play out to.

I'm telling you, it could be one *helluva* training session and inevitably, one time, I lashed out at the ball and caught Billy square on the eye!

He had a 'keeker' for days and that was the end of the cross-ball tactics for a while.

I had passed the test and, let's face it, it's not often you get to punch your own manager in the eye and get away with it.

With Peter and Roy fighting it out for the number-one jersey I was propelled into the reserves and directly under the influence of Frank Connor.

And *what* an influence.

Frank was completely hands-on, insisting on doing the rub-downs with his players and always looking at ways to motivate you and inspire you. He worked you hard and, being an ex-keeper, he especially spent time with me out on the training pitch as he did, in fairness, with Peter and Roy.

His influence on the reserves was immense and I defy any of us who played under him at that time, guys like Charlie Nicholas, Danny Crainie, Mark Reid, John Halpin, Alan Sneddon, Peter Mackie and others, to say anything contrary to the fact that we all looked up to him and respected every word that came out of his mouth.

Playing reserve football at Celtic was, in a sense, no different from the first team in that it was ingrained in us that we *had* to win football matches. Nothing less would do and so it didn't matter whether it was a bounce game at Montrose or a Reserve League fixture against Rangers. Losing was not an option.

That said, there was a game against our greatest rivals that didn't exactly go to plan.

If I remember rightly, John Clark took charge of the reserves for this one, a League Cup tie, and selected a side that was more youth-oriented.

Rangers took advantage of that situation by fielding a team

that included first-team regulars like Alex Miller, Jim Denny and a few others. Their experience was crucial as we succumbed to a 7–1 defeat and, I have to say, this was my first competitive game at any level against Celtic's greatest rivals.

To his eternal credit, John Clark took complete responsibility for the reversal.

As we sat disconsolately in the dressing room after the match, John came in and said, 'Just get yourselves into the showers. This was my fault, not yours. I picked a side that was too young to take them on.'

To be fair, it was the making of that team as we grew in strength and came to understand the value of performance on our way to winning the Reserve League title.

That was great preparation for getting into the First XI. By the time you got your chance you knew that the 'Celtic way' was to win and, hopefully, with some style.

It tied in with my psyche and my resilience and Frank Connor was a big reason why that was a part of my make-up.

Frank's team talks made you think that reserve football was just a bridge to the next level. He would spend the time telling you why you *had* to be in the first team. It was only a matter of time – you had the ability, that sort of thing. Not only should you be playing for Celtic – you should be a first pick!

It was all great motivational stuff, years ahead of its time and the sort of thing José Mourinho gets credit for nowadays.

Years later, when my son Andrew was trying to make his way in the game at Albion Rovers Under-19s, he came in one night from training and I could tell by the way he was talking that Frank Connor, who was in charge of the Rovers youth set-up at that time, was responsible for making him feel like he was the next Diego Maradona.

Andrew never did make his living from the game but I can tell you that I felt as proud when he won a couple of Under-17s caps for the Republic of Ireland as I did at any time in my own playing career.

Quite rightly, his caps and Irish international jersey are framed and proudly displayed on a wall in his house.

Frank Connor's influence extended over two generations of Bonners.

Another advantage for us – and this is certainly one not enjoyed at Celtic today – was that the reserves played all their home fixtures at Celtic Park.

At that stage of your development, running out of the tunnel on to the pitch and getting the 'feel' for the ground meant that the possible psychological fear of being on the big stage for your home debut was taken away from you.

In addition, the reserves generally played their games at the same time as the first team and, sometimes, if Celtic were, say, away up at Aberdeen or Dundee, a decent crowd would roll into the ground to see *us* play. Midweek fixtures could also set up a nice audience for us as well.

Training with the first team, playing for the reserves and working with Frank Connor helped me to adjust to the new level and certainly speeded up my development, and when Roy Baines left the club in early March 1979 to go back to Morton I was installed as the number-two goalkeeper behind Peter Latchford.

That was a healthy vote of confidence from Big Billy and, at the time, I needed it. For, if things were going well out on the pitch and at training, the same could not be said of my domestic life.

Don't get me wrong, living in Muirend with Uncle John and Aunt Bridget Mary was fine and they were extremely generous but Glasgow wasn't Donegal. For a start, I missed Denis, and the rest of my family as well as friends, dreadfully.

By and large, Denis and I had been inseparable since coming out of the womb and had grown up together cheek by jowl.

We loved our football and shared our friendships with our cousin, Connell Boyle, and another fella called Sean Walsh.

Sean was a Dubliner and his father, a Burtonport native, had a holiday home up at Cloughglass. We were roughly the same age and, one summer, when I was about twelve and laying a pipe track down from Tullyisland (another job for the ol' fella) I remember spotting him as he stood and watched Denis and myself hard at work.

I know for a fact that his father spoke to the ol' fella and fixed up for Sean to come down to the pier the following day when we were fishing. From that awkward start has come a friendship that has endured for over forty-three years and, along with Denis and Connell, we were known as the 'four amigos'.

There was no Sean or Connell in Glasgow either.

We had no phone in Castleport House and, although Donegal is hardly Australia, it felt at the time that my home county was just as far away.

I had never experienced this before: separation from a family that had been the core of my life and the places that I loved and that I had, inevitably, taken for granted.

Yes, my dream was to be a professional footballer and, yes, I was willing to make any sacrifice to see that happen, but there were definitely times in those early days when I felt everything was in the balance.

There was a day and one particular training session at Celtic Park when we had split into teams behind the goals.

It was nine against nine and the games were great, played at high intensity among quality players. I was having a nightmare, well out of sorts, and Billy McNeill noticed. He more or less told me to snap out of it. As he put it – 'If you don't get your act together then you'll be back on the first boat to Ireland!'

It was a hard time and I am not ashamed to say that, alone at night and lying in my bed in Uncle John's and Aunt Bridget

Mary's, I would, very softly, cry myself to sleep. They had three sons, Patrick, Denis and John. Denis, who was in his late twenties, still lived at home and, while we got on very well and enjoyed each other's company, I wouldn't say that I confided in him too much about my personal feelings.

With communications being limited, I started to get letters from home. Maura Monaghan was another great friend from my schooldays and she began writing to me and then, in turn, even asked her friend Margaret Sweeney to do likewise.

I didn't know Margaret at the time but those letters became so important to me even if they were just full of trivia. It didn't matter – they represented home.

My ritual would be to get up in the morning, have a shower and some breakfast and then wait for the post before leaving for Celtic Park.

I would gather up my kit, stow away the precious epistle and make my way down to the bus stop to catch the 64A which would carry me from Muirend to the city centre and then pick up another bus to get out to Parkhead.

On those buses I would devour the letters the way you imagined soldiers in the trenches read something from home over and over again.

They weren't novels and there was nothing sensational or ground-breaking in them but they brought an immense peace of mind to me and I sometimes wonder if Maura and Margaret realised their value.

Those tales from home, the normality of it all, well, it's not inappropriate to say that they saved my sanity and with their help I was able to stay determined and focused across the Irish Sea and in this strange city of Glasgow.

What was that word I used earlier – *adaptable*?

Once again, I had to adapt, and quickly, for precisely one week after Roy Baines left Celtic I made my first-team debut.

WELCOME TO CELTIC!

Big Billy had been switching between Peter and Roy throughout the winter and neither seemed to be making the position his own.

In particular, Peter had endured a nightmare in a fifth-round Scottish Cup replay against Aberdeen in early March, gifting the Dons two goals that were enough to see them through to the semi-finals of the tournament.

Still, it was a surprise when Billy sidled up to me after training the following Friday before a weekend League game at home to Motherwell and said, casually, 'I'm putting you in tomorrow.'

And that was it.

No preamble.

No explanation.

I was to become the first Republic of Ireland goalkeeper to play for the club since Frank Collins in 1921 and I was to do so on 17 March 1979 – St Patrick's Day.

As I mentioned earlier, communication between myself in Glasgow and the family back in Cloughglass was limited, so the irony was that I couldn't tell them the big news.

In addition, there was a postal strike in Ireland so the mail wasn't getting through and a telecommunications strike meant that I couldn't have contacted anyone at home in Donegal.

They would have to read about it in the Sunday papers where, thankfully, their relative locality to the Scottish coast meant that they had access to the two big weekend newspapers, the *Sunday Mail* and the *Sunday Post*.

Uncle John, though, was another matter and as soon as I relayed the news to him he immediately sent the feelers out around the Irish community in Glasgow. The upshot was that, within twenty-four hours, word had got around and there was a sizeable support from those, like myself, who had left our homeland and settled in the city.

I woke up on the Saturday morning to see that there had been an overnight snowfall. This was nothing new that year as Celtic's League fixtures had been decimated.

Between 23 December and 3 March, the team had only played two Scottish Cup ties as postponement followed postponement after yet another early morning pitch inspection.

It did cross my mind that the Motherwell game could be another casualty so I was relieved when I got to the ground to see that the straw that had been laid down the night before by our groundsman, Joe Docherty, was being lifted having done its job.

The stage was set for my debut.

My pre-match routine would not vary from what I usually did for reserve fixtures.

It's hard to imagine nowadays but, back in 1979, there was no pre-match warm-up out on the pitch. Basically, you did all your stretches in the dressing room.

I wanted to have a little bit of handling practice, though, so I took myself off into the shower area where the first-team bath was and started throwing the ball off the solid concrete walls and jumping up to catch it. A photograph actually exists of me doing it on the day although, for the life of me, I can't remember anyone having a camera with them let alone the presence of a photographer in the Celtic Park dressing room.

There I am, though, a big old stick of an Irish teenager

wearing nothing but a pair of jockey briefs leaping as high as I could and clutching the ball.

I guess it must have taken a bit of an edge off the nerves!

In the Celtic changing room that day there was the experience of club captain Danny McGrain who was easing back to his best after a long injury lay-off. Andy Lynch was also there. He had been captain in Danny's absence and was always an influence when he played the odd reserve game with me.

Andy talked a lot during a game and he would always go on to me about making the number-one jersey my own. I could only do it myself etc. etc. etc.

Comparative new signings Davie Provan and Murdo MacLeod were also there and what an impact they had made since arriving in the autumn.

Roddie MacDonald and Shuggy Edvaldsson, they of the powerful headers, were my centre of defence pairing while Roy Aitken and Tommy Burns could also lay claim to the fact that they were established first-team players at twenty-one and twenty-two respectively.

Lastly, there was the irrepressible Johnny Doyle who was as passionate about Celtic as any supporter waiting for us out on the terraces and, of course, the man who had seen it all, Lisbon Lion Bobby Lennox.

In the middle of all that was the eighteen-year-old Irish goalkeeper and yet, despite that wealth of experience from my team-mates and my probable naivety, I don't recall anyone making a case for advising me or taking me aside for a word in my ear.

It was business as usual even with the kitman, Neil Mochan.

Neilly was a former Celtic player of some note in the 1950s and a real character. Along with masseur Jim 'Steelie' Steele and physio Bob Rooney, they were the last link with the Jock Stein era having, in Neilly's case, played with him and then, along with Sean Fallon, formed the perfect quartet of backroom boys that assisted Jock throughout the glory days of Lisbon and all.

He was notorious for laying out the wrong kit, say an outsized jersey or one that hadn't been washed, but I came to realise that was his way of geeing you up pre-match.

A bit of banter would ensue, all good-natured, of course, and he even did it on my debut, leaving me with the wrong colour of jersey and necessitating a quick replacement.

That wasn't unusual for Neilly as he once threw me a high polo-neck jersey to wear at training. I think it belonged to his 1953 Coronation Cup colleague, goalie Johnny Bonnar – I was scratching for weeks!

The lack of a warm-up on the pitch had another spin-off.

It meant that the first time I saw the famous 'Jungle', the North Stand terracing that faced the tunnel and where a huge, raucous rump of the Celtic support gathered on a match day, was when I emerged with the team being led out by Danny McGrain.

What a feeling that was!

The tunnel had never looked more imposing as I took my place behind Danny and waited for the referee to give the order to take to the pitch and, when he did, there was the chorus of 'good lucks' going on among the players.

This was it.

I clutched my bag in my left hand, held a match ball in the right and followed Danny McGrain out into the daylight as a genuine Celtic first-team player.

If it were only to happen once in my life, it was a moment that I would never, ever forget.

I'd had the advantage of playing on the Celtic Park pitch a fair bit during that first season but that was with the reserves and to attendances numbered in hundreds at best.

Here now were 16,000 Celtic supporters roaring us on to the pitch and, although that number pales in comparison to the figures they get today, or even the crowds that I would go on to play in front of, it was still a sizeable audience to face when making a debut.

And my appearance must have come as a surprise to them.

Having only decided to throw me in on the Friday, Big Billy wouldn't have known of one by-product of the act.

The match-day programme had already been printed on the Thursday so I wasn't listed in the squad for the match – that honour went to Peter.

As is so often the case in these situations, the actual match was a bit of a blur for me.

We won 2–1, thanks to a brace from Bobby Lennox, but the ninety minutes flashed past so quickly.

I like to think I must have done something right since the *Sunday Mail*'s Don Morrison started his match report the following day by saying that 'Young Irishman Pat Bonner looked good enough to suggest that Celtic have found themselves a tip-top goalkeeper.'

That would please the folks back home in addition to their shock at seeing me listed in the Celtic first team.

It can't have impressed Big Billy, though, as he put Peter back in for the next two games.

The second one was a 2–1 loss to Hibs, so for the midweek fixture against Motherwell (again!) I was back on duty.

This time the game was at Fir Park and under the floodlights. Motherwell's ground had a strange alignment to it, to say the least. The pitch sloped from left to right longways and from right to left sideways! It meant that a cross ball could actually end up six inches higher at the back post than it would under normal circumstances.

From my time in GAA I'd learned the tactic of leaping early and trying to get the jump on your opponent which was why I misjudged my timing and the flight of the ball at a corner when we were 3–1 ahead. Gregor Stevens was on hand to nod the ball home.

Bobby Lennox then extended our lead but five minutes from time the home side pulled one back. We edged it 4–3 at the finish but, to be honest, it was a game that hadn't gone well for me.

On a personal level, I was dealing with my emotions although I don't believe in any way that it affected my game. My grandmother, Maggie, passed away three days before the match and her funeral had taken place that day.

I knew my responsibilities, but the truth was that I couldn't get away from Glasgow although the thought of not being there to help comfort my family and pay my respects to a woman who had always been a big part of my life certainly haunted me for a while.

I'm fairly certain that I never even told Big Billy.

Anyway, Peter regained his place for the next game and kept it right up until the end of the season when he was instrumental in an amazing Monday-night game against Rangers at Celtic Park.

It was our last fixture and nothing less than a Celtic victory would give us the title. The lads came from a goal down and the loss of Johnny Doyle to a red card before running out 4–2 victors.

I was in the stand that night, savouring the atmosphere and the intensity of the match, but, having only played the two games, I didn't really feel I had done enough to justify being a part of the celebrations.

Still, I went down to the dressing room afterwards where the party was in full swing and George 'Toby' McCluskey's father was taking photographs.

It was enough to give me a taste of it, though – a hunger to experience this sort of occasion as a regular.

This is what it meant to play for a top club like Celtic. It was the night when 'Ten Men Won the League' as it was dubbed by the supporters and every one of these players was making history.

That's what I wanted – to play a part in moments of Celtic history!

It had been a big year for me.

Leaving home, the unsettling time in Glasgow, the step-up to a completely different level of football and the chance to make my debut – all of this had happened in twelve months.

I was, as a consequence, less daunted as I returned for pre-season training although my journey back could have proven to be a little bit more hairy.

Celtic's pre-season generally kicked off in or around the middle of July and so there I was, this young Donegal lad, on the books of Celtic and on my way back to the club by bus and boat, passing through predominantly Unionist towns like Castledawson and the like, with red, white and blue pavement trimmings and banners the length of gable ends portraying King Billy stretched between poles above the streets.

There I was, sharing that journey with hundreds of Orangemen returning to Scotland after the annual 12 July celebrations in the North and genuinely not having a clue about the festivities. I'd never seen anything like it in Cloughglass!

Just as well I wasn't, as they might say, 'a well-kent face'!

The 1979–80 season was another year of learning and I would say that this was the season when, in my eyes, Frank Connor really came into his own.

I only played reserve football all that year, although, as second-choice goalie, I trained with the first team, but Frank was always working me hard and building my confidence up as much as developing my game.

He was also in charge when we went out to Viareggio in Italy for a youth tournament as well as a similar contest in Haarlem, Holland.

These tourneys were the making of us as Celtic players and virtually anyone who developed in the first team over the coming years was with Frank when he took us into Europe.

Then again, how could your game not develop when you played against the cream of young Italian football or were on the same pitch as Ruud Gullit, as we were in Haarlem?

He, even in those days, stood out a mile.

Already well-developed in his physical appearance, he shone out to anyone who watched him perform and I just knew he would be one to really make it. Within a year, he would be signed full-time at Feyernoord and en route to an incredibly successful career. I could never have believed, however, that we would line up against each other years later in the Euro Championship and the World Cup.

There was also my first experience of travelling abroad in continental competition as back-up to Peter Latchford.

The European Cup campaign that season took the club out to Albania to face Partizan Tirana in the first round.

I was to return there a couple more times over the next twenty years and see the changes but nothing can take away my first memories of that closed country.

For a start, we never saw any women at all in the streets or working in the hotels and everybody seemed to dress in a drab blue-grey uniform. From the vantage point of our bus on the way in from the airport, manned gun turrets were easily visible up in the hills.

There was a controversial moment when it looked as if Danny McGrain wouldn't be allowed into the country because he had a beard although that was just about smoothed over and, when we all went out for a walk one night, Johnny Doyle attracted a crowd of about forty to fifty locals as he was strutting around downtown Tirana in a pair of white shorts and a white T-shirt.

Apparently, that was something sensational although not as interesting as training on the pitch the night before the match with a full house there to watch us be put through our paces!

Fascinating place but very strange.

Unlike Dundalk, where Celtic were drawn in the next round.

That game was pure box office back home in Ireland and, with the lads scraping a 3–2 win at Celtic Park, there was much to play for in the second leg.

It was a personal highlight for me to be on the bench that night in my home country and the ol' fella travelled up to the game with local councillor David Alcorn and a couple of other Burtonport men, pub-owner Frank Kelly and pride of the constabulary, Jim Brennan. He swore he would never do it again, though, as, in his words, they '… visited every pub from Dungloe to Dundalk!'. The home side had resisted the pressure to move the game to the national stadium at Lansdowne Road in Dublin and had kept the tie at Oriel Park even though it meant constructing temporary stands to accommodate the numbers.

With the scores tied at 0–0 and the home side only needing a goal to go through on the away aggregate, Tommy McConville missed a tap-in sitter at the back post with only five minutes left to play.

I remember seeing Peter scramble across his line to block the shot but Tommy fired wide when scoring looked easier.

It took me back to the night in 1976 when I had gone to see our local side Finn Harps play Derby County in the UEFA Cup. This was the Derby of glorious talents like Colin Todd, David Nish, Archie Gemmell, Kevin Hector and Charlie George.

One of their players wore white boots.

I mean, *pure white boots* – nobody wore white boots in 1976 but there they were and the studs were set in a circle on the sole which allowed him to swivel with his foot firmly planted in the turf. I'd never seen anything like it before and wouldn't again until a few months later, when our 'bible', *Shoot!* magazine, advertised a pair for sale.

The Harps were our heroes but they were no match for County who won 16–1 overall and 12–0 back home at the Baseball Ground.

I guess a sign of what was to come occurred not long into the match when one of the Derby forwards picked up a pass thirty yards from goal, dropped a shoulder, moved to the side and unleashed a thunderous strike towards the Harps goal.

I was standing immediately behind the net where Gerry Murray was playing and I watched him dive low to his right and catch the ball in his midriff.

It was a decent save but Gerry stayed prone on the ground for a while as one of the defenders got the ball and kicked it into touch. Apparently the force of the shot had left him winded and it was quite a few minutes before he could get up and get on with the game.

Jesus! I thought. *Who the hell could hit a ball THAT hard?*

Dundalk were a different proposition to the Harps and, having just scraped past them, my education continued when Celtic drew one of the biggest names in the game in the quarter-finals, Real Madrid.

Imagine, if the Irish side had put us out and *they* had got to face the champions of Spain.

I don't think *that* game would have been at Oriel Park!

Of course, they weren't the Real of the past or, indeed, the more modern *los galácticos*, but they were still a tasty outfit boasting home-grown players like Camacho, del Bosque and Santillana as well as German powerhouse Uli Stielike and English winger Laurie Cunningham.

The game was a sell-out for a crowd of 67,000 in Glasgow and in a recent conversation I had with the great Vicente del

Bosque he told me that the memory of playing in front of that crowd on that night is etched in his mind forever.

Not bad for the only man to date who has managed his club and his country to success in the UEFA Champions League, the European Championship and the World Cup.

He may have remembered that George McCluskey and Johnny Doyle got the goals in a 2–0 win but he might not recall that it was Alan Sneddon whose shot was spilled by the goalkeeper Ramón, for Toby to bag the opener before then supplying a pinpoint cross for a Doyley header, of all things.

Along with another reserve, John Weir, Alan was a close friend of mine in those early days and naturally I was delighted to see him play his part in a famous victory.

Ultimately, it wasn't enough as Real won 3–0 back in Madrid but it could have been so different had George McCluskey been able to finish in a one-on-one with the goalkeeper at 0–0.

Of course, these were the fine margins at that level.

I continued my apprenticeship in the reserves up until the end of the season and I have to admit to a niggling worry that started to plague me.

I had been at Celtic now for two years; made my debut at the age of eighteen and then for the next year didn't really get another sniff at the first team – I also assumed my contract was almost up.

At the season's end I decided that I had to speak to Big Billy to find out what the club's position was with me.

Frank Connor, the higher level, the first-team training rituals – all of these had made me a far better player than the one who had arrived off the boat, clad in that duffel coat, clutching a bag with all my worldly possessions only a couple of years before, but was it enough to convince Billy McNeill that I merited being kept on?

To be sure, the club had not signed another goalkeeper so I felt a certain comfort that I was still the only back-up should

Peter hit a bad spot or pick up an injury, but, other than that, I knew nothing of what the future held for me.

I waited until after training one day and, I tell you, there's nothing worse than hanging about and hanging about waiting to see your manager.

Billy had, as he always did in those days, taken a lively part in the session and now he was alone in the dressing room, having showered, and was getting himself together. I remember he was combing his hair in the mirror and not looking directly at me as I crept awkwardly into the changing area.

'Boss?'

'Aye, what is it?' he said, again without looking away from the mirror.

'Can I talk to you?'

'Aye, what is it?' he repeated.

'Well, my contract is up at the end of the season now and I was wondering whether I was ...'

He cut me off abruptly.

'Oh no, no. You've an option on that contract for another year and we'll be taking you up on it.'

I was pretty startled.

To begin with, I didn't even know there *was* an option. I never got to see a copy of the contract that I signed back in May 1978.

You see, that was how the football business worked in those days.

Anyway, I had just heard what I wanted to hear from Big Billy.

And then, as if all the stuff I had been through – the toughening up with Billy's training sessions, the loneliness, crying myself to sleep of a night – and that steel in my upbringing of digging in and working hard came out as I said to him, 'But I don't want to be here only playing in the reserves. I want first-team football, Boss.'

I don't really know why I said it and I can't even remember his response – if he responded at all – but I guess I wanted him to feel that I had something to offer and a determination to succeed.

I look back now and think that both he and John Clark saw some value in me and that they had confidence in my ability, but, just as with Declan McIntyre's injury back in the days of the Inter-Provincials, just as with Roy Baines's decision to go back to Morton, like most goalkeepers I needed a happenstance to occur.

It arrived in the early part of August 1980.

I don't think I'd been up to training on this particular day but news reached me that Peter had broken his hand during the session and would be out for the start of the season. That meant that I might have a run of games to play starting with a glamour friendly at Celtic Park on the Monday night.

Danny McGrain was celebrating his testimonial season and the visitors were Manchester United.

Right then, it didn't get any bigger for me.

Manchester United with Gordon McQueen, Joe Jordan, Lou Macari, Sammy McIlroy, Martin Buchan and more.

United had a big pull in Donegal – they still do – and only a couple of years before, as with every other football-daft boy in the country, these guys were stickers in my Panini collection. You would swap, trade and sell them to your pals but here I now was lining up against them.

Just before the match, Danny had a word of warning for me.

'Watch yourself with Joe Jordan.'

Of course, Danny McGrain had played with Joe at the highest level and I'd followed him since his days at Leeds United so we both knew how dangerous he could be in the box.

Early on in the game, a cross came in from the right. There wasn't much in it and it would be a fairly routine catch but still, my instincts were on alert.

Concentrate.

Get the timing right.

Keep your eyes on the ball.

Take it cleanly and then ...

Joe Jordan smacked into me like a runaway horse!

I held on to the ball as I hit the ground but I swear to God every single bone in my body was shaking.

In all my football life, even in GAA, I'd never felt a smack like it.

I thought Danny was warning me about Joe's prowess with headers or his ability to get beyond a defender but I hadn't prepared for this!

And there he was, standing over me, minutes into a pre-season friendly for Christ's sake, and giving me a huge grin with those famous missing front teeth (or, rather, without them) and having the time of his life.

You had to wonder who'd had the guts to take the big fella's teeth out.

Actually, he did me a favour as I went on to have a decent game in a 0–0 draw.

The game went to penalty kicks and, even though I got to Steve Coppell's strike, we lost 3–1.

It was a great night made all the more memorable by the ovation given to our respected captain but also to Lou Macari who was, like Danny, carried shoulder-high around the pitch to tumultuous applause.

Once again, I marvelled at the Celtic support and their capacity to dish out the plaudits even when a look at the record books tells you that Lou played less than a hundred games in the green and white hoops.

He was, of course, a man with whom I was destined to come head-to-head in later years, but that's a different story.

As I stood there, drinking it all in, I couldn't help but feel that this was my time.

This was what I had waited for – a chance – an opportunity to stake a real claim for that number-one jersey.

I had served my apprenticeship and now I really felt part of the team.

I felt that I ... *belonged.*

Pressure was always going to be a factor when you played for Celtic and they went into that season of 1980–81 having lost their title as champions to Aberdeen.

The Dons hadn't won the top-tier division since 1955 and Celtic had seemed to be edging towards a successful defence when a late downturn in form allowed Alex Ferguson to pick up his first Scottish Premier League title as a manager in the run-in.

I knew that I was going to be in place, at least for the first few games of the season, and I also knew I would have to make my mark.

We started with a home game against Morton who, although a part-time outfit, were the thorn in the side of many a Scottish club.

In a narrow 2–1 victory, I'd been called upon to make a quick double save. Morton full-back Jim Holmes fired in a shot that I did well to get down to but only knocked it out as far as striker Ally Scott. I scrambled to my feet quickly and, as Scott hit the ball full on, I was able to flip backwards and push his effort over the bar.

It was an important moment in the match and I was pleased that, not only had I contributed to our first points of the season, but I felt I had also laid down a marker with myself that I could really play at this level – that I deserved to be in this company.

In a season of firsts, I made my senior derby-day debut when Rangers came across the city towards the end of August but it didn't click for us that day.

Having said that, we were heading for a share of the spoils at 1–1 in the final seconds having had a Murdo 'goal' chalked off for offside, when Rangers won a throw-in in front of the Jungle.

I was at the stage where I just wanted the game to end. It had been an enjoyable experience but I just wanted to get back into the dressing room and reflect on my first taste of the big Glasgow berby, if not as a winner then certainly not as a loser.

Willie Johnston went to take it and he was renowned for his long throws into the box so Davie Provan stood right in front of him.

Johnston just threw it to the side to Alex Miller who, in turn, let the ball bounce before firing a fierce drive from about thirty-five yards that flew past me into the net.

It was a hard one to take, especially since it was Rangers's first League win at Celtic Park in six years and, believe me, the only thing worse as a Celt than losing to Rangers is losing to Rangers at home.

The disappointment around the ground and rolling down from the terraces was so palpable that I could almost taste it as we trudged off the park.

You make a mental note to yourself in these situations that you don't want to go through *that* kind of feeling too often.

The experience of some of the veterans, in particular Danny McGrain, helped to guide us younger players and pick us up for the following weeks as we then set off on an unbeaten run that took us through to November.

This was the month when everything seemed to be going in reverse.

A month when we would only win two out of five League fixtures and lose to Rangers, Aberdeen and St Mirren.

Apart from the result, the game against the Dons would infamously go down as the day Aberdeen midfielder Gordon Strachan was attacked by a supporter who leapt out from the crowd.

Gordon was a great player who wore his heart on his sleeve but a real nuisance on the park. He always got into stuff that didn't involve him and that passion plus, let's be honest, the fact that he was playing in a great team meant that supporters of other clubs hated him.

In saying that, you can't condone somebody jumping out of the crowd and assaulting a player.

That's just not on.

Gordon, of course, had that red hair which I always felt was an indicator of someone with passion but a fiery temper to boot. In that respect, he mirrored Tommy Burns and in those days both of them had some real battles in the middle of the park.

I reckon Gordon respected those qualities in Tommy and that was why they worked so well together when the wee fella was in charge of Celtic many years later down the road.

Tommy was never slow to react to any given situation and never afraid to stand alone with an opinion, even in front of Big Billy.

There was an occasion, back in the spring of 1980, when I was still playing understudy to Peter, and, just ahead of a Scottish Cup semi-final against Hibs, Billy had taken us all away to Seamill Hydro, the faithful Ayrshire retreat for Celtic since Jock Stein's days, to prepare for the big game.

I loved Seamill – I still do.

Neilly Mochan would take us away for long walks along the seemingly endless beach at the back of the Hydro, all the way around to the golf course and back up the main road again.

I couldn't help but think of Donegal as we strode for miles letting the smell of the salt water fill our nostrils, the dry wind smooth our faces and the wet sand from the retreating tide pummel against our feet.

At the Hydro itself, we were guaranteed privacy, conditioning and a certain amount of freedom to do some light training.

It's still a popular place to go for many of us older players and, years later, I would take the family down at Hogmanay and we would bring the New Year in with Tommy Burns and his family.

Tommy loved it, too, although, on this particular occasion it was to be more memorable than usual.

After dinner one evening, Billy invited us all into the large front room of the hotel and sat us all down. Celtic had lost their last two games in the League to Aberdeen and Dundee United and that run had to be halted against a Hibs side inspired by George Best.

On this particular night, Billy held Bobby Lennox up as an example of the kind of player he was looking for, suggesting that certain people were not pulling their weight and didn't have the sufficient dedication or, for that matter, fitness that Bobby, in his mid-thirties mind, had in abundance.

The message was clear and nobody took the criticism personally ... well, nobody apart from the bold Tommy.

Raging to the roots of his red hair, he couldn't control himself and sprang to his feet taking the offensive with Big Billy.

'Was he saying that he wasn't pulling his weight or was as fit as Bobby Lennox?!' Tommy demanded.

Billy shrugged and muttered something to the effect of 'if the cap fits, wear it' ...

... at which point Tommy's temper broke and, when that happened, it was like witnessing the eruption of Vesuvius!

He jumped to his feet and went toe-to-toe with Billy who then grabbed his red-headed midfielder by the throat and pinned him up against the fireplace.

He might have had sixteen years on Tommy and a few extra pounds around the waist but Big Billy was as intimidating as they came and if I'd been a betting man then my money would have been on the Celtic manager in a square go!

Players jumped in to separate them and John Clark was doing his best to act as a buffer but eventually Tommy was told to get upstairs and get packed.

Eventually, the situation was defused and, of course, the following Saturday Tommy Burns came off the substitute's bench at Hampden to help his team to a 5–0 thrashing of Hibernian and a place in the Scottish Cup Final.

Big Billy was never a man to bear a grudge especially if it was to the betterment of his teams.

Our form improved a bit with three straight wins in December and then came a tricky visit to Aberdeen just after Christmas.

Denis and Connell were over for the holidays and decided to travel up to the game with a local supporters' bus. They also decided to keep their connection to me a bit of a secret.

Which was just as well – the game wasn't my shining hour and a half and to complete the misery of a 4–1 pumping I had brought down Don's forward Mark McGhee for a penalty kick scored, inevitably, by Gordon Strachan.

It's a long way back from Aberdeen, especially in a bus full of disgruntled Celtic supporters, and Denis and Connell lay low as they listened to more than a few of the boys suggesting that … 'that Bonner's f*****g useless by the way. McNeill needs to bring Latchford back!'

Thankfully, it was not a view shared by Big Billy and, in fairness, that defeat was the last in a run that took us all the way to the title on a warm April night at Tannadice Park in Dundee and a 3–2 victory over United.

Champions of Scotland again and in my first full season as number one. It just doesn't get any better.

A great deal of that success was due to the rise of another debutant in Celtic colours – Charlie Nicholas. I was just the goalkeeper but Charlie was the top man – the 'Prince of Goals' as the press called him.

An exceptional talent in the classic mould of a Celtic centre-forward, he had the ability to put the ball in the net from anywhere and that year of 1980–81 was when he laid down a marker to the quality that he had in spades.

He also had that vital ingredient – confidence.

Charlie believed in himself on the park and was fairly sure of himself off it as well.

He epitomised that early 1980s attitude in Glasgow and would take to the town on a Saturday night to enjoy himself along with friends.

A stylish character, you could set your watch by his fashion sense; he had a bit of a following around the town and would set the trend in clothes and hairstyles for a lot of the local lads.

I remember the pair of us heading over to Dublin one time to receive a couple of awards from the Irish Celtic Supporters' Club.

Champagne Charlie, another press anointment, had also become famous for not wearing socks as he strode around in the most fashionable shoes money could buy. This was some-thing that Big Billy could never come to terms with but Charlie couldn't care less.

Anyway, when we were in Dublin he decided that he wanted a pair of white Chelsea boots to go with his outfit and so he dragged me through every bloody shoe shop in the Irish capital looking for the perfect footwear.

We drew a blank but, just as I was about to suggest we headed back to our hotel to get ready for the evening, the bold Charles spotted another outlet.

'Eh, is that not a ladies' shoe shop?' I asked.

That didn't matter a whit to Charlie. In he goes and rummages around a collection of shoes and boots designed for the female sex, convinced that he was about to find the perfect footwear to debut at the supporters' shindig that night.

Thankfully, he didn't find them but it was typical Charlie. He was all about 'the look' regardless of gender. If a pair of women's Chelsea boots looked the business on his sockless feet then he couldn't get them on quick enough!

Ach well, Spandau Ballet were probably wearing women's shoes and all!

Incidentally, we made a mistake with the awards and I ended up with Charlie's and he ended up with mine!

We never got around to swapping them. I think Danny McGrain told us not to bother and whatever Danny said was law.

I've still got it.

I couldn't help but like Charlie and, of course, the Celtic support fell in love with him.

Charlie scored goals and the one he grabbed against Rangers in April, the Saturday before the Dundee United midweek match, virtually guaranteed the championship for us in that all we now needed was one point from the visit to Tannadice.

Charlie brought a great deal to the party that year and not just for the likes of myself breaking into the team. I always thought that veterans like Danny McGrain were buoyed up to see fresh talent (and what a talent) getting their chance, and as club captain he would bring his experience to bear on Charlie.

With the fame, though, comes the recognition and I remember a visit to Seamill again that season when Big Billy announced that he and John Clark would be spending the evening with the more experienced first-team players such as Danny and Bobby Lennox, Johnny Doyle, Tom McAdam etc. etc., taking a quiet drink in the bar.

He suggested that the younger players, myself, Danny Crainie, Charlie, Tommy, Jim Duffy and a few others should take off to town and go to the pictures to unwind a bit.

The 'suggestion' was by way of an order and a bus had been laid on for us so we headed for the cinema in Ardrossan.

Charlie, of course, dressed like a pop star but I had finally discarded my old duffel coat and, given my new-found status as a first-team regular, splashed out on a fantastic sheepskin coat. The sort of garment you saw on the backs of big-time managers and *Match of the Day* commentators.

I loved that coat!

Anyway, we'd left the picture house, I can't even remember the film, and were all standing at the bus stop waiting to get our coach back to Seamill as pre-arranged.

We were fooling around like young fellas, enjoying the craic and the chance to get away from the pressures of the game for a while, when, from out with a local pub, a couple of boys showed up.

Instantly, we were recognised and, given that we were in a part of Ayrshire where Celtic supporters were as rare as mermaids, we started getting stick from this duo who clearly had no affinity for the Celts.

The situation started to escalate as one of them, in passing Jim Duffy, landed a punch and, to be sure, we weren't just going to stand there and let that happen. So the inevitable happened and the next thing I knew we were all going at it with our fists and, I like to think, holding our own.

Certainly, Charlie was no slouch and the rest of the lads could handle themselves as well.

I was in a set-to with a fella who was lying on top of me. In turn, Charlie was on top of *him*! Wary of the old 'Glasgow kiss', I was holding him really close.

Eventually, the charter bus arrived and most of our group managed to scramble on to it as if it was the escape plane in the film *Where Eagles Dare* before shouting at me to join them.

I rolled my would-be assailant over but I couldn't break free as he had a real firm hold of my prized sheepskin. There was only one exit strategy so I slipped backwards out of the coat and jumped, defrocked, for the safety of the bus.

Oblivious to the fact that I had left the scene, the fella was still flaying away at the chunky sheepskin while we were all roaring with laughter.

But what about my coat?

I *had* to retrieve it. The sheepskin was the best coat I had ever worn so, possibly without really thinking it through, I jumped back off the bus, clouted him in one swift movement, pulled on my precious sheepskin and hared it back to the lads for our getaway.

They, of course, loved it!

It was exhilarating and hilarious but not the sort of thing that you would want to see in the papers.

Back in the day, there were no mobile phones which was a relief because that's the kind of thing nowadays that has somebody filming and then uploading it so that, by the time you get back to your hotel, it's all over social media.

Somehow, we all kept it under wraps for about five or six weeks but when Big Billy found out, he hit the roof.

I still thought it was ironic, though, that we were the troublemakers while the better example would have been to sit in the bar downing a few pints and chasers.

I wouldn't have been risking my sheepskin either!

BEING NUMBER ONE

Looking back now, that season of 1980–81 was a big one for me for a number of reasons.

Front and centre, of course, was being an ever-present in a Celtic side that were the champions of Scotland but not long after that event I made my full debut for the Republic of Ireland.

I had actually been a part of the Irish squad in 1979 but, along with John Devine, that was more of an experience for the two of us as we never made it to the bench. It did, though, take us into the orbit of one of the biggest Irish idols of his time, Johnny Giles, the former Leeds United midfielder, who was the Irish manager.

Then, in 1980, I'd travelled to Toulon in France for an Under-21 tournament.

Straight up, I have to say I hated that event with a passion. Mainly because it was in June and I felt that this cut into my holiday time when I longed to be back in Burtonport.

I guess I still hadn't fully adapted to being away from Donegal and all I could see was that this bloody tournament was keeping me from where I wanted to be – home.

Perhaps that's why my actual recall of the competition is practically nil although I think Diego Maradona played with the Argentina side.

My full Irish debut arrived just after the finish of the season and took place in Poland.

Back in the day, the Republic seemed to play a lot of friendlies against the Polish. Maybe there was a secret agreement with the respective football authorities as Pope John Paul II had visited the shrine at Knock, County Mayo, in 1979!

He was a goalkeeper at one point as well – but more of that later.

Anyway, in keeping with notable dates such as my Celtic debut on St Patrick's Day, I lined up for the Republic of Ireland for the first time in the Zdzisław Krzyszkowiak Stadium, Bydgoszcz, on 24 May, 1981 – my twenty-first birthday.

A date that I shared with Denis and, having had a chat before the match with the famous Irish commentator Jimmy McGee, and telling him that it was a special day for the Bonner family, he went on to wish Denis a happy twenty-first on my behalf across the airwaves.

I'm betting Denis had a better day than I had.

We were a goal down within ninety seconds and went on to lose 3–0.

To be fair, we were a bit disjointed at the time.

It was the end of a long, hard season.

Some of the regulars had dropped out and to get to Bydgoszcz we'd had to endure a nightmare five-hour journey by bus.

All in all, not the best of circumstances.

Over the next five years, myself and Gerry Peyton would alternate in some of the international fixtures whereas Jim McDonagh, who kept goal for Everton and Bolton around that time and preferred to be known as 'Seamus', was pretty much the first-choice for the big games.

For those first few years I didn't really feel a part of the Irish squad.

Most of the players were based in English football and, as a representative of the Scottish game, I felt I had to prove myself time and time again.

he ol' fella, back in the day.

The man with the first Bonner football boots,
Dad's brother Packie Joe. He died too young.

Myself and Denis – the early years!

A rare photo of my grandmother and mum with myself and Denis.

Mum with the Bonner clan.

Keadue Rovers Seniors 1977 with the legendary Manus McCole.

The pride of Donegal – the County youth side that took me to Dublin and the Irish Youth set-up.

Irish Youth side 1977-78. It was around this time that I first met Sean Fallon.

17th March 1979 – Debut Day and I go through a pre-match warm-up in the shower area. Can't believe somebody took a photograph!

etting in front of an Andy Ritchie header at Cappielow Park, Greenock v Morton, 1981. I made my eatest domestic save in this game.

ith Ann and a couple of the lads on our wedding day. My best catch ever! *Left to Right:* ank McGarvey, AB, PB and Roy Aitken. *(Daily Record)*

The Four Amigos 1981: Ready to take on the world. *Left to Right:* Denis, Sean Walsh, Connell Boyle, P

The Four Amigos now. Still taking on the world, but older, wiser and yes, heavier. *Left to Right:* PB, Denis, Sean, Connell.

he heat of the battle, 1983. The 2-1 win was Celtic's first New Year's Day victory at Ibrox since 921. *(Daily Record)*

Relaxing with a beer after winning my first Scottish Cup medal, 1985.

Up against Billy Stark. Soon to be a team-mate and a lifelong friend.

Left to Right: Jim Stewart, PB, Paul Mathers. Even in our UEFA work, I make sure I remind Jim about Love Street, Paisley, 1986. *(Daily Record)*

Then again, of course, there was the 'Donegal' thing.

I wasn't a Dubliner. I was from the rural backwaters and, as I've mentioned before, we do carry that wee chip on our shoulders. Something that my wife-to-be, Ann, would hear about as we had been seeing each other since just before the Christmas of my first full season.

Uncle John and Aunt Bridget Mary had moved back to Ireland but, thankfully, there was always another relative on hand to provide support so I had moved over to Simshill and was now lodging with Uncle Dan and another Aunt Bridget, my mum's sister. They had a son, Danny, who was twelve years old and he and I shared a bedroom.

I don't imagine any twenty-year-old footballer does that nowadays but Danny and I got on well enough so there was never a problem.

Above us in Simshill lived John Di Paolo and, being about my age, we soon buddied up and occasionally went into town together.

To be honest, I hadn't really been much of a one for doing the nightlife and although I still liked to think of myself as anonymous, clearly playing week in, week out for one of the biggest clubs in the Britain meant that I was getting to be a wee bit better known.

Not quite Champagne Charlie, of course, but enough to make me wary of my surroundings.

Anyway, this night John and I headed into town and in one of the local nightspots out at Shawlands we bumped into a crowd of girls, including one called Ann Kerr, who John knew quite well. We got chatting, as you do, and they seemed like a nice crew.

On another occasion we all met up for a more formal night out and then after that I plucked up the courage to ask Ann for a date.

Being a first-team player, I had been given a car by club sponsors Douglas Park. They held the franchise for Vauxhall but, such was the pecking order at Celtic Park, most of the senior players got first dabs at the more upmarket Cavalier while Charlie and I were given the less glamorous Chevette to cruise about in.

I'm not even sure Charlie could drive, and I think his was eventually towed away from his parents' house, but I held a full licence and fancied impressing Ann with my brand new car so I arranged to pick her up at her house down in the Southside of Glasgow.

Ann was two years younger than me and the middle child of Tommy and Jess, along with sisters Joan and Lynne. Naturally, being the father of three girls, Tommy was quite protective of his daughters and Ann had only told her mother that she was going out on a date with me. She also told her what I did for a living, and with whom, which was sure to impact on Tommy, a dyed-in-the-wool Rangers man who regularly went along to Ibrox.

Come the big night then and Tommy notices that his middle daughter is getting ready to go out and so he enquires.

Ann tells him that she's going out for a drink with a fella called Pat Bonner.

'And what does he do?' asks Tommy.

'He's a professional footballer.'

'A footballer?'

Tommy seems quite taken with that.

'Who does he play for?'

At which point Jess says with a smile, 'You haven't heard the worst part yet!'

'He plays as a goalkeeper' – she pauses – 'for Celtic.'

Tommy, to his credit, has never heard of me and there follows some real confusion when he thinks that his middle daughter has been duped into going out on a date with that 'Peter Latchford fella. Is he no' married?!'

Of course, I knew nothing of this conversation, which was just as well.

There's a school of thought that 'meeting the parents for the first time' is one of the most nerve-wracking moments in any relationship. In my book, right up there with a first-team debut in front of 16,000 supporters but I thought I would at least impress with my shiny new Vauxhall Chevette!

Anyway, I pulled up at the house and rang the bell. Jess answered and told me that Ann was upstairs, almost ready, but running a bit late.

I would get used to *that* over the years, incidentally!

Jess invited me into the house and I tried to stay cool as she ushered me into the front room.

It's always a concern that a father or mother could, understandably, not like the idea of their daughter dating a footballer but I told myself that it was unlikely that Ann had told them what I did for a living.

Fat chance!

Or so I realised as I went into the room and there was Tommy Kerr, the man destined to be my father-in-law, sitting with his back to me, a huge red, white and blue scarf tied around his neck and a whole heap of Rangers programmes strewn across the floor!

Well, that fair broke the ice!

In fact, glancing down at his collection I noticed there was one for an Old Firm match and I was on the front cover ... letting in a goal!

I guess if your prospective son-in-law is going to play for Celtic and you're a Rangers man, you need a sense of humour.

Life was good.

I was happy with the way my career was heading and, although I still missed home, even I could see that my immediate future lay in Glasgow so I did what any aspiring young professional would do – I bought a house.

Jeez, I was twenty-one years old and I couldn't really go on sharing my sleeping arrangements with my younger cousin so I moved into a small semi-detached in Newton Mearns.

Not just a home, but a place for the rest of the 'four amigos' to crash when they came over to visit me. The boys were over one time when we realised that, typical of the living arrangements of a few devil-may-care young fellas, the kitchen was out of basic provisions.

There was a mini-mart a few minutes down the road so Connell and I took off for that to stock up the larder. I was up the back of the shop looking in bewilderment at a stack of tinned meals while Connell was casting his eye over a range of brown and white bread.

Suddenly I heard the shout ...

'Haw Packie – Packie?'

I looked round from my tins.

'What kind of a bread is this, Packie?'

'Come again, Connell?'

'I'm not sure what kind of bread we want, Packie!'

At which point I turned to see the Asian owner of the shop shaking his head and muttering before taking issue with myself and Connell.

'You come in here to insult me?!' he asked with some justification.

I hurried down to the counter offering my hand as I did so before trying to explain that 'Packie' was short for Patrick. To the folks back home I would always be 'Packie'.

I still am although I was never sure that I managed to convince the poor shopkeeper of the innocent misunderstanding.

For a good while afterwards I just went to Tesco!

*

We kicked off season 1981–2 as champions and were motoring well in the first few months when tragedy struck our united dressing room.

Johnny Doyle had only recently moved house and it was on

the night of 19 October that, in attempting some household rewiring, he was killed outright by an electric shock.

Doyley was a real character.

Intimidating, to be sure, and the kind of guy who liked you to know that he was around the place, he could, in parts, be quite heavy-handed with some of the younger players particularly when it came to the subject of religion.

'You been to Mass?!' he would thunder at some young fella who may well have been polishing his boots and possibly wasn't even Catholic.

Without it being a warm relationship, I got on well with him and was pleased to notice once that he had picked out myself, Charlie and Danny Crainie as young Celts with a big future.

He styled himself as 'the man', a position he maintained even after Frank McGarvey arrived at Celtic Park.

I felt that Frank, like Doyley, had a fair opinion of himself, considering that *he* was the 'king of the jungle', and when you have real wind-up merchants like Tommy Burns, Davie Provan and Roy Aitken added to the mix then they could set the pair of them at it hammer and tongs all day long on the issue.

There was a time, on a trip away to Aberdeen, as the coach had just pulled out from Celtic Park, when Frank and Doyley started their personal battle of wills. This time, it got physical and they went at each other in the aisle of the bus like a pair of rutting stags. Frank had Doyley in a headlock, refusing to yield, and the wee fella had grabbed Frank's crown jewels from below.

'Who's the man now, Doyley?'

'I'm the man, Frankie. I'll always be the man!'

'You're no' the man, Doyley. There's only room for one!'

'And that's me, Frankie! I'm the man!'

I swear they stayed locked that way all the way up to Pittodrie Stadium, neither one giving ground to the other while Big Billy and John Clark just sat at the front of the bus not bothering with them.

I think they thought it amused the rest of the squad and worked off any pre-match nerves – certainly, it was more entertaining than the wrestling on *World of Sport*!

On another occasion, I drove into the parking area in front of the stadium and saw the wee fella standing in front of his green Audi (everything was green in Doyley's world) and Johnny and his wife were having a bit of an argument.

I sidestepped it, but when I got into the dressing room the word was out – Doyley was not to be wound up today; there had been a bereavement in the family.

That's when I found out that Doyley's pet cockatoo had choked to death by chewing the curtains in the front room – seriously!

If I remember rightly, it was Tommy Burns who mimicked a parrot-like squawk when Doyley was getting changed into his training gear half an hour later.

Only he could get away with it!

Johnny had enjoyed some great moments in a Celtic jersey but, in truth, he had been in and out of the team in recent times and had a few run-ins with Big Billy.

In addition, he had turned down moves to Hearts and Motherwell that season.

I guess he just couldn't play against Celtic having been such a part of the history of the club.

It isn't cheap or corny, then, to speculate that it might just have been fitting that Johnny Doyle left us all as a Celtic player.

His funeral was difficult to come to terms with. You just didn't expect a team-mate to pass away and in such tragic circumstances. Tommy Burns, I remember, was all but inconsolable as Doyley had arrived at the club when he was breaking through and they had a shared passion for all things Celtic but his death reverberated around us all at the club.

Little wonder, then, that we lost our very next match after Johnny's death, going down to Hibs 1–0 at Easter Road, our first League defeat of the season.

We could, however, afford to concentrate on the domestic games as we had already exited Europe at the hands of Italian giants Juventus.

Boasting the talents of Zoff, Gentile, Tardelli, Bettega and, of course, my compatriot Liam Brady, nobody had really given us an earthly against Juve but somehow, in a tight first leg in Glasgow in September, we had prevailed 1–0 courtesy of a Murdo MacLeod goal.

As we walked off the pitch after the ninety minutes, I shook Liam's hand and we headed towards the tunnel.

He was a god in Ireland, a cultured midfielder who starred for his country and had the belief to take this ability over to Turin and try his hand at the continental game. I desperately wanted to make an impression on the most revered Irish footballer of his generation.

As we approached the tunnel area, I suddenly saw a Celtic supporter virtually hanging off the side of a wall and verbally abusing Liam with all he had in his vocabulary.

I wasn't sure how good the linguistics were with the rest of the Italian side but you didn't need to be fluent in English to understand that, according to this bold boy, Juventus were a pile of crap and right at the heart of that crap was the overrated Liam Brady.

I remember thinking, *Jesus, don't be winding these fellas up now. That's all we'll need for the second leg.*

And so it proved.

On a personal level, I had one of my best games to date in the Celtic goal but it wasn't enough to stop us going down 2–0 to the Italian champions and that *overrated* Liam Brady was right at the heart of that victory.

Our paths would cross at a later date but, for the moment, I was quite happy that he praised my performance in the Irish newspapers.

If we couldn't make headway in Europe, then we would have to put our backs into retaining the title and it was clear that the challenge to do so was coming from the north-east clubs of Aberdeen and Dundee United rather than Celtic's traditional rivals, Rangers.

In many ways, this was a harder season than the one before, due, in no small part, to losing both Frank McGarvey and Champagne Charlie as our main strike force to broken legs in the second half of the campaign.

George McCluskey came to the rescue and Toby had a great year, finishing as Celtic's top striker for the season. Thankfully, he was on the pitch for the final League match against St Mirren at Celtic Park.

A 3–0 thumping at Tannadice the week before, while not quite derailing our ambitions, ensured that, to clinch the title in front of our own fans, we would have to beat the Paisley Buddies.

Aberdeen were sticking to us like a limpet mine and, were we to fail against St Mirren, even as much as a draw, then a 5–0 victory for the Dons against Rangers at Pittodrie would see the League pennant heading to the north-east.

At half-time that day, Aberdeen were, incredibly, already 4–0 up and we were goal-less with the Saints. Big Billy, of course, tried to keep the Pittodrie news out of the dressing room but that was never going to happen.

The nerves were palpable and you only had to look out at the faces on the terraces to know how the afternoon was developing.

There was a young fella called Frank McAvennie playing up front for St Mirren and he was busting a gut to put the ball in the back of the Celtic net. We almost had a private duel going on between us and I had to be at the top of my game to defy him.

Five years later, when he joined us from West Ham, I good-naturedly reminded him that he'd done his utmost to ruin that afternoon for the Celtic supporters.

I think he was just trying to make a name for himself!

Anyway, Toby stepped up to the plate and his goals, either side of a Tom McAdam header, saw us home 3–0 and become the first Celtic side in eight years to win back-to-back titles.

Let me tell you, there's nothing quite like winning the League at home in front of your own supporters on the last day of a long, hard season, especially when it looked as if it could be slipping away from us – the margins again.

Celtic director Tom Devlin used to be driven down to the matches from his home in Edinburgh by a good Donegal man, Tony Gallagher, who was reared in Dungloe. When Tony came into the Celtic dressing room after the match, he found me in tears.

God, there was pressure on us that day and, although, as I say, it's the greatest feeling to win the flag in front of your own fans, the thought of failing in front of them and feeling their disappointment raised the stakes considerably.

I did think back to that night in 1979 when I didn't feel a part of the title celebrations but now I was in a triumphant Celtic Park dressing room splashing champagne. I belonged there and was a part of the club's history.

Satisfying? Yes.

Emotional? Definitely.

That's the powerful thing about sport.

In the close season of that year, I decided it was time to take a holiday.

Being at Celtic had taken me all over Europe and I even had the USA stamped on my passport for a pre-season tournament out in New York in 1981 with Seattle Sounders, New York Cosmos and Southampton, but I had only been out of Ireland once on an actual holiday and that was with Denis and my two sisters Mamie and Ann.

I liked America and fancied seeing it a bit further down the coast and catching some sun, so my girlfriend Ann and I booked a condominium down in Fort Lauderdale, Florida, along with her parents, Tommy and Jess.

Family duty meant that I had to spend some time in Burtonport, where I had to persuade my parents that I really needed a holiday away from everything and not spending the summer, as I always did, in Donegal; so I suggested that Ann and her folks flew out first, settled into the condo and I would join them later.

Well, I was the big international flyer, wasn't I? Quite at home with global travel …

In addition to my luggage, I had two bits of paper. One had the address that I was to eventually get to and the other had the phone number of the condo, of which I had only seen a picture when we booked it.

It was a simple route … Dublin–New York–Tampa, where I would make a phone call and Ann and Tommy would pick me up.

I first ran into trouble at JFK Airport in the Big Apple.

When I got to immigration I discovered that I had lost the first piece of paper with the address on it so I couldn't satisfy the customs guys as to where I would be staying in their country.

'You don't know where you're going, man?!'

'Eh, well, I know I'm going to Tampa and Fort Lauderdale, Hollywood Beach?'

That didn't cut it and, before I knew it, I was sent to room full of migrants which looked like a United Nations meeting.

There was only one other white fella in the place and, lo and behold, he was Irish.

If the accent wasn't a giveaway, then the mighty hurling stick he had packed with his luggage certainly was so I had a chat with him.

'Ach, I'm over to do a bit o' work for the summer and play a wee bit o' hurling as well.'

'Ah, good luck to you now.'

Once we had wished each other well, I was called forward by a customs official.

He had my passport, opened, in his hand.

'So you were here last year, man. Where did you stay then?'

'Eh, the St Moritz in Manhattan,' I answered, realising that if they thought I was a high-end criminal then staying in one of the most luxurious hotels in America would pretty much convince them.

Where would a fella from the 'Rosses' get that kind of money?

It occurred to me now that I was going to be late for my connection with all the red tape going on and, undesirable that I was, they had lifted my bag away as well.

I eventually cleared immigration and found my bag on a huge trolley stacked with luggage. I raced through the airport, thinking that my flight had gone, but when I arrived at the gate I still had an hour to departure. The great international traveller had reset his watch to the wrong time!

At least now I was back on track. Eventually, I arrived in Tampa and now all I had to do was to find a telephone and ring Tommy and Ann.

I must have rang that bloody number twenty times and *still* no one picked the damn phone up at the other end.

I spent the night stretched across a few chairs with my leg propped up over my bag to deter any thieves and dozed away.

Apart from the cleaners, who were shooting me some mystified looks, I was the only eejit in the whole airport.

What the hell was I to do?

I hadn't reckoned on Tampa being a six-hour drive from Fort Lauderdale.

I had exactly $50 on me and the first currency exchange I went to wouldn't cash a European cheque.

It could have been the lack of sleep, the jet lag, the long journey or just a fever but I started to speculate about how I could survive in America if I couldn't get out of Tampa.

I'll go and get a job washing dishes or something, I thought.

Donegal, you see – resilient!

After a fitful sleep, I woke up realising that I would have to find an open exchange that *would* cash my cheque which, thank God, I did and so, now armed with $120, I booked a flight to Fort Lauderdale.

I was now two days overdue and there was no way for Ann and her parents to contact me.

I found out later that she and Tommy had spent both days driving up to Fort Lauderdale Airport and then visiting all the Greyhound bus depots in the area, hoping that I would eventually roll into town.

When I did get to Fort Lauderdale, I jumped into a taxi.

An old couple on the plane had told me that Hollywood Beach was about half an hour away by car and I just had to hope that my remaining $30 would cover it.

My plan now was to get to the beach and walk around until I recognised our condo so I said to the driver ...

'Can you take me to Hollywood Beach, please?'

After all, how many Hollywood Beaches could there be?

He looked at me from behind his sunglasses, smiled and replied ...

'Do you mean Little Hollywood Beach or Big Hollywood Beach, man?'

The old heart fair sank but I had no Plan B so off we went.

I didn't take my eyes off the meter and when we got to one

of the Hollywood Beaches and my bill heading towards the $25 mark, I told the driver to stop on the road that passed behind a row of about a million condominiums.

I got out, ran between two condos and headed down to the boardwalk.

The sun was at its peak, hotter than a barbecue, and, naturally, everybody was out on the beach in swimsuits and the like, working on their tans. I was standing out a mile in my heavy travel clothes and big shoes with litres of sweat pouring down the back of my neck.

Nope, didn't recognise any of the condos.

Back into the taxi for my remaining $5.

If your man was getting a tip, it was going to be in quarters and dimes!

On we pressed for another thirty yards or so and stopped again.

I kept that up until we reached the $29 mark at which point I knew the game was up. I got out of the taxi, handed the driver my very last dollar and waved him off.

A big ol' Donegal lad, standing behind a row of condominiums, facing on to Hollywood Beach in the middle of a boardwalk, sweat running down my back and thinking …

This is it. I'm stuck here with no money. I'll need to get a job in the kitchens. The only Celtic goalkeeper in history to miss pre-season because he was working his passage back to Scotland in a Florida restaurant!

After a couple of minutes with that daunting thought, I dejectedly picked up my bag, slung my jacket over my arm and randomly started to walk down the road where I turned left between a gap in the row of houses.

That was when, unbelievably and out of nowhere, I suddenly saw Jess looking out at me through the window of our condo.

Sandpiper Condominium – never to be forgotten and a name that I will take to the grave with me!

You talk about the luck of the Irish.

After all the hassles – customs and immigration – missing bags – wrong time – poverty of dollars – lack of communication … I had alighted at the very place I wanted to be purely by chance.

Turned out the phone wasn't working in the condo!

After that, we had a great holiday but, if I hadn't experienced international travel with Celtic Football Club and the Irish national team, I might well still be washing dishes in Florida!

Anyone who plays for Celtic gets the opportunity to go abroad because, for over fifty years, give or take the odd season, the club has competed in European football in various competitions.

If there is one regret I have about my career it's that we never really made the kind of progress that we should have on the Continent.

When I think that we were jousting successfully with the likes of Dundee United and Aberdeen in those early years, both of whom made it to European finals and, in the case of the Dons, winning the European Cup Winners' Cup in 1983, then I can't understand why we didn't have the same level of success.

There was the odd notable scalp such as Ajax of Amsterdam in the autumn of 1982.

They were a fantastic side and we drew them in the first round of the European Cup. Johan Cruyff was in his second spell at the club and, although thirty-five at the time, still had the presence and authority out on the pitch to dictate a game.

In the first leg at Celtic Park we somehow managed to hold on for a 2–2 draw but the truth is Ajax destroyed us!

Two Danish internationals were at the heart of it all – Søren Lerby and Jesper Olsen. Lerby controlled the midfield while, down the flanks, Olsen gave Danny McGrain possibly the toughest ninety minutes of his career.

And yet, we were still in it come the final whistle as the Celtic support rose as one to salute the Dutch side.

I always think that the Celtic philosophy back then was the same one that Billy had inherited from Jock Stein – don't think too much about how they play; let's just play *our* normal game.

And yet, for the return leg in Holland, Big Billy posted a specific instruction to defender Graeme Sinclair. It was only the small matter of a man-marking job on the great Cruyff.

Sinky was told to stick so close to the Dutch master that he could tell you his brand of aftershave.

Only months before, he had been playing for Dumbarton and, having impressed against us in a Scottish Cup tie, Big Billy had brought him to Celtic and this was his night to man-mark one of the greatest football players on the planet.

Ajax had moved the match to the Olympic Stadium to suit the large crowd as the Celtic support alone numbered around 3000.

We had the opportunity to train at the stadium the night before the match which was something that I always loved. It gave you the chance to get a feel for your surroundings, the grass, the position of the floodlights as well as a quick bout of crossing and shooting from the strikers.

While we were out I noticed that the pitch seemed to slope from the eighteen-yard line all the way up to the goalmouth. It wasn't a huge gradient but it could be a useful tool so I mentioned to Charlie that, if he saw the Ajax goalkeeper, Piet Schrijvers, a few yards off his line then a decent chip shot would be almost impossible to save.

Schrijvers was a Dutch international keeper but he wasn't the tallest of men.

This was Charlie's year.

He was at the height of his pomp having returned from the broken leg the season before and, if anything, was a better player than before the injury.

And so it was, on one of our few forays up the pitch on the night, Graeme Sinclair took a superb pass from eighteen-year-old

Paul McStay, made his way up to the penalty box, where he was robustly tackled but the ball broke to Charlie, who evaded two tackles before playing a one-two with Frank McGarvey, then clipped a shot above Schrijvers and into the net.

It was a brilliant goal.

A typical Charlie Nicholas goal.

To have the skill and the mental agility in the heat of the moment to remember my suggestion before pulling it off was yet another sign of a great player.

I was in decent form myself and remember it as one of my best performances for Celtic.

That was useful as Eoin Hand, international team manager, was up in the stand watching. He had already picked me for the Republic but this was the first time he had actually seen me playing for Celtic.

It was real backs-to-the-wall stuff, as it so often was when we travelled away from home on European duty. A deflection from a shot in the second half brought Ajax level on the night and with the two away goals they were odds on to go through.

Then Big Billy pulled his masterstroke by sticking George McCluskey on in place of Davie Provan.

With two minutes left of the ninety and us on the precipice of tumbling out of Europe, Danny McGrain attempted a long-range effort that bobbled around the edge of the box before being slipped to Toby who, quick as a whip, placed a shot past Schrijvers to give us the victory no one had anticipated.

It's probably my best memory of European football, along with watching 3000 Celtic supporters cavorting about on the terracing off to my right-hand side when the final whistle sounded.

It was a great achievement for Billy as well although the overall memory of it is somewhat soured as we went out in the next round to Real Sociedad of Spain – a decent side but hardly Barcelona.

If the European adventure was over then, at least I got to pick up my first domestic cup medal a few months later.

Celtic have always had a fractious relationship with the League Cup throughout their history. The club have lost as many finals as they've won. I'm happy to say that I played in one of those victories when we faced Rangers at Hampden three weeks before Christmas.

I'd always dreamed of playing in a major cup final.

The setting always seemed to be just right – the weather beautiful, the pitch playing like a carpet.

The 4 December 1982 must have been one of the wettest days of the year, possibly the decade. In atrocious conditions, Charlie – who else? – had us 1–0 up early in the match before a Murdo MacLeod thunderbolt doubled the lead and saw us comfortably in control.

I wasn't best pleased with a Jim Bett free-kick from twenty-five yards just after half-time that sailed over the wall and into the net on my right-hand side, but we managed to see out the rest of the match to take Celtic's first League Cup in eight years – and what would actually turn out to be their last for fifteen years.

I was soaked through, of course, and nowhere near dry when I followed Danny up the stairs at Hampden to receive the cup, but it's funny how a win in the Glasgow derby and a trophy to boot makes you forget the dreadful conditions.

Disappointingly, the League Cup was as good as it got for us that year as we were pipped by Dundee United to the title on the final day of the season after Aberdeen knocked us out of the Scottish Cup.

If there was anything to be had from the last game it was the fact that we came from being 2–0 down to Rangers at Ibrox to turn the match around in the second half and win 4–2.

Charlie took a couple of penalties and, between those, goals from Tom McAdam and Frank McGarvey completed a legendary turnaround.

Those penalties were to be the last competitive goals Charlie would score for us in that era but, contrary to popular belief, it wasn't his last outing in a Celtic strip before he left the club.

Big Billy came into the dressing room one day after a match, close to the end of the season, and told us that we were scheduled to play a friendly in Ireland before we could all down tools for the summer break.

This was a surprise, as were the opposition – Finn Harps at Finn Park.

I got an even bigger shock when, as the rest of the squad groaned about another game after a long, hard season, Billy announced that it was all my fault. Apparently, part of the deal included in my transfer to Celtic was that the Hoops would visit Ireland and play against the Harps; now, five years on from the signing, we were to honour the arrangement.

Fran Fields!

Of course, that's why he was cutting about with Jock Stein that day I signed.

Crafty so-and-so made sure that there would something in it for Finn Harps.

I didn't know anything about it but I could see how it all came together. My only regret was that Keadue Rovers got absolutely nothing out of my leaving for Celtic apart from a set of strips.

I guess you needed a smart operator like Fran to make these sorts of things happen.

Anyway, on a lovely Donegal day and in front of a capacity crowd of 10,000 at Finn Park, Baleybofey, Frank, Charlie, Murdo and Toby found the net in a 4–0 win that seemed to keep everybody happy.

We all had a fair idea that it was Charlie's last game but we weren't to know that it was Toby's as well as he would leave for Leeds United before the start of the following season.

I remember Billy McNeill berating Paul McStay as he supped

a pint in the bar at the Great Northern Hotel after the match. Paul would have been barely nineteen at the time and I guess Big Billy wanted to impress on him the dangers of the evil brew to a professional sportsman.

Charlie was the man whom Celtic should have been building a side around and, with others like Paul and Danny Crainie pushing for places, the future seemed to be quite bright.

Yet, Charlie Nicholas was off to England and, if that wasn't news enough, Big Billy's decision to quit Celtic and head for Manchester City at the end of May had the headline writers scrambling around to come up with the goods.

It was a changing time and a disturbing one as well and, once again, I would have to 'adapt', as would everyone inside the Celtic Park dressing room.

STEPPING UP

BILLY MCNEILL'S SUDDEN DECISION TO LEAVE CELTIC PARK was a complete shock to all of us.

There had been absolutely no rumours that he was contemplating his future and I, like a lot people, imagined that he would be the manager of Celtic for years to come – it just seemed a natural fit.

Billy *was* Celtic.

His style was to lead from the front, chest puffed out, and take the club's fight to anyone out on the pitch.

He managed as he had played.

I remember him standing on the touchline one day, during a match, going toe-to-toe with referee Andrew Waddell after questioning a decision the official had made and refusing to back down in front of a packed house. Typical Billy – no quarter given; and the man who stepped into his shoes would need to bring that kind of leadership and self-belief to the club.

I was in Ireland when it was announced that our new manager was David Hay.

In essence, that was good news as he was a club legend reared in the Celtic tradition of attacking football and success, although, if I'm going to be honest, I remembered him more when he patrolled the midfield for Chelsea in the mid-1970s.

Of equal pleasure to me was that Frank Connor was coming back but, this time, as an assistant.

If I harboured any reservation it was that Davie was only thirty-five although he wasn't a rookie manager, having taken Motherwell up to the Scottish Premier League in 1982 before quitting the club.

Of course, he was going to have to do it all without the talismanic Charlie who, having the pick of FA Cup-holders Manchester United, League champions and League Cup holders Liverpool or Arsenal, had chosen to head to north London in the next stage of his career.

It seemed a strange choice; we all thought he'd be joining up with Kenny Dalglish at Liverpool and they had already shown how productive they could be together when playing for Scotland, but he was getting front-page coverage for his move and it was pure box office when he quickly returned to Scotland for a pre-season game against Hearts.

I hadn't seen Charlie since the Finn Harps match so I drove through to Edinburgh, paid in at the gate and stood among the Hearts supporters who, naturally, 'welcomed' him back across the border.

I was intrigued about the whole issue of Charlie moving south and, in particular, how he would perform in the glamour of London. I had absolutely no doubts that he would take England by storm – he was *that* good – and yet, well, the Arsenal boys played with a swagger as if they weren't quite taking the whole thing seriously and there was Charlie trying hard to fit in. I have to be honest and say that I left Edinburgh with a certain sense of apprehension for my friend.

Still, it was for Charlie to find his feet.

My job was to consolidate my position to a brand new manager for the first time in my career.

And it started well for Davie and Frank in the early months of the season.

Although losing narrowly to Rangers in the Glasgow Cup

Final, we had dominated the match and, crucially, had gone on to beat our rivals in the first League encounter of the season at home in September.

I always think it's vital to win that one when you're the manager of Celtic or, indeed, Rangers.

Then came October and a stream of unsatisfactory performances when we couldn't win a domestic fixture in six attempts and fell to Sporting Lisbon 2–0 in the first leg of our second round UEFA Cup tie out in Portugal.

A 0-0 draw with Hibernian in the League Cup on Wednesday, 26 October, saw us wake up to headlines from Davie, promising changes to his line-up.

That Thursday night, I was escaping from such pressures, sitting in Tommy and Jess's house, watching *Top of the Pops* with Ann and discussing our wedding that we had set for the following June.

Like most footballers back then, you got married in the close season!

The phone rang and moments later Jess told me that I was to get over to Aunt Bridget's house.

At first, I thought it was Uncle Dan but when Ann and I got to the house I was given the devastating news that my father had passed away suddenly in Donegal.

He was only sixty-one and, although not in the best of form in recent times, I doubt anyone, least of all he, suspected that he was in any imminent danger.

Typically, he had been working away in the garage as was his custom and putting the finishing touches to some windows that he was making for Ray Ham's new house. He had, of course, built the house, block by block, and convinced Ray, who would go to the bank on the strength of my father's word, that the right decision was to construct his own property to a certain specification.

Having completed the job and reset his tools in their allotted places, he made his way back to the house and then went up to the bedroom for a short nap before supper.

He never woke up, slipping away peacefully in his sleep as the Atlantic broke against the rocks just yards from Castleport House and as the dusk descended over Donegal.

My father would never get to see the heights of my career. He had enjoyed the early success that I had been a part of with Celtic and I know, as a lover of all sports, he would have taken the greatest pleasure in seeing me as part of an Irish squad competing on the biggest stage of all in the World Cup.

Dad, slight in stature but a giant of a man in so many other ways, was taken from us at what I would consider to be an early age.

On informing Davie Hay, I was immediately told to get back home to Ireland as my friends and relations gathered to mourn. The benefit of such a large family is the comfort and solace we can take from one another in times of greatest need as well as providing support for my mother, Grace.

I had a Ford Capri at the time which wasn't exactly designed for the comfort of three people but nonetheless myself, Ann and Aunt Bridget climbed into it and took off for Ireland.

My head was a mess, reeling from the shock of the news.

It's the mundane things that can get to you at a time like this and so I fought with a petrol pump at a local filling station as I was convinced that it wasn't working properly and I desperately needed fuel to get me home. I still feel a little sorry for the assistant whom I berated about the faulty pump and who stepped outside to show me that it was fully functioning.

The trip was a long one, weighted with the sadness of the occasion. We rarely spoke on the journey, just content to sift through our own memories of my father.

As I mentioned, the ol' fella wasn't the largest of men, standing five-foot-ten in his stocking soles on a good day, but he was a powerfully built, broad-shouldered individual, undoubtedly honed by years of solid, unrelenting graft, with the largest hands that I have ever seen on a human being.

What came back to me were those moments out in a boat fishing or of him and Uncle Dan going for a drink or when Denis and I had laboured for him as he built the houses.

I had a fear of heights, still do, but Denis was a mountain goat who thought nothing of standing on the roof of a detached two-storey job and merrily banging nails securely into wooden rafters.

I reckon he was the blue-eyed boy with the ol' fella on those occasions, as Dad would only shake his head at me as a nail flew across the roof from my trembling attempt to hit it square on!

As with any relationship between young men such as myself and my brother wanting to make their way in the world, we would clash with the ol' fella and possibly his old-fashioned view of life, but it was never a drawn-out saga and, of course, as I get older, I look back fondly at the gifts he gave to me that have guided me along the way.

Andrew Bonner was laid to rest on the following Saturday morning in the soft Donegal earth of Cruit Island cemetery.

Despite his period of work in Scotland, Donegal was very much an integral part of who my father was and his identity.

I remember in my early days at Celtic that he came over one time and came out to the Park.

I was getting showered after training and so he sat out in the foyer on a battered old green settee that probably dated back to Jimmy McGrory in the 1930s, keeping his own counsel and minding his own business.

When I eventually joined him he said to me, quietly, 'Who's that fella over there?' And pointed to John Clark.

I whispered to him John's name and expected to hear him talk about the great Lisbon Lions but he shook his head and raised his eyes to the ceiling before saying, 'I don't care much for him, you know. He's been passing me this many times and never once said, "How are ye?"'

Ah, that's the Donegal way, you see.

Nobody ever passes anyone without a nod or a wink and a bob of greeting.

The ol' fella just couldn't understand it and John – well, he was a quiet man as well and not pronc to saying hello to everyone who crossed his path.

Of course, in traditional Irish style, the observed wake drew many such stories about the ol' fella by those who best knew him.

There was one from a few years back when he had gone out for a drink with a neighbour, Donnie Ward. The ol' fella was a bit light in the pockets at that time so he asked Donnie if he could borrow a ten-shilling note so that he could 'dress the table' with a drink.

Donnie was obliging and the two whiled away the night until it was time to come home.

Just as they reached the point where they were to go their separate ways, Donnie reminded the ol' fella that he was into him for the ten shillings and tensions rose between the two until my father put an end to the 'discussion' by hitting Donnie a clout!

That was the kind of community Andrew Bonner was raised in.

If there was something to be said, he said it.

If action was to be taken, he acted.

The ol' fella was never anything less than honest.

Over the coming days, Denis and I would stand at the wake watching the various mourners drifting in and out and occasionally nodding at each other before whispering, 'Did the ol' fella not take a crack at that fella over there?'

For some reason, Celtic's League game on the day of the funeral, against Hibernian, was being broadcast live on RTÉ.

Keen as I was to support the lads, I wasn't too sure about the etiquette of tuning into the football just after we had buried our father but, when we asked Mum, her response was spot on: 'Your father would have done the same himself.' And so we settled down in front of the box like it was the Mexico World Cup Finals all over again.

The difference this time, though, was that Denis, myself and the lads were nursing a few whiskeys. That was my first drop of the Jameson's and cousin Connell, at the grand old age of twenty-three, had his first ever drink, which was to his liking as he polished off a bottle of Drambuie.

As I sat swilling the glass around until the viscosity of the whiskey coated the inside, I thought back a couple of years to a time when the ol' fella was in Glasgow and I took both himself and Uncle Dan to the famous Albert Bar down on the Langside Road.

It was a seminal moment.

I had never taken my father for a drink back in Ireland and so, I sat both men down, went to the bar and came back to furnish the table with the classic combo of a half-pint of lager and a half o' whiskey.

Satisfied, in a kind of coming-of-age moment, I went back to the bar and ordered myself the most insipid drink I could think of, a half-pint of lager shandy. I was a professional sportsman, after all, serious about my craft and not given to boozing.

No sooner had I sat back down at the table when the ol' fella looked disdainfully down at my glass and then up at me before saying, 'So, you're drinking now, are you?'

Six words only, but loaded with meaning.

The message was clear: you're fella enough now to fetch a round in but don't be taking this up as a hobby.

What would he have made of my settling down with a Jameson's and watching the Celtic play?

Thankfully, Peter Latchford, who took my place, and the boys put in their best performance of the month with a 5–1 victory.

My father's death was a traumatic event for me.

The death of a parent, particularly at only sixty-one, always *is* traumatic, but, in my case, it underlined to me that I had left my home to make my way in the world and was separated from that home when I was, perhaps, needed most by my family.

I didn't really get the opportunity to mourn my father properly as I had to return quickly to Scotland with the return leg of the Sporting tie due on the following Wednesday and I suppose my mind was hard set on getting on with the game.

If it was set at all.

On the way back and about ten miles out from home, at a place called Doochary, I had the choice of two roads to take me to Larne. The first was the obvious route, an artery towards one of Donegal's biggest towns, Letterkenny, but for some reason I took the less used road to the left.

I would almost never choose that direction but for some reason that I still can't fathom, we set off in an effort to make the boat on time.

Not too far down a way, the road narrowed a bit, making it awkward for two cars to pass each other. Perhaps I should have pulled in to let the fella coming towards me squeeze past but I was not myself that day. I maintained my momentum, refused to yield ground and there was a sickening explosion as our respective wing mirrors clashed before fragmenting into pieces.

We both kept on driving away from each other and not a word was spoken in the Capri but, from the back, I made out the audible gasp coming from Aunty Bridget and it made me ashamed of my actions.

It was, to be sure, a strange time but, thankfully, I had the football.

I *always* had the football.

The game, the inevitability of the next match, the need to put my personal grief to the back of my mind and focus for the good of the club and the passionate support, very probably kept me afloat amid the anguish.

And yet, as we all lined up in the tunnel a few days later before kick-off against Sporting, there was a little moment that was emotionally intense and typical of my friend, Tommy Burns.

He was just behind me in the line and, as I prepared to walk out to a 67,000 Celtic Park crowd and a big night of European football, Tommy whispered to me, 'Let's do one for your ol' fella here, eh?'

It was a beautiful moment and even in the recall of it now I still feel the shiver at the back of my neck.

And Tommy Burns was true to his word.

At 2–0 down from the first leg, Celtic put on the greatest display of football in my time at the club to destroy a very decent Sporting Lisbon side 5–0.

Tommy himself got the ball rolling in four minutes when he opened the scoring from a Frank McGarvey cross before Tom McAdam and Brian McClair put us three to the good ahead of half-time.

The away-goals rule meant that one counter from Sporting would put them through but even though it took until the last five minutes for Murdo and then Frank to put the tie to bed at 5–0, there was never any doubt in my mind that we were going to win the match.

It was a wonderful performance, reminiscent, I felt, of the old Celtic, and would linger long in the minds of anyone who was there on the night.

There had been a League match the year before when we had thrashed Motherwell 7–0 at Fir Park and, at the end of it, I overheard the veteran defender Joe Wark, who had been chasing the boys around the pitch for ninety forlorn minutes, say as he walked up the tunnel that this was the best side he had ever played against.

Personally, I would class the Sporting Lisbon night as being better and it was also good to see Davie Hay getting the acclaim as well.

He'd been getting it tight through the press for most of October and if he didn't realise the pressures of being Celtic manager before, he surely did now so the Lisbon result was fairly crucial to him.

Within days of the game I was back out at Ann's parents' house where I was now a regular feature.

I enjoyed the company of Tommy and Jess and, at this time, in the immediate aftermath of my father's passing, their consoling support was indispensable to me.

And yet, I wasn't prepared for a gesture from Tommy that, in Glasgow football terms, was seismic.

He took me aside in the house one day for a quiet word.

As mentioned, Tommy had been a Rangers man all his days, proud of his team. It amused me a bit that, when he attended Rangers–Celtic matches around this time and I was getting the customary stick from the 'Gers supporters, he would be high up in the stand saying things like 'Ach, maybe he's not such a bad lad. He's no' a bad keeper' and other platitudes but never once telling his mates that one of his daughters was engaged to be married to the big Irish so-and-so guarding the Celtic goal.

That would have been the utmost treason.

We would have many a friendly joust about those matches after the event and it never affected me that he was a Rangers supporter.

It is, after all, surely just a football game.

But, on this particular day, he took me into the front room where we could get some privacy and informed me that, henceforth, he would be coming up to Celtic Park to watch me play and give me his undivided support.

His Ibrox days were over and he was true to his word.

For the remaining years of my career, my father-in-law would attend as many Celtic fixtures as he could accompanied by Connell and my son, Andrew. He even went on to follow the Republic of Ireland national side when I became a fixture under Jack Charlton.

– You have to put this in context.

There is nothing bigger in the world of football than stopping following the side you were reared on, nurtured by and to whom you owed your allegiance by suddenly doing an about-face and starting to attend the games played by their biggest rivals.

When you put Celtic and Rangers into that equation, it's even more startling. I used to tell him later on that it was all a cunning plan for me to miraculously transform Rangers supporters into die-hard Celts!

Don't misunderstand me here. I'm not saying that Tommy became a season-ticket holder who would throw on a hooped jersey before heading off to stand in the Jungle. He was more of a 'neutral' Celtic supporter who maintained a balanced judgement of every game yet still wanted Rangers to tear up most opposition in front of them, but his single-minded clarity and voluntary support for me were very precious.

It was not a view that, I know, was well received within the outer reaches of his family but Tommy was unanimous in his decision. He knew that, in effect, he could perhaps try to fill some of the void that my father had left, by stepping into his shoes and giving me his support.

It is a gesture that I have never forgotten.

The victory over Sporting Lisbon led us to Nottingham Forest in the next round and a classic Battle of Britain clash.

The first leg was down in England and televised by the BBC.

Typically, Celtic weren't expected to do well against a side from south of the border, or so the popular thinking went … in

England; but we showed up on a hard pitch and a frosty night to put in a spirited performance to earn a 0–0 draw.

Frankly, I hadn't been in the best of form around that time but I was happy, early on in the match, when I got out to block an effort from renowned Forest striker Garry Birtles as he bore down on the Celtic goal.

Once we had secured the draw it was all back to Celtic Park and seemingly we had the advantage although, crucially, we had not scored an away goal.

Certainly, charismatic Forest manager Brian Clough talked us up as favourites but, on the night of the return leg, he showed us just why he had won back-to-back European Cups in 1979 and 1980.

He played down Forest's chances and cashed in on our naivety.

We were still playing the 'let-them-worry-about-us' tactics and, although we had a couple of decent penalty claims in the match, two second-half goals from Steve Hodge and Colin Walsh were enough to leave Murdo's eightieth-minute strike in a packed goalmouth a mere consolation.

After the highs of Sporting Lisbon, we had been dealt a lesson by Nottingham Forest – they had won both of their previous away ties in the competition.

In Europe, you have to score when you're on top – especially if you're away from home; as former European Cup winners, Forest knew that and were the masters of the discipline.

As if to rub it in, we found out later that Brian Clough had taken his entire squad off a bus and into the pub that Davie Hay owned in Paisley on their way up from England the night before.

That took a fair bit of cheek.

I bet he charged the drinks to the house as well!

The European nights were perhaps the highlights of Davie's first season as Celtic manager.

Our League form was inconsistent and we never really got a decent challenge going to match eventual champions, Aberdeen. The Dons even held the upper hand over us in the Scottish Cup Final, 2–1 after extra-time.

The controversial moment in that one came in the thirty-eighth minute when Roy Aitken became the first player to be sent off in the showpiece final since 1929.

He had put in a typical Roy challenge on Aberdeen striker Mark McGhee and, as ever, wee Gordon Strachan had got himself involved and was talking to referee Bob Valentine.

Then we were down to ten men as well as trailing 1–0.

Of course, it's always dangerous to count out a Celtic side and when Paul McStay struck with five minutes to go for the equaliser, I genuinely felt it could be our day.

That all came to a halt in extra-time when the duo from the first-half controversy struck again and, from a wee Gordon cross that I had misjudged and made the mistake of coming for, Mark McGhee bulleted a header past me.

Hampden disappointment for the second time that year.

Extra-time disappointment for the second time that year as we had lost the League Cup Final 3–2 to Rangers as well.

That was another stirring comeback as we were 2–0 down on the hour mark until Brian McClair pulled a goal back. Ninety seconds into injury time and an Ally McCoist tackle on Murdo resulted in a penalty as awarded by Bob Valentine – yup, him again!

Mark Reid was a quiet fella and I remember once, before a game against Morton during Billy McNeill's time as manager, when Big Billy was going out of his way to praise our opponents' left-back Jim Holmes. Rumours abounded that a deal was imminent to bring him to Celtic Park and, as Billy raved about him in the dressing room, I could see young Mark, who played in the Holmes position, sink further and further into the bench. It was demoralising and frankly embarrassing.

Yet Mark Reid obviously had the nerves of a tightrope walker as, on this day, he stepped up at Hampden in the League Cup Final to place the ball past Peter McCloy and draw us level at 2–2.

The penalty action wasn't over, however, and in extra-time Roy sent Ally McCoist sprawling in the box.

I had gone the wrong way for Ally's opening penalty but, this time, I guessed right and got down well to stop the kick; but before I could move to muffle the ball completely, the Rangers striker pounced to knock in the rebound.

This would be the first season without silverware at Celtic Park in six years and that, of course, brings a certain pressure on the club's manager.

Davie was eager to press forward with the next campaign which was, possibly, why he called me on the night of 15 June. It's not so unusual to get a phone call from your boss, I guess, but on this occasion I found it a bit odd.

I was tucked up in the Normandy Hotel in Renfrew with my friends as it was the night before my wedding to Ann.

'It's Davie Hay,' said one of the boys as he handed me the phone.

Davie wanted to nip over to see me and the Normandy wasn't exactly just a moment's drive from his house.

I was flattered.

Here was the boss with all the pressure on him, making his plans, dealing with expectations, getting to work on making up for a barren season and he would still find the time to go out of his way and wish one of his players the very best as he embarked on life's biggest adventure.

I wasn't expecting a cheque but I was more than a bit surprised when he arrived clutching a paint-fresh contract.

Mine was up for renewal and although I hadn't exactly been playing hardball, I was looking for a better deal, somewhere around the £350-a-week mark.

To put that into perspective a little, it is a mark of Davie Hay's quality that, from a basic £250, he had stuck another £100 on to my wages in recent times and I was getting used to the extra cash.

It was the kind of issue that I felt would be resolved in the pre-season period but Davie, possibly acting under the orders of the Celtic board, was here to sort the matter out on the eve of my wedding.

I signed it, of course.

Well, we weren't married yet so it was still, technically, *my* decision!

The mysteries of the Celtic Park treasure chest have been the subject of speculation down through the years.

I guess I was happy with what I was earning as I never opted to move on but in terms of even the most modest businesses in 1984, the wages distribution network at Celtic was more akin to 1884!

At the time, the office was run by three people: former player Jim Kennedy (nicknamed 'Pressie' as he had played at the height of JFK's tenure in the White House) and two girls named Irene MacDonald and a young Tracey Bailey.

And that was it.

Which is astounding when you consider the amount of staff required to control the finances, day-to-day running etc. etc. of a modern club like Celtic in today's business world.

They dealt with everything that washed ashore into Celtic Park and wages were no exception.

The drill was simple.

Every last Tuesday morning of the month, Irene would catch a bus from the ground into the city centre and head over to the offices of Celtic chairman Desmond White.

Once there, she would sit patiently as Mr White looked at the list of wages and proceed to allot the required cash into the waxy pokes that served as the wage packets. Once he had completed that process, Irene would collect up all the pay pokes, place them into the heavy-duty black leather bag she carried with her and head back out to catch the returning bus to Celtic Park.

As Irene sat on a double-decker clutching the entire monthly payroll of the management and playing staff of Celtic FC, we would all be gathered up in Joe's Kitchen, tucking into a full Scottish breakfast after our usual hard 'Tuesday on the Track' training.

Once we were fed, we would make our way back down to the ground where one of the lads would keep an eye out for Irene's bus.

She always alighted on to London Road right in front of the stadium and would then make her way back to the office, whereupon she would proceed to hand out our wages to us, player by player, in alphabetical order when we presented ourselves at the window of the office.

Not surprisingly, the wage slips were all handwritten.

Security?

Ah well, there was a fella who went by the nickname of 'Flax' and I don't think anyone knew his real name. He owned a newspaper stand in the middle of the city and he would very often accompany Irene back to the ground on the bus.

Flax dated from Jock Stein's time, was probably a personal friend of the big man and, when you consider that he couldn't walk without the aid of a stick, it would be fair to say that our money was not exactly being protected by G4 Security.

The wage structure at that time was also governed by bonuses. These were the essentials that you would use to pay off overdrafts and such things.

Successful European nights, beating the Rangers, winning a cup or two – all of those events would boost your Celtic Park pay poke.

Handwritten slips, cash wages and heavily waxed envelopes – that was the system that Celtic employed for your monthly remuneration back in the day.

And a day that really wasn't that long ago.

Of course, you didn't think about your bonus when you went into the big games.

We were at Celtic to win trophies and medals, the significance of which was brought home to me in February 1984.

I had been out for dinner with Ann and her family, celebrating Tommy's fiftieth birthday, and then returned to the house to find that I had been burgled. There wasn't much to take but I felt we had been targeted as the biggest losses of all were my first two championship-winning medals, a reserve League Cup medal and a carriage clock that all participants received from Danny McGrain on the night of his testimonial in 1980.

Bizarrely, the clock turned up in a house not a minute's walk from our place and the reserve medal was also returned to me courtesy of the police, albeit in a form that suggested the burglar had jimmied with it for a while.

Unfortunately, some thirty-plus years on, the championship medals have never been found, although, if you're reading this now and feel the urge, then they can be sent to my publisher's address on the opening pages of this book – no questions asked!

What I would have given to add a European medal to my collection. By the winter of 1984, I felt we were improving on the continental front.

The Nottingham Forest game had been a lesson but that was played in a more British fashion so we felt that we would always present a challenge to more European sides. Such was the case with Rapid Vienna of Austria whom we faced in October of that year.

They had Austrian international and legend Hans Krankl playing up front for them and he it was who scored a vital third goal, three minutes from time in the first leg of our European Cup Winners' Cup tie out in Vienna.

It had been a nasty, niggly affair that match with Frank McGarvey going off after a horrific tackle/assault from Reinhard Kienast and then our striker, Alan 'Rambo' McInally, who had replaced Frank, being red-carded with a quarter of the match to go.

Still, we had an all-important away goal in a 3–1 scoreline with Brian McClair hitting the net and felt, as we always did, that it would be a different affair at Celtic Park.

And it was – but that had little to do with the football.

Although, that aspect of it was fair enough on our part.

Brian McClair and Murdo had us 2–0 up by half-time, ahead on the away-goals rule, and when Tommy Burns slotted in a third after the Rapid goalkeeper spilled a Frank McGarvey shot, the tie was over.

The Austrians felt hard done by, especially after that goal as they thought there had been a foul on the keeper, and so Reinhard Kienast got in on the act again by punching Tommy on the back of his neck in the box.

For his trouble, he was sent off although, bizarrely, we weren't awarded a penalty.

When a spot-kick did come, about twelve minutes from the end, it was in our favour as goalkeeper Karl Ehn attempted some more retribution on the maligned Tommy.

As Swedish referee Mr Johansson discussed the matter with his linesman out on the touchline, close to the Jungle, and with the Rapid players in close attendance like a baying mob, a bottle flew out from the terraces.

Rapid defender Rudolph Weinhofer fell to the ground, clutching his head. A credible later account by a Red Cross ambulance man who was on duty attested that there were no marks or blood of any kind on Weinhofer's head.

The whole thing descended into so much farce that it's often forgotten that Peter Grant missed the penalty but somehow the game concluded with about fifteen minutes of added time and we were through to the quarter-final stages of the tournament.

Or so we thought.

Rapid appealed and although they were fined twice to the total tune of £10,000, UEFA ordered the Celtic Park result null and void and scheduled a third fixture at a minimal distance from Glasgow.

That turned out to be Old Trafford and on the night of the fixture it was 'mayhem Manchester' as thousands of our supporters headed down for the match.

My overriding memories of that game are, first of all, my utter surprise at how poor the playing surface was for one of the biggest clubs in world football and, secondly, the only goal of the match scored by a guy called Peter Pacult.

We had spent the opening fifteen minutes hammering down on the Austrians but, once again, our naivety at that level caught us out as Rapid counter-attacked swiftly from one of our corners.

Pacult took off from his own half, breezed past our only defender, Danny McGrain, and bore down on me in goal.

I have to say now that it never occurred to me to haul him down but perhaps I should have, as he rounded me before sliding the ball into the net.

We huffed, we puffed but it just wasn't to be and the 1–0 scoreline was a bitter pill to swallow.

That year, we really felt we could do something in Europe and it was even more galling to see Rapid Vienna, whom we all considered to be a poor side, go all the way to the final.

Thankfully, Everton beat them 3–1 to take the trophy but the whole experience was a bitter one for us. We felt cheated out of a tournament that we thought we could win.

And the pressure was on as our League form once again trailed eventual champions, Aberdeen.

If there was to be retribution, it was to be found in the Scottish Cup and, for its one-hundredth final, we would face Dundee United. Pivotal to our reaching the occasion were the two goals scored in a 3–0 semi-final replay against Motherwell by Davie Hay's biggest signing to date.

It was a statement of belief in our manager that the club had backed him with a £400,000 cheque to tempt promising Scottish striker Maurice Johnston to the club from English First Division outfit Watford.

A flamboyant individual, he arrived with a point to prove and became an immediate presence in the Celtic dressing room. Never short of confidence in his ability, Mo set out to prove his worth as the kind of forward so revered by the Celtic support. He was on the pitch that day at a rain-soaked Hampden, partnering Frank McGarvey up front.

It was a game that Roy Aitken almost missed.

Roy was never injured, never hurt, but on the day of the final he needed an injection into his back to be anywhere close to fit. His inclusion would turn out to be an important factor in a match that looked to be getting away from us at 1–0 down.

Davie Provan had sung a sublime free-kick into the top corner of United's net to bring us level on seventy-six minutes and, with time running out, Roy took a hand in proceedings.

My fellow former Irish Youth player Pierce O'Leary was a Davie Hay signing as well and, when he replaced Paul McStay as a substitute, Roy moved into midfield.

From a determined run down the right-hand side, Roy Aitken delivered a dangerous cross into the box and Frank McGarvey threw himself at it to direct the ball away from veteran United goalkeeper Hamish McAlpine.

It was a classic Celtic moment but United still posed a tangible threat and it took a Pierce O'Leary header off the line in the final minute to ensure that we never had to go to extra-time. A ball was flicked on from a corner, went over my head and was sailing into the net when Pierce made his vital intervention.

In truth, Pierce never played that many games for Celtic but his contribution that day, at that particular instant, certainly altered the story of the match and the immediate history of the club.

Davie Hay had his first trophy as Celtic manager on the same day that I won my first Scottish Cup medal.

Frank would always have dreamed about scoring the winner for Celtic in a major final and it was another example of his ability as well as that never-say-die attitude he exuded throughout his time at the club.

Unbeknownst to him, though, it was all about to come to an end as Davie showed why he was regarded as the 'Quiet Assassin' in the game.

Despite scoring a goal that arguably kept Davie in his job, Frank was released by the club at the end of May. It was, of course, the kind of decision that managers so very often have to make but Frank McGarvey leaving Celtic Park was as big a shock to us as Big Billy's departure had been in 1983.

However, Davie Hay was determined to add a Scottish League title to his list of managerial honours and had decided that his chosen strike force for the coming season would be Brian McClair partnering Maurice Johnston.

LOVE STREET AND THE DOUBLE

FRANK MCGARVEY'S DEPARTURE FROM CELTIC WAS A SIGNIFICANT change to a tight-knit group of Celtic players with whom I had formed close bonds.

Tommy was obviously high on that list as was Danny McGrain whom I think we all looked on as a mentor. How could you not like and admire Danny? He fought back from two career-threatening injuries, including a fractured skull, as well as playing at the peak of his abilities, when he was regarded as one of the best full-backs in the world yet living with diabetes.

Roddie MacDonald was a member of the group even though Billy had sold him to Hearts in 1981 but he lived close to us in and around Newton Mearns and was a good friend.

As was Dominic 'Dom' Sullivan, also an elder statesman to us in a sense as he aged with Danny and perhaps gave Celtic his best years between 1979 and 1983. In my opinion, Dom was an underrated player although Big Billy valued him highly enough to manage him at Aberdeen before bringing him to Glasgow.

Together, we socialised at each other's houses and, naturally, our wives were a part of that fraternity. In time, our families would grow together and continue the shared friendship to this day.

From that perspective, the summer of 1985 was a very important one for Ann and me.

On 14 June, our son, Andrew Patrick Bonner, entered the world. Typically, he was born in the close season.

Well, it's all about timing, isn't it?

It was a huge moment for both of our families as well and I wouldn't have missed it for the world – even though I almost did!

Ann was in labour at Paisley Maternity when I decided to nip out to the car with my father's rosary beads in my hand and indulge in some quiet, reflective prayer dedicated to the safe, imminent arrival of our baby.

I guess that I focused more on the 'quiet' aspect rather than the 'reflective' bit as I fell into a heavy sleep before waking up in a panic and legging it back to the hospital just in time to witness the safe delivery of Andrew, named, of course, after my father.

Wherever he was, I was quite sure the ol' fella would have been shaking his head at my near miss.

This was a good time for me both personally and professionally.

I was settled down, married and now a father for the first time and I think that sense of security can transmit itself into your working life.

It stands to reason that happiness off the pitch can only help the job that you do out on the pitch and, by season 1985–6, I felt in a good place.

Davie Hay was the type of manager who would encourage you in the dressing room. He would come down to me and tell me that I was going to be one of Celtic's best goalkeepers and that I was going to play a big part in the club's history.

Little things, in a sense, but they had a desired effect.

Everybody likes to be told that they're doing well and that the future has a rosy haze about it and I remember one day, just jogging around the Barrowfield training ground that Celtic used and feeling, well, content.

This would be a seminal campaign for the club.

The Scottish Cup was all well and good, but the goal, as always, was to be the champions of Scotland.

Hearts had emerged as the surprise leaders of the pack that year under the guidance of player-managers Alex MacDonald and Sandy Jardine. We had endured a mixed campaign up until the turn of the year but a confident 2–0 win over Rangers on 1 January hinted at the potential of the team.

It was always good to be the winner in the Glasgow derby but the next match against Dundee United at Tannadice was a warning shot across the bows and, for me, a crisis.

I had been struggling with my back and although I can't say that was instrumental in us being 4–1 down at half-time, just prior to the interval the back went into a complete spasm.

When I got back to the dressing room I told our physio, Brian Scott, that I could barely move.

In 1986, teams did not have a second goalkeeper on the bench as they do nowadays and Peter Latchford was away on reserve duty, yet I just knew I couldn't go back out on to the pitch.

Scotty was unequivocal. He started to massage and manipulate the affected area but told me I had no choice other than to play on in the second half. Somehow, I got through the next forty-five minutes and without conceding another goal!

Perhaps the United boys felt secure about the points but I knew when I came off at full-time something would have to be done.

I had been fairly lucky with injuries up until that point although I did have to undergo a hernia operation in 1983. That was at the Bon Secours hospital in Glasgow, an establishment run by nuns. I remember one day during my recuperation the Scottish Cup Final was scheduled to take place and I had left explicit instructions to Ann and everybody else in my family as well as friends that I was planning to spend the afternoon resting in bed and watching the match between Aberdeen and Rangers.

Celtic had put me in a private room and I was really looking forward to an undisturbed showpiece occasion on the box.

And so, there I lay, wondering what it would be like to play in a Scottish Cup Final, trying to work out the formations of both sides, enjoying the pre-match build-up when, just as both captains lined up in the tunnel with their teams around 2.55pm … there was a tap on the door.

I tried to ignore it but it was persistent and getting a little bit louder with every successive knock.

Eventually I shouted 'Come in!' and from behind the door appeared a tiny nun. I thought she was there to change my sheets or adjust my pillows but it turned out she was from a closed order that had a convent down in Helensburgh, a few miles west of Glasgow.

There was a slight hint of the Irish in her accent as she explained that she was in for an operation herself and wanted to meet and have a wee chat with Packie Bonner of the Celtic.

That 'wee chat' lasted for well over two hours and, gentleman that I was(!), I had no alternative but to turn the television set off as she talked and talked and talked. I missed the whole game and that included extra-time!

She may well have been in the congregation a few days later when I went to Mass in the little chapel housed within the hospital.

Certainly, when I went in, I was the only layperson in the chapel. It was like a scene from *The Sound of Music* and there were all these nuns sitting either side of me as we squeezed up in a pew.

I had always been taught reverence in the Church.

You didn't make a move to leave or otherwise until the priest had moved away from the altar after his final blessing, so I was taken a bit by surprise during the final hymn when a young nun, possibly even a novice, nudged me in the ribs and whispered almost in prayer, 'Would you sign me bible for me, Packie?'

Wow! All reverential protocol had been broken and, even now, I often wonder what happened to that nun or, indeed, that bible.

I thought I would go to hell for putting an autograph on the holiest of holies.

Anyway, that operation had been successful but I wondered if I would now need to go under the knife again and at such a crucial juncture of the season.

The injury was a mystery and the treatment was frustrating. I would go over to Celtic Park and, while the rest of the lads headed out to training, I would stretch out on a massage bench while Scotty would strap an ice pack to my back.

It didn't seem to be working and the trouble with that kind of injury is that it can get into your head a bit.

Equally, you start to think that people don't actually believe that there's anything wrong with you and so I would look at Scotty or Davie Hay and wonder if they thought I was at it!

I was sent for X-rays and was diagnosed with ankylosing spondylitis, a form of arthritis that was incurable but controllable.

A fella called Mick Davies was brought in to help me.

Mick was a fitness fanatic and believed 100 per cent in the power of physical stretching so he set out a programme for me as well as a regimen of exercise to get me back to peak condition.

That would have ramifications the following year but, for the moment, I concentrated on the stretches and was happy to note that they were beginning to work.

In fact, within two weeks of Mick's prescription and techniques, my back problem was completely gone – and I was soon back in the team!

Essentially, I missed two months of the season but was now available for the run-in of the campaign.

Peter had been deputising well but when the boys were

knocked out of the Scottish Cup by Hibs at Easter Road in an end-to-end 4–3 defeat, Davie brought me back into the side.

I had spent part of my recovery period watching the games the lads were in and this gave me a rare perspective on how we were performing. I was assessing the team and was itching to get back in and make my own contribution.

Hearts had maintained their form and were still favourites to take the title. That, and the form of Aberdeen who had won the League Cup and were in the hunt for the Scottish Cup, meant there was a perception, in the press, that Celtic and Rangers weren't the force in the land that they once had been.

From my point of view and, I think I can safely say, that of the lads with whom I trained and played, we recognised that there may have been a bit of a dip in form but there was a determination to knuckle down and get on with it.

Besides, the Old Firm were still solid gold at the box office, the hottest ticket in town, and I returned in time to play in one of the most remarkable Glasgow derbies of the modern day at Ibrox.

The weather was atrocious. Rasping wind, horizontal rain – a real dreich Glasgow day – and as a consequence conditions made 'good' football difficult to play but in terms of entertainment there was little to beat this match.

We were 2–0 up when Willie McStay was sent off and we then conceded a goal but, still, 2–1 at half-time was a decent position to be in.

Tommy restored our two-goal lead just after half-time but, in an incredible eleven-minute period, Rangers scored three goals to put themselves 4–3 ahead.

However, our ten men were in no mood to give up the fight and twenty minutes from time Murdo equalised with a fantastic strike from long range to tie the match at 4–4.

Hard to believe that with a quarter of the game still to play no more goals were scored. Both teams came off the pitch to a standing ovation.

Naturally, no goalkeeper is happy to concede four times in a single match but at least our outside shot at the title was still on and that hard-fought point would be crucial at the end of the season.

It would be fair to say that nobody expected anything other than Hearts being crowned champions on 3 May 1986. It was the last day of the campaign and the Edinburgh side required only a draw from their match at Dens Park with Dundee.

We were the only side who could take the title from them but needed to beat St Mirren, in Paisley, by four clear goals and hope for a slip-up at Dens Park.

The boys had been on a great run, unbeaten in sixteen League games, having won the last eight on the bounce. Pleasingly for me, we hadn't conceded a goal in the last four matches.

So, we were very confident about getting a result from Love Street even if we couldn't determine the outcome of the Hearts match and we were a man down in the squad. Alan 'Rambo' McInally called off on the morning of the game with an illness.

Davie Hay's pre-match team talk was one of the briefest he ever gave in his time at the club and consisted mainly of taking us through copies of the press cuttings that virtually anointed Hearts as champions.

We were 4–0 up at the interval and had managed to score one of the best goals that I can ever remember in my time at the club.

Danny started it on the edge of our own box, winning the ball before passing to Paul McStay who then slipped it to big Roy who, in turn passed it back to the onrushing Danny again. When he released Brian McClair down the right, his cross was turned in by Maurice Johnston.

At half-time, news came through that it was 0–0 at Dens Park and Hearts were still in the driving seat.

As I sat quietly in the dressing room, I thought back to 1982 when Aberdeen were 4–0 up against Rangers and we were still being held at home by St Mirren, requiring a win. That day, the news had inspired us but, for a while, it definitely unnerved us as the Dons were clearly going all out to put pressure on our challenge. I wondered if the Hearts boys were feeling that pressure now.

They *had* to know what was happening in Paisley and although 0–0 was enough for the title ... well, one goal from Dundee could cause panic.

Brian put us five-up early in the second half and then it was the waiting game.

When you're a player out on the pitch you get used to the noise of the crowd. Cheering would always follow a goal for either side and I was used to that crescendo of sound even when I conceded.

The spontaneous cheer, well, that's something else altogether.

Until my dying day, I will always remember the shock I felt when, after a move up the pitch that ended with Jim Stewart clutching the ball in the St Mirren goalmouth, this explosion of sound suddenly roared out from behind him and then, like a huge wave, from different groups around the stadium until it came from every single Celtic supporter in the ground.

I have seen the footage many times and it always has the same effect on me, as does even relating the story now.

The hairs on the back of my neck stood to attention as I took in the news, the *only* news that it could possibly be – that Dundee had scored at Dens Park.

We would later find out that it was a fella called Albert Kidd, second-half substitute and a Celtic fan to boot, who had done the damage by scoring the first of his two goals that day – with just seven minutes to go.

In the very last moments of the season – with Hearts just seven minutes or so away from their first top-tier championship in twenty-six years – Kidd had pounced and, ninety miles down the road in Paisley, we were champions.

It was surreal.

I remember looking over at the St Mirren team. Frank McGarvey was playing for them, having moved back to the Buddies after his departure for Celtic the year before.

He was out on the pitch on another unforgettable day in Celtic history, but, sadly for both him and his family, he was not a part of it in the way that he would have loved to have been, but that's the game, isn't it?

What was even more surreal was getting back into the dressing room and there, as large as life, was Alan McInally, fully recovered and ready for his cameo in the spotlight. Seriously, 'Rambo' would strike a pose every time he opened his microwave and the light came on – and this was even before his years at Bayern Munich!

Jim Stewart, former Rangers player, was in goal for the Saints but powerless to stop the Celtic onslaught. Jim would later work and travel with me in our capacity as UEFA technical advisers and, believe you me, we surely talked a lot about 3 May 1986.

Davie Hay had finally brought the title to Celtic Park and in the most dramatic of circumstances. He was the coolest man in the ground that day, almost as if he just *knew* something special was to happen.

The story goes that there was cheering at Ibrox that day where Rangers were playing their final match of the season but that was due to confusion about who had scored. The home support thought it was *Walter* Kidd of Hearts and that we were being denied the title. Apparently there was a hushed silence when the actual news filtered through.

For most of my career to that date, Celtic's biggest challenge for domestic honours came from Aberdeen and Dundee United.

Dubbed the 'New Firm' they had, under Alex Ferguson and Jim McLean respectively, taken up the challenge for the best team in the land winning titles and cups between them.

When I had signed for Celtic, Rangers were champions and treble winners as well, but that was 1978 and, since that high, they had faded, not having won the championship in any of the seasons since I had come into the Celtic first team.

All that was to change in 1986 when they brought in Graeme Souness as player-manager.

It was a significant statement of intent, as was the shopping list of players whom Souness would bring to Ibrox.

In a short space of time, England internationals like Terry Butcher and goalkeeper Chris Wood would form the spine of Souness's Rangers and, over the years, other players of high quality such as Trevor Steven, Ray Wilkins, Trevor Francis and Gary Stevens would join them.

The lure of Scottish football, of course, was the opportunity to play in Europe, something that English clubs could not offer as they had been banned from continental club competition since the Heysel disaster in 1985.

And I would have to say that the Ibrox pay structure must have been a powerful incentive as well. Rangers also had Ibrox in pristine condition and modernised beyond the reach of any other club in the country so expenditure could be turned towards the squad.

Their first challenge was to usurp us as champions.

I remember one of the Celtic directors, Chris White, was quite withering about the Rangers cheque-book policy.

'They're trying to buy success. It will never work,' he said to me one day as yet another international rolled through the doors of Ibrox.

It was a policy that would soon take effect on Celtic, however, and, in a sense, the buying of ready-made players as opposed to nurturing them, which had always been the Celtic way, became the norm.

The press were loving it and suddenly the prospect of Rangers and Celtic scrapping it out at the top of the Scottish game was back in fashion.

We were the champions but I felt we were classed as the underdogs when we met Rangers in the Scottish League Cup Final in October 1986.

Here now was the litmus test of what Rangers were about, according to the newspapers.

The game was a fairly ugly spectacle for the reputation of the sport and I felt we let ourselves down badly at the finish. Rangers had taken the lead in sixty-four minutes but a wonder goal from Brian McClair had us right back in it, but then, six minutes from time, big Roy went up for a ball with Terry Butcher in our box and when they hit the ground, referee David Syme awarded a penalty kick. Peter Grant and I were incensed and, as a result of our protests, we were both booked. Davie Cooper scored and Rangers held out for a 2–1 victory.

What most people remember, however, is that Maurice Johnston was yellow-carded for a second time and as he left the pitch in full view of the Rangers support and the watching millions on television, he blessed himself.

An act, in similar circumstances, that I would imagine he would not look to repeat a few years down the line in his career.

It's an anomaly that only in Scottish football is the blessing considered a provocative gesture and on that occasion all hell broke loose on the full-time whistle.

Davie Hay, ice-cool Davie, who rarely lost it at all, got into an argument with Syme and had to be escorted from the pitch by a posse of police.

As I say, we let ourselves down a bit but, if I'm honest about it, we certainly thought we'd been cheated by a bad penalty decision.

Davie later publicly stated that if it was down to him, 'Celtic would apply to join the English League'.

It was heat-of-the-moment stuff but a template had been set and, although we had played some good football throughout the season, we surrendered the title to our rivals before the end of the campaign.

The policy of buying players for success was upon us and I was delighted when Davie brought in Mick McCarthy from Manchester City for £500,000 during the close season.

I knew Mick from our time spent in the Irish international set-up and I knew what this tough centre-half with the Yorkshire accent could bring to our defence.

So did Davie Hay – but he was never to find out for himself first hand as, before the season kicked off, he had been sacked as manager of Celtic. It seemed bizarre that the club would let him spend that kind of money on a player before giving him his jotters.

I went down to see Davie just after the event. He was, quite naturally, somewhat bitter about it all and I also felt his pain. I had enjoyed working under him as he gave me confidence which, in my opinion, is the key to all that you strive to do in any walk of life.

Davie was a quiet motivator who created an environment for players to flourish in their own way.

How much did I rate the man?

Well, he was the only manager I worked with whom I made a point of going to visit after he had been sacked so I guess that must tell you something.

In his place now was Billy McNeill.

Big Billy was back!

The stakes could not have been higher for the club in the summer of 1987.

Celtic were about to enter their centenary year and the

possibility of ending that year without a trophy, *any* trophy, was unthinkable.

The returning Cesar didn't have his problems to seek, either.

Some of the players, myself included, were out of contract and very quickly we lost Maurice Johnston, Brian McClair, Murdo MacLeod and Alan McInally as well as Danny McGrain, who finally retired from top-flight football at the age of thirty-six.

The manager had to move quickly and did so, bringing in Chris Morris, Andy Walker and Billy Stark in a short space of time.

For my part, I was never going to be difficult to deal with as I enjoyed being at the club and wanted to be a part of the centenary campaign.

I had stuck hard to Mick Davies's fitness regime to the point that Tommy and myself, as well as a few others, would run through a programme before training at Barrowfield.

Ann and I had gone home to Donegal over the summer as well and I had continued my pre-season fitness while I was there through long walks and running for a few miles every day.

I returned to Celtic Park a week earlier than usual, specifically to work with Mick. We would venture down to Queen's Park where he had identified a steep hill that we would race up and then jog back. For most of that week we continued doing hill-runs, followed by all-out sprinting sessions and body work.

And it really paid off as I felt that I was peaking in my fitness. I had never been so in tune with my body.

From my normal position of staying in with the pack at training, I now found myself leading the early pre-season runs around Strathclyde Park and feeling exceptionally sharp.

With that degree of fitness comes a mental strength that takes you to another level of performance altogether.

Big Billy was returning to a different Packie Bonner from the one he had left four years before.

I was now a married man and father, had established myself as first-choice goalkeeper at the club and, in addition, I was an internationalist as well.

Billy McNeill was an intimidating character but I felt a lot more confident about dealing with that now and, indeed, we would have the odd argument out on the training ground wherein I would end up telling him to try and play in goal.

One of the big changes was the arrival of Tommy Craig as assistant to Billy.

Tommy was a graduate of the SFA Largs coaching courses who thought not just about the way his teams played but also about the opposition. We were on a pre-season trip to Sweden that summer when Billy was called back to Glasgow to deal with a tribunal hearing on Brian McClair's move to Manchester United.

Tommy Craig took us for training and we spent a number of days working on a particular method he had devised to shut down the opposition attack right from their own penalty box.

Nowadays, they call it a high-pressing game and it was the first time we had been coached on how to defend properly *as a team from back to front.*

I had just started my own coaching badges with the SFA and it fitted perfectly into my thoughts as a key member of our defensive strategy so, naturally, I took a particular interest in the theory behind it all.

In a sense, it pretty much went against the Celtic philosophy of all-out attack but it was a more balanced way to play a match.

The Irish national team, now under Jack Charlton, had a similar approach – 'Put them under pressure' – although not necessarily with the same offensive tack as the Celtic ethos.

In all my professional career to that date, we had never really worked on this part of the game and it opened my eyes. The moral is that you never stop learning in this game of ours. Every day is an education.

I know that all of the players were equally as impressed and it was a tactic that we took into the biggest season of our careers.

Celtic's centenary year was the stuff of folklore.

From losing a vital third of our team in the close season, bringing in a new manager albeit for his second stint at the job and facing a Rangers team hell-bent on building a squad of winners, it was deemed as almost miraculous that we went on to win a League and Scottish Cup double, Celtic's first since 1977.

Big Billy had persuaded the board to invest in the team and to supplement the attack he brought in Joe Miller from Aberdeen and Frank McAvennie from West Ham United.

These were pivotal signings, loaded with intent.

Joe was a crucial element in the Aberdeen set-up and it was thought that the Dons would refuse to sell him, particularly to a rival club, but the deal was too good for them to turn down.

Frank had been the top goalscorer in England a couple of years before and his signing was a definite coup for the club.

What a presence he was in the dressing room! A larger-than-life character with an infectious personality that soon permeated Celtic Football Club.

Roy Aitken had intimated to Billy that we needed a real big-name player to join us and Frank McAvennie could have had that printed on his business cards.

He wasn't everybody's cup of tea, especially up in the board-room, but he was a huge part of what we achieved that season and, in my book, one of the best centre-forwards I ever played with in my career.

Frank could score goals with either foot, was a great header of the ball, had huge energy levels and thought nothing of defending if he felt it was for the good of the team.

He loved the Rangers games. Let's face it, we all did, but to Frank they were the centre of the universe. A heaving cauldron of passion that was ideally suited to his personality.

Our record against our old rivals that year was truly the form of champions – three victories, one draw in the League.

Although, due to a virus that struck me around August and an injury that I picked up just before Christmas, I only played in one derby that season – but it was a vital one.

We turned up at Ibrox on 20 March in control of our own destiny, knowing that a victory would put us six points clear of Rangers at the top of the table.

It was an enthralling encounter, one of the most enjoyable derbies in my career. I'd had a couple of decent saves. One came from an Ian Ferguson drive, which I managed to turn away for a corner, and then a fierce shot from Ray Wilkins, which I thought I had touched over only to see it bounce back off the bar, at which point I had to hurry back and smother the rebound.

Paul McStay, without doubt our most outstanding player that season, had a terrific match and put us ahead in the second half with a fantastic first-time volley from the edge of the box but Rangers equalised when a shot came through a ruck of players from Danish player Jan Bartram. I saw it late and dived quickly to my left but it came in close to the post.

Eleven minutes from the end, though, we got our reward when a Tommy Burns corner was met with a misdirected header from Anton Rogan and cannoned in off the chest of Andy Walker.

That was typical Anton!

A couple of years earlier, I had been at a dinner dance in Belfast when I was approached by somebody to tell me that Celtic were signing a young fella from Northern Irish club Distillery and that he would be popping in that night. Could I possibly meet with him?

I said, 'Surely,' but, as the night wore on, there was no sign of the guy. Eventually, this fella wanders into the event wearing a pair of overalls. He'd obviously just come from his work and was completely covered in paint and not just on his clothes, either. I reckoned there must have been more paint on the boiler suit, his face and his hair than could possibly go on any wall.

'Ah, I'm coming over there to Glasgow soon to join you. Me name's Anton Rogan,' he said, offering me a well-painted hand and with a big smile on his face.

I hoped he was a decent player because he sure as hell wasn't going to make a career as a painter and decorator!

I liked Anton a lot and considered him to be an undervalued player in the squad, possibly because he wasn't a glamorous figure to the support but, then again, there weren't many players who came out of the inner city of Belfast and played for Celtic.

Things had a way of happening to Anton.

We lost a match one time at Celtic Park and Big Billy fair flew into the dressing room afterwards to get laid into us. Such was his rage that, on seeing a spare boot lying on the floor, he kicked it in a fury. If you are David Beckham, it hits you on the corner of the eye and you have a distinguished scar for the girls to rave about.

If you're Anton Rogan the boot flies above your head, smashes into an ancient fan heater that had resided in that corner attached to the wall since Billy McNeill was a reserve player and, as the contraption explodes, all the dust and dead wasps and flies that have gathered in it for years come pouring down on to your head!

Anton, Mark McGhee and I occasionally went fishing just outside Glasgow. Fishing was and still is a relaxation for me. The White Cart River certainly wasn't like the sanctuary back in Donegal that I prized so much in my life, but it did the trick.

In certain areas of the river there was peace, solitude, the chance to be at one with nature and perhaps be lucky enough to pick up a few trout.

We hadn't long spread out the length of the bank, almost crawling to the water's edge in case we frightened the fish away, and were just settling down to a quiet day's fishing when we heard this almighty roar coming from upstream.

Mark and I dropped our rods and took off, fearing the worst for our friend; yet, when we reached him, there was Anton, up to his waders in the stream, rummaging around the boulders like some old grizzly bear!

He told us he was just 'tickling the fish'.

Apparently he'd quickly got bored by the more 'traditional' way of catching trout. Of course, this was nothing new for our Anton whose threshold of boredom was usually no longer than twenty minutes. He has a tattoo of his name on his arm but it's missing the last letter because he got bored during the session and decided to leave!

The centenary season was a magical period and I know it's easy to say this after the event, but I do remember thinking at the time that there was something tangible about it all – a feeling of everything being as it was meant to be.

For that whole season I felt as if we were just actors playing our parts in a drama that was bigger than the actual story of the season.

People talk about that Celtic 'mystique'. Big Billy always did and certainly there was a powerful flow to it in season 1987–8.

We never felt that it was all over until the final minutes.

Take, for example, the Scottish Cup semi-final that year between ourselves and Hearts.

This was a game in which I felt I was about to be sent off.

With the teams tied at 0–0, Brian Whittaker crossed a high ball into the area which was sailing towards the goal-line. I went up for it under the crossbar looking to make a comfortable catch when Hearts defender Davie McPherson barged into me from behind, taking me out of the play and letting the ball nestle in the back of my net.

It couldn't be a goal.

Davie had made no attempt to play the ball and instead had pushed me out of its flight path.

It was a clear case of obstruction but I was absolutely staggered to see referee Kenny Hope point back to the centre spot having awarded the goal.

I was beyond furious and the next time the ball came into the box and Kenny was up with play, I let him know about it in no uncertain terms.

I knew Kenny well.

He often came across to Ireland to officiate at some of the friendly internationals we played in and it wasn't unusual for him to come for a couple of drinks with myself and the squad in a Dublin hotel after the match.

But, on this day, at that moment, I let rip with a raging tirade against him and Kenny Hope stared at me. In the passing seconds I could actually see his eyes change as if he was looking at me for the very first time and he reached for his pocket.

It wasn't very often that I lost it on a football pitch and I still maintain the decision to give the goal was an outrageous one but I had lost my discipline and was cursing and swearing directly at a referee.

In the event, Kenny booked me for dissent, which was a relief although the sense of injustice was still palpable.

Perhaps it flowed through the team as, with ninety seconds left to play, substitute Mark McGhee shot through a ruck of players and into the back of the net ... 1–1.

In most seasons that would have entailed a replay but not with this Celtic side, with this group of players.

From the resumption, the lads took the game to Hearts and were rewarded in the final seconds when Andy Walker hooked a Mark knockdown high into the net.

It was a classic Celtic moment. A testament to the fact that this was a season when we would not be denied.

And so we were in the Cup Final and also had the chance to clinch the title in front of our own fans when Dundee rolled into Glasgow a couple of weeks later.

Officially, there were 60,000 at the game but I reckon you could have stuck another 10,000 on to that figure. I had never seen a crowd like it and when we wrapped it up with a 3–0 victory they surged on to the pitch to celebrate. We ended up coming back out on to the ledge at the front of the directors' box to join in the celebrations.

I have no doubt that it was the best campaign of my career at Celtic. The only thing I wanted to do now was add my second Scottish Cup winner's medal to the collection but there was a problem.

Although I had stuck faithfully to Mick Davies's stretching programme, I had noticed that it was having less and less of an impact on my back. About five minutes after I had completed the exercises, I would start to feel a stiffness at the base of my spine. It meant that I found it difficult to stand and listen to Billy issuing instructions on the training ground.

I would be stretching and moving about, possibly giving the impression that I wasn't taking it all in, which Big Billy wasn't best pleased about, as you can imagine.

Scotty would say to me: 'Listen, don't let anyone tell you that you have a disc problem. You have ankylosing spondylitis and it's controllable.'

That may well have been the case but now I was finding that the pain was travelling down the side of my leg and giving me discomfort.

It all came to a head the Tuesday before the Cup Final when we were training up at Barrowfield.

Once again, I was having an issue with the back stiffening up but now, in addition and probably as a direct result of that as the pain was travelling down the sciatic nerve, my calf muscle tightened up like a snare drum.

It was like having a rock in my shoe and extremely uncomfortable.

Scotty was full of reassuring noises about teasing it out as he was convinced I had just pulled a muscle, but on the day of the final itself, with us down at Seamill as usual and my calf showing no signs of improvement, I knew a decision had to be made.

After breakfast, I put my kit on and went through a fitness test – which I promptly failed. I couldn't even stand on my toes.

Looking back, I'm not even sure if it was myself or Scotty who told Big Billy that I was out of the game but I do remember taking myself away out to the back of the hotel and sitting on the wall that looks down towards the beach. All alone, still clad in my training gear, on a beautiful spring morning and with the lash of the waves coming ashore, I stared out to sea with tears in my eyes.

To miss a Cup Final was always devastating but to miss *this* Cup Final in *this* year was especially heartbreaking.

Peter Grant was also missing out. He'd broken a bone in his foot the month before and, although he had made a remarkable recovery, the match against Dundee United was coming along too quickly for him.

Together we would watch the lads do what they had been doing all season – taking the game to the final minute and coming out on top.

I've said it before and I'll say it again – we were only actors playing out a part that season.

Once again, we found ourselves a goal down in the second half but, with a quarter of the game to go, Frank drew us level.

He was the man for the big occasion and with everyone around Hampden checking their watches and thinking about extra-time, Frank it was who stole into the box and buried a shot into the United net.

The cup was ours and what a party we had. We all finished up in Mark McGhee's house later that evening, players and wives altogether, singing and dancing into the wee hours. The season was over. Lads from home in Donegal, close friends, Neil Campbell, his dad Charlie and Patsy 'the Yank' Boyle got the call to come along, too. They would talk about it for years. How could it get any better, celebrating with Frank McAvennie and Jenny Blyth!

More importantly, the centenary double was ours as well and I still meet people to this day who regard the squad from that season as the best they saw in their time as supporters.

And it could not have been achieved without Big Billy.

On the first day that I returned to Celtic before the start of that season, I saw him striding down through the corridor at Celtic Park, chest out, rubbing his hands together and giving the impression that all was well.

That *he* was back in charge!

The club needed a lift.

They got it quickly and look where it took us.

Who knows what could have been achieved in the years to come? But there would only be one more triumph under Billy McNeill, a Scottish Cup and no more League titles.

The seeds of that despairing period, I feel, lay in the immediate aftermath of the clinching of the double.

Actually, in the bus, on the way back from Hampden.

Big Billy knew what the next move was – Celtic had to build on this campaign.

He had told the board that Rangers would not take that season lying down. That they would come back stronger and that Celtic must prepare to meet that challenge all over again.

As he and Tommy Craig sat on the bus with the Scottish Cup

on the front dashboard, they plotted their next moves in the transfer market.

Allegedly, top of the list were two experienced players of the highest quality – Peter Beardsley and Chris Waddle. Beardsley had just won the English League title with Liverpool and Waddle was the star man at Tottenham Hotspur but neither would get their chance in European football due to the ongoing ramifications of the English ban from the Continent.

This would be the card that Big Billy would play to tempt these players north, just as Rangers had been doing for a couple of seasons.

Yet, as it turned out, only one player was brought into the club during the close season and that directly affected me, but before any of that happened I was off to Germany for the 1988 European Championship with the Republic of Ireland.

BREAKTHROUGH WITH BIG JACK

JACK CHARLTON WAS APPOINTED AS MANAGER OF THE REPUBLIC of Ireland in February 1986. It was a bold move by the FAI and a break with tradition.

The story goes that former Liverpool manager Bob Paisley was considered to be the favourite and, as the members of the committee broke for lunch, he had the job in the bag. By the time they got back, though, they had looked at another Geordie. Jack Charlton was not only in the frame, he was the choice candidate.

I first felt his impact when I headed out with the Irish squad to that tournament in Iceland that I mentioned at the start of the book.

Usually, the squad gathered in Dublin and those players who had been born in the capital were allowed to go and stay with their families while others, like myself and English-born players such as Tony Galvin, Gerry Peyton and Chris Hughton stayed at the hotel.

At those times, Sean Walsh would come to the hotel and keep me company and we would take off, on the odd occasion, up towards the Dublin hills or invariably to a local hostelry for a 'bottle or two of club orange'. I would have a wee bit of fun passing *him* off as Tony Galvin to anyone who asked for our autographs.

Sean was very obliging. A shy lad, who just didn't like to refuse, and so, to put the record straight, if you did get Tony's signature back in the day, then it might not be entirely genuine and for that both Sean and myself would like to apologise profusely!

Ah, come on – we were just young fellas!

All of that stopped when Jack Charlton took over.

He had played in the greatest Leeds United side ever and studied under manager Don Revie who believed firmly in establishing a family feel among his players.

All activities, either inside or outside of the hotel, were done together with everybody. Nobody was left out and this was the philosophy that Jack Charlton believed in and so, from here on in, there was to be no fragmenting of the group.

If one player wanted to go out for a coffee, we all went along as well, under the watchful eye of the larger than life team physio Mick Byrne and the kitman, little Charlie O'Leary.

In time, it fostered a camaraderie in us all and undoubtedly was a cornerstone of the success we achieved.

David O'Leary had, as I said, opted out of the end-of-season trip to Iceland and that was a decision that big Jack would remember. As it happened, we won the only international trophy that Ireland has ever won on that trip but it was really about Jack Charlton assessing us and seeing what he had at his disposal.

My caps tally up until that period was poor.

There were a couple of highlights such as the night World Cup winners Italy came to play a friendly out at Dalymount Park in Dublin. That was an incredible evening with the old stadium bursting at the seams and the Gardaí controlling the crowds with a kennel's worth of Irish wolfhounds!

The supporters were practically on the pitch and sitting on the roof of the stand, and every time I looked off to my right I could see this huge old Irish wolfhound, seriously about the height of a horse, standing to attention and on his lead waiting for the first sign of trouble.

I often wonder just what the hell the sophisticated Italians, kings of the world, made of it all. Especially when they came out to inspect the pitch pre-match with their Armani suits on covered by expensive beige mackintosh overcoats. They were like touring film stars and Deputy Dawg and his pals were there to protect them!

I had also realised a dream to play at Wembley Stadium where we narrowly lost 2–1 to England in 1985 but, the reality was that, between 1981, when I made that debut against Poland, and 1986, by which time I was twenty-six, I had only started nine games for my country.

That was another thing that changed under Big Jack.

I most certainly did not have the best of tournaments out in Iceland but Jack Charlton saw something in me and, even though he never actually made a direct statement to me, it soon became apparent that I was his first-choice goalkeeper.

I played in all of the qualifiers for the European Championship of 1988.

Interestingly enough, Scotland were in our group and we faced up to them in February 1987 at Hampden.

This was a big occasion for me.

I played my club football in Scotland.

I would, potentially, be up against my Celtic team-mates as Roy Aitken, Paul McStay, Brian McClair and Maurice Johnston were in the Scottish set-up. Scotland were very much the favourites as they had home advantage and had drawn 0–0 with us back in October in Dublin. And yet, when I look at the team we put out on the night, there was no shortage of quality based on the clubs from which we had drawn the pool of players.

Big Jack always joked about jumping around Irish graveyards in the dead of night looking at names on headstones from which he could find another Irishman to play for him.

In defence we had Paul McGrath and Kevin Moran, both Manchester United. Mick McCarthy was still at Manchester City and Ronnie Whelan played for the English champions, Liverpool, as did Mark Lawrenson, Ray Houghton and John Aldridge. Tony Galvin was at Spurs, Frank Stapleton was also a Manchester United player and, finally, Liam Brady, ex-Arsenal, Juventus, Inter Milan, Sampdoria and, at that time, winding down his Serie A career with Ascoli, was in midfield. Everywhere you looked there was a wealth of experience at the very highest level of the game.

Oddly enough, we were billeted in the Macdonald Hotel which, even on a stormy night, is about a two-minute walk from my house.

It felt like the whole Irish team were coming to my home – my townland, as we would say in Donegal, and it was a personal visit for a few days.

We would go for our usual walks (all together, of course, as per the Big Jack template), this time through Rouken Glen Park which was directly adjacent to the hotel, and I would point out to the lads where Ann and I took Andrew to play on the swings.

Actually, I half expected to see them there along with Tommy Burns's wife Rosemary and their kids.

On the night, a Mark Lawrenson goal was enough to win us the game and, crucially, prove to us that we could get results on the road.

At the end of the campaign, the group that also comprised Luxembourg, Bulgaria and Belgium was tight. We were at the top of the table, having completed our programme of fixtures, but the final match saw Scotland go out to Bulgaria. The Scots couldn't qualify but if they could beat the Bulgarians then we would go through.

Andrew was only two at the time and he stretched across my arms as I sat back in a chair at home watching the match. If my son had any notions about sleeping, they were dashed late on in the game when Hearts midfielder Gary Mackay swept an unbelievable shot into the Bulgarian net and Andrew ended up about six feet in the air!

There were ten minutes left to play and I had to talk to somebody – *anybody* – or I would burst, so I phoned Connell at work and proceeded to give him a running commentary on the rest of the match.

Once the news had finally sunk in that we had qualified for our first ever major international tournament, the press got on the phone and asked me to come down to the airport with a bottle of champagne that they had supplied and greet the Scottish party.

I guess it made for a decent story.

And so to Germany and a group consisting of England, Holland and the Soviet Union but, first of all, I needed my sabbatical back in Ireland. Big Jack had given us all some time off so I returned to Donegal for a few days before I was due to meet up with the Irish squad in Dublin. I needed this time to prepare myself for the biggest stage that I could potentially be playing on and a great part of it was spent with Toney Gallagher.

Toney was family, as his father, Owney Gallagher, was Dad's uncle.

Owney had been a remarkable fella back in the days when I was growing up. He had multiple sclerosis and spent a lot of time in this enormous black wheelchair. It was very much a design of its time with a huge handle at the back and, in many ways, looked like a go-kart.

Certainly that was what Denis and I used it for on those occasions when Owney, perched on a seat outside his house on a beautiful summer's day, allowed us to push it up to the top of the hill close to his house and career back down in it at breakneck speed. All the while, Owney would just shift his head back and laugh uproariously at our devil-may-care attitude.

Little did he know the number of times that myself and Denis ended up overshooting and ploughing into a nearby field.

He was an enormous influence on us and his house was very much the meeting place for many of the local fellas, including my dad, who would come over for the craic. Many a game of cards was played, all around the table, with Denis and myself watching on in amazement, listening to the stories and the wit.

Toney had inherited his father's appetite for life and he was always someone I could turn to whenever I felt the pressures building up all around me.

There was only one place to go, then, when I returned home and, for a pleasant week, Toney took me out on his boat so that I could fish and just yarn away with him about the past and the shared bond we had for this particular part of Donegal.

I can think of no better way to prepare for a major life event than that and so, relaxed by my few days of unwinding, I headed off to join up with the lads and the great adventure we were about to undertake.

The German efficiency was no myth as we were whisked away almost immediately on landing in Stuttgart without all the rigmarole of customs and passports.

I was sharing a room with Gerry Peyton and we were like a couple of schoolkids on their first trip abroad when we discovered, to our delight, that the hotel backed on to the football pitch where we could train.

This was brilliant.

You could get changed in your room and make your way down to training so we got our gear on, stole into kitman Charlie O'Leary's room and nicked a football to take out on to the pitch.

As we kicked a ball at each other, testing the bounce of the grass, we were suddenly joined by Big Jack and his son, John, who had taken a wander to familiarise themselves with their surroundings.

'What you doing?' he asked casually.

Gerry and I thought we had been caught by the headmaster out of hours but when we explained that we were just getting a feel for the pitch, he did the most extraordinary thing.

Jack Charlton, manager of the Republic of Ireland, pointed to his son and said: 'Right, give the ball out to the young fella there and we'll try a couple.'

With Gerry and I taking it in turns to go in goal, John Charlton lobbed the ball towards the penalty box and Big Jack, dressed in his tracksuit and his training shoes, would catch the ball full on the volley and rocket it towards us.

It took me back to the Keadue Rovers days as the lads wandered in an hour or so before a match and an informal game of cross-it-in would ensue out on the pitch with all of us still wearing our jumpers and jeans before we changed into our strips.

With Jack Charlton, you came to expect the unexpected and this was typical of a man who could create the most relaxed of environments for his players.

Of course, the big game was the one against England.

Here was a fixture that had caught the imagination of the Irish public. There was always a wee bit of mischief in putting one over the English, given our history, but this represented the most important match that the Republic had ever played. Our first in a major international tournament.

Big Jack wasn't really a coach as the definition would be today. He was a manager – a manager of players – and it was his job to get the very best out of that group of players.

Our training sessions were basically warm-ups, shooting practice when Gerry and I worked our butts off, and then playing a game.

In Jack's opinion, if you had to be coached at this level in the art of passing, ball control, technique etc. etc., then you really weren't an international footballer. He told us once that if he explained ten things to each one of us then there was a fair chance that nobody would be thinking the same thing out on the pitch, but if he told all of us just three things then it was more than likely that we would all be on the same wavelength.

Simple philosophies and tactics that worked very well for us during this period.

As we sat in the hotel, just before we headed off to the Neckarstadion ahead of the English match, Jack went into his team-talk.

We would all be stunned to learn later that Glenn Hoddle had been left on the bench which was a bit of a relief, I think, for Big Jack, because he was paranoid about that ball over the top that Hoddle could deliver just about better than anyone else and that would let the supreme poacher, Gary Lineker, in on goal.

Lineker was the obvious threat but Jack thought that Peter Beardsley was just as dangerous and talked about him at some length even though the gist was simple. He pointed out that the defenders weren't to let Beardsley turn with the ball as that was a favourite manoeuvre of the Geordie striker. He would try to find space and run at his marker either to play a penetrating pass or simply get a shot away.

'If he picks up the ball then nail 'im and if he gets past one of you then the second man has to come in fast and get the tackle in. DON'T LET HIM RUN!'

With the best wishes and tactical thoughts of Jack Charlton we walked out on to the pitch on a beautiful summer's day in Stuttgart for what I would consider to be the biggest game of my career up until that time.

We were the underdogs, certainly in the group, but also in this game.

Ireland had never been to a European Championship before and it was the proudest moment of my life when we all turned towards the flag of our country as 'Amhrán na bhFiann' ('The Soldiers' Song') rang out around the stadium.

The preliminaries over, we lined up in formation and there was England staring at us.

The England of Lineker and Beardsley, Bryan Robson, John Barnes and Chris Waddle etc. etc. and behind them, at the opposite end of the pitch to me, was Peter Shilton.

The last time we had shared the grass, Peter was already a well-established England international, playing out his time at Stoke City before that move to Nottingham Forest, and I was the interim goalkeeper for Finn Harps, seventeen years old and clinging to a dream that I could, somehow, some *way*, break into the professional game. Finn Park with a respectable crowd, curious to see an English First Division side with a smattering of star names take on their local boys before the real business began in earnest.

As I mentioned before, we had exchanged handshakes at the end of the match, but I was quite certain that was not the lingering memory for Peter Shilton that it was for me.

And now here we were.

The last line of defence for our country – the highest honour you could have in the game – and playing on the biggest stage available in European international football.

Wasn't this why I had pursued my dream of professional football so strongly?

I thought of the ol' fella.

He would have been here for this one, completing the circle from the mini-transit van we used for transportation and the open-air changing rooms behind a bush that was our lot when he followed Denis and I through Keadue Rovers right up until the five-star hotel accommodation, air-conditioned coaches and well-pressed team kit that was the green, white and gold of our country.

Oh yes, he would have definitely been here for this one.

And I thought of Ireland.

My roots, my identity.

It was common enough craic around the time for people to point fingers at our players and make fun of the Yorkshire, Cockney and Scottish accents that proliferated in our dressing room playing under the 'Geordie' manager, but every single member of the Irish set-up, from gaffer to players to kitman and physiotherapists, was totally and utterly committed to representing the Irish flag and people out on the field of play.

This was where we could make our mark.

And we did so within ten minutes when Ray Houghton looped a header beyond Peter Shilton and into the net.

The Irish contingent in the stadium went absolutely crazy. They had hoped and now the realisation of that hope was unfolding before them.

We were 1–0 up against England, one of the favourites for the tournament and, well, *England!*

An early lead is a double-edged sword as it can calm the nerves a bit but, equally, it can shift the focus for a while and asks the question – 'Defend that lead or try to increase it?'

In the game of cliché, the popular notion is that you are never more vulnerable than after scoring and, like many other clichés, there is an element of truth to it.

Ronnie Whelan would crack the English bar later on in the match but for the greater proportion of those ninety minutes we were up against it.

I am often asked what, in my opinion, was my best game in an Irish jersey and I always reply, 'England, 1988.'

The stature of the opposition is a factor, of course, but, from a purely football perspective and that of a goalkeeper, my eye was in that day.

At times, it seemed to be a personal duel between myself and

Gary Lineker who also clipped the bar, but there were other English players who peppered our goal with shots and headers such as Robson, Barnes and Neil Webb.

Glenn Hoddle emerged from the bench and, just as Jack feared, he started to flight those balls over the top that could cause any defence in the world to look static.

Ironically, after the game, Big Jack slaughtered me in the press saying that I should have come for Hoddle's penetrating passes. However, I stood my ground with my manager as Glenn had the ability to clip that diagonal pass, from the middle of the pitch, over Mick McCarthy's shoulder between himself and Chris Morris, to the predatory Lineker.

I *couldn't* come for that kind of ball. It would have put my goal at risk.

It really was one of those games where practically every time I was called into action I made a block or a parry or even held on to the shot culminating in a last-minute save when I deflected a header from six yards out around the post. It truly was Ireland's day – ninety minutes that would go on to define the next decade for Irish international football.

And at the end of it all, we emerged with a victory.

Jack Charlton, thirty-five English caps as a player, brother of Bobby who was arguably the greatest English striker of all time just as *he* was the linchpin of an England team that had won the World Cup – that same Jack Charlton had taken a side of Irish underdogs and given them their biggest scalp in international football – Republic of Ireland 1 England 0.

This was the result that transformed the Irish nation and their relationship with football.

Up until that time we had always enjoyed a core of support and there were lads, like Sean Walsh, who followed the team wherever we played.

Sean wore a distinctive green Aran sweater that you could

pick out from about ten miles away. He maintained that his lucky green jumper, worn to every single Irish international match regardless of the temperature, was the reason we enjoyed such a run of success. This was Sean's time as well as a lot of the fellas who we got to know as they followed us around Europe on our various trips and I was happy that they were getting to enjoy something really big.

But the England result was the catalyst, I believe, for turning the whole country on to the Republic of Ireland football team. It also put us at the top of the group alongside the Soviet Union, our next opponents, who, to the surprise of many, had beaten the highly fancied Dutch 1–0.

The Soviet game was to take place in Hanover and, to my mind, was a tougher fixture than the opener against England. This was before the break-up of the Soviet Union which meant that they had a huge pool of players from which to select a squad.

I had already seen the kind of quality they had at club level a couple of years before when Celtic had drawn Dynamo Kiev in the European Cup. After being held 1–1 in Glasgow, we went out 4–2 on aggregate after a 3–1 defeat on a bitterly cold evening in Kiev.

Vasiliy Ratz, Igor Belanov and Anatoliy Demyanenko were the star men for the Soviet champions and when you added to the national side the likes of Oleg Kuznetsov, Aleksei Mikhailichenko, both of whom would eventually play at Rangers, and the man whom I considered to be the finest goalkeeper in the world at that time, Rinat Dasaev, then here was a side capable of winning the European Championship.

If the England game was my finest display for the Republic then I feel that the game against the Soviet Union was the finest we ever played as a team with that particular group of players.

In fact, I honestly believe that, had we won that night after leading at half-time through a spectacular Ronnie Whelan volley before Oleg Protasov equalised with fifteen minutes left to play, we would have gone on to the final of the tournament.

Why wouldn't we believe that?

Ultimately, holding on to Ronnie's goal and the victory would have put us into the semi-finals.

I was furious about losing the goal. It was, after all, the first we had lost in eight consecutive matches. We had been on that good run but also, in the immediate aftermath, I wondered if I could have done more to prevent it.

The Soviets played a long ball out to the right-hand side of our box and Belanov, with his foot fairly close to Kevin Moran's head, had looped it onwards into the path of Protasov. My instinct was that I was not going to get to it first but, in that split second, the Soviet forward controlled the ball and drilled it between my legs and into the net.

I repeatedly slapped the turf in disgust.

Anyway, the result meant that we only required a draw against Holland to progress to the semi-finals but, before that one, I had a reoccurrence of my back spasm.

It was, as these things so often are, the most innocuous of events that brought it on. I was washing my hands in the bathroom that Gerry and I shared when it happened.

I cried out to Gerry, who was lying on his bed, 'Oh no ... my back has gone!'

It was like half-time in the Dundee United match from 1986 again so I immediately sought out the Irish physio, Mick Byrne, and we started some stretches but even they were having little impact.

I was faced with a stark choice.

This was the morning of the Dutch match, a 3pm kick-off, and I went out for a fitness test as did Paul McGrath but I clearly wasn't fit. I told Mick that I was going to see Jack who was bil-leted a couple of floors below us in the hotel. Mick must have phoned down because, when I arrived at his room, the door was ajar as though he was expecting me.

I knocked, but there was no reply so, very gently, I pushed the door open and there he was, Jack Charlton, already on his way to being an Ireland legend and he was washing his socks in the washbasin of his bathroom.

'What you want?' he said without looking up.

'Jack …' I started tentatively as I didn't think he was a man who took bad news well, '… my back has gone into spasm. I don't think I can play today.'

There was a seemingly interminable pause while I watched the manager of the Irish national football team squeeze the soap out of his wet socks.

'Listen …' he spoke without lifting his eyes up from the basin, '… if you don't play this afternoon, you will be letting yourself down. Not only that, you'll be letting me down and, worse than that, you'll be letting your country down. Now, f*** off.'

As motivational speeches go, it was brief and to the point – and I got the point!

I crept back up to my room to recommence the stretches.

There was about an hour to the team briefing and lunch so I kept at it with the words of Big Jack ringing in my ears. Given the circumstances, I was a little bit late for the meeting and, when I arrived at the restaurant downstairs, the squad were already seated.

To this day I still don't know what Big Jack had told the lads about me but, as soon as I entered the room, every single one of them burst out laughing!

I sheepishly went to a chair and sat down.

I suppose a combination of the stretches, a little bit of rest, Mick Byrne's healing hands and, I have to say, the boiling heat

THURSDAY November 12 1987

Daily Record SPORTSFRONT

REAL MACKAY!

BUBBLY BOYS . . . Scots goal hero Gary Mackay is the centre of attraction as Eire goalkeeper Pat Bonner (right) toasts the Scotland team with champagne at Glasgow Airport last night. Pat's Celtic team-mate Roy Aitken joins in as head waiter.
Picture: ERIC CRAIG

BULGARIA..0 SCOTLAND..1
MATCH REPORT—PAGE 46

ENGLAND IN EURO STROLL
MATCH REPORT—PAGE 47

Gary's Irish jig..

By ALEX CAMERON

SCOTLAND'S Gary Glitter—goal ace Gary Mackay of Hearts—jetted home last night to a hero's reception at Glasgow Airport.

Andy Roxburgh's super sub sent millions of armchair fans into a fireside frenzy with his sensational late winner against Bulgaria in Sofia...

And sent Guinness sales soaring in Dublin as he provided the Republic of Ireland with their passport to the European Championship Finals in West Germany next summer.

It's their first ever major finals and manager Jack Charlton said: "I'm overjoyed for my lads and didn't Scotland do well."

"For a long time it

looked as if both sides would settle for a 0-0 draw, then Gary Mackay lifted us into the finals with a super goal.

"NOW INSTEAD OF SENDING THE SCOTS A CASE OF CHAMPAGNE AS I PROMISED I'LL SEND THEM TWO!"

First to toast Scotland's success was Celtic and Eire 'keeper Pat Bonner. "It's unbelievable, I think all the Irish will get drunk tonight."

"It's fantastic for Jack Charlton and for some of the older players, like Liam Brady and Frank Stapleton. They have given Ireland tremendous service and have never had the chance to play in a major finals.

"This will also give us a

chance at last to show other people that we have some good players."

It was a dream debut for 23-year-old Mackay.

The Hearts midfielder was only called into the squad as a late-minute replacement on Sunday.

"This has been the most incredible day of my career," said Mackay. "I can hardly believe that I am here in the first place but to win my first cap and score a goal on my debut is just unbelievable.

"It was marvellous to get the chance at half-time when Paul McStay was injured but scoring the winning goal is a dream come true for me."

Jubilant Scots manager Andy Roxburgh admitted that the 1-0 win — Scotland's first away from home for 22 months—had given him "great pleasure."

EDITED, PRINTED AND PUBLISHED IN SCOTLAND

Published by Scottish Daily Record and Sunday Mail (1986) Ltd. (041-248 7000) and printed by British Newspaper Printing Corporation (Scotland) Ltd., Anderston Quay, Glasgow G3 8DA. Registered at the Post Office as a newspaper. © Scottish Daily Record and Sunday Mail Ltd. 1987. A Mirror Group newspaper.

Heart's Gary Mackay scored the goal for Scotland against Bulgaria in November 1987 that took the Republic of Ireland to Euro '88, so it seemed only right to greet the midfielder as he stepped off the plane in Glasgow. *(Daily Record)*

B, Peter Grant and Tommy Burns in relaxed mode.

A rare picture – Celtic goalkeeping training. *Back Row, Left to Right:* PB, Joe Corrigan, Gordon Marshall, Brad Friedel. *Front Row, Left to Right:* Shay Given, Stewart Kerr.

Beginning of the Centenary Season 1987-88 and new bhoy Mick McCarthy and I are under starter's orders from Physio, Brian Scott. I can't remember who won the race! *(Daily Record)*

988 and Anton Rogan was always game for a laugh. *Left to Right:* Mark McGhee, PB, nknown and Derek Whyte. *(Daily Record)*

lasgow City Chambers 1988 and the Civic function to mark the Centenary of Celtic Football Club. yself and some great faces and names from the Grand Old History.

Euro '88 and I climb above Ruud Gullit for a vital punch.

My best ever International match – Euro '88 v England and I'm about to stop Gary Lineker scoring…AGAIN! (*Press Association*)

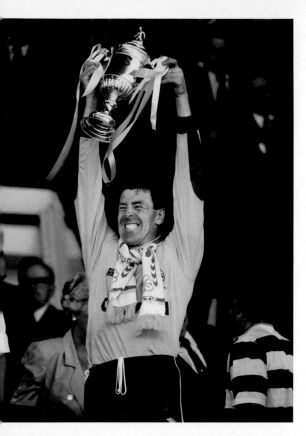

This one's not getting away! Lifting the Scottish Cup, 1989.

Hampden in the Sun' and the joyous feeling of winning a Scottish Cup against Rangers, 1989.

At my Donegal sanctuary – back among the lobster pots just before my life changed at Italia '90. (Trevor McBride)

1990 and recording the World Cup song with the Irish squad and U2 drummer, Larry Mullen. As a singer, I'm a great goalkeeper but that didn't stop me joining in!

yself and David O'Leary before the penalty shootout. Little did we both know how the next few inutes would change our lives.

Italia '90 v Daniel Timofte and Romania. This is the moment.

It wasn't just meeting the Holy Father that was special. He knew who I was and my position in the team. "I was a goalkeeper as well", he said.

The greatest manager with whom I worked. Myself and Jack Charlton out on the training ground 1990.

in the Parkstadion, Gelsenkirchen, all combined to provide a remedy for my ailment and by the time we got to kick-off, by some miracle, I was able to play.

We still played our aggressive tactics even though it was extremely hot, which I think surprised Holland. I remember Mick McCarthy challenging the fast-rising Dutch star Marco van Basten for a high ball. They both fell in a heap and as the play raged up the other end, Mick was still lying on the striker with his hands around his neck and van Basten pleading for mercy!

Don't get me wrong, we weren't dirty and the Dutch had as much physicality about them as they did artistry, but it was one of those games when the stakes were high so no quarter could be given.

With eight minutes left to play and us looking as though we could get the precious point we required, Ronald Koeman attempted a volley from a Paul McGrath clearing header. He misfired the ball into the ground and it spun in front of substitute Wim Kieft who somehow adjusted his body to redirect a header.

It looked as if it was going wide but such was the spin from the volley that the ball careered back towards the goal and crept inside my left-hand post even though I was at full stretch.

It was devastating and by today's standards would perhaps not have counted, as I thought Marco van Basten, who was making his way out of the box, was in an offside position. Then again, he may have been deemed as not interfering with play nowadays.

However, the goal stood and we were out of the competition.

It was no disgrace to lose to a top outfit like Holland who then went on to win the tournament. They had a collection of great players such as Koeman, Frank Rijkaard, captain Ruud Gullit, van Basten, Arnold Muhren and goalkeeper Hans van

Breukelen whom I had faced once before back in 1983 in that second-leg UEFA Cup match against Nottingham Forest.

Yet, there was a sense of dejection about the whole thing.

On reflection, we had been beaten by the eventual winners, had drawn with finalists the Soviet Union in a game I thought we should have won and, of course, we had beaten England. Not bad for a squad of players making their debut in a prestigious international competition.

When we got back to the hotel, we bumped into Johnny Giles and the former footballer-turned-journalist Eamon Dunphy.

Eamon had an abrasive style about his writing but I had always got on well with him and, naturally, Big Jack knew him from his time as a player. After a drink at the bar, he invited both men to join us for our evening meal in a private room. No sooner had Eamon entered the room and taken a seat at the Irish table than Liam Brady rose from *his* seat and left the room. Mick McCarthy wasn't too far behind him in doing the same thing. It was a clear statement.

Eamon had written about Liam in the past and had not been particularly complimentary. The following day he didn't hold back on Mick either in his column in the press. I have got to say that when I read it I was stunned by some of his comments; in my opinion, Mick had a great tournament and never let the team down.

I assumed it was a sense of loyalty that made Mick follow Liam out of the room and I often wondered if that came back to haunt him when he was in charge of the national team, in those periods when things were not so good and the press were taking a stand on his tenure.

Anyway, despite our obvious disappointment, the Irish stock was high everywhere else and the welcome for us on returning to Dublin was quite unbelievable. Huge crowds lined the streets as we travelled on the bus back to a civic reception. As I said, I think this was a catalyst for a change in priorities and how the Irish public viewed football and their national team.

It would, naturally, be just a taster for what we were all to experience after the 1990 World Cup.

Two things really stand out for me.

On the night we got back to Dublin, Big Jack, Mick McCarthy, myself and our wives went out for a Chinese meal in Malahide, a village approximately ten minutes from the airport.

Once we had finished, we decided to head down to Duffy's Bar and have a couple of beers to round off the night. It was utter mayhem and the subject of that mayhem was Jack Charlton himself. He was greeted like Jesus Christ on Palm Sunday and, to be honest, he and his wife Pat really had to leave as it was so overwhelming.

The Irish were taking this firm but likeable Geordie to their hearts.

Mick, myself and the girls stayed on a while. Sean Walsh and his parents, Terry and Danny, came down to join us and what a night it was!

The second thing was, around that time, Ann and I and Andrew, who had just turned three and was in his pram, were still in Malahide.

Out for a stroll one day, we nipped into a café to get a sit-down and a coffee.

It was fairly busy, but we managed to get a table and were sipping our coffee and just having a bit of a natter when an older lady, sitting across from us with her friend said to Ann: 'Ah now – there's a Scottish accent.'

Ann looked over and smiled before answering: 'Yes, I'm from Glasgow but my husband here is from Donegal.'

The second lady suddenly beamed a broad smile.

'Oh, you must be right proud of Packie up in those parts after the football?'

We both nearly choked on our coffee before Ann got in with: 'To be honest, no. Unfortunately, he is my husband!'

Both ladies gasped in astonishment and then took a right hard look at me before we all burst out laughing.

Actually, I was quite relieved that I still had a bit of anonymity, especially in Ireland.

I had an experience in Glasgow once, down in a Southside restaurant when Ann and I were courting and had dropped in for a spot of lunch. I was establishing myself in the Celtic first team and was surprised that a few boys came up to me for a bit of craic and some autographs. It carried on for a wee while until Ann and I left the restaurant at which point the waitress came running out to me, calling at the same time:

'Mr Bonner! Mr Bonner!'

I got my pen back out, ready to sign a menu or a piece of paper, but when she caught up with us she said, breathlessly, 'You forgot to pay, Mr Bonner.' And she presented me with the bill!

The Malahide coffee-shop incident did show me, though, how much the success in Euro '88 had penetrated the whole country. If a couple of older ladies who, perhaps, had never watched a football match in their entire lives, had got caught up in all the excitement of the Irish team and our exploits abroad, what did that say about the rest of the country?

My back was still an issue, though, and so within days of my return to Ireland, Mick Byrne sent me over to Martin Walsh, a doctor who specialised in that area of the body.

I was no sooner in his surgery when he asked me to touch my toes from a standing position. This I did and in the very instant that I was bent over he simply said: 'Packie, you have a disc problem. I can tell that by the way you bend on one side.'

I was stunned.

The thinking back in Scotland was all based around the ankylosing spondylitis but the X-rays that I had in Ireland now proved that I had a disc injury and one that would require an operation.

Mick Byrne had been in touch with Scotty back at Celtic Park and as soon as Big Billy heard the news I was ordered to get the first flight to Glasgow so that they could get the operation organised immediately.

Such was the urgency that I had to cut short my holiday in Donegal and catch a plane from Carrickfinn airport, leaving Ann to drive our car back to Scotland.

I was to find out later that, no sooner was I airborne, than Ann crashed the car into a ditch and had to be pulled out by a tractor. Thankfully, neither she nor Andrew, who was strapped into the back seat, were injured but it fair shook her up.

Back in Scotland, I checked into the Nuffield McAlpine Hospital and, to be honest, with a sense of foreboding.

Clearly, this disc deterioration had been working on me for some time and although I had absolutely no choice but to have the operation, I couldn't help but wonder how it would all work out.

I didn't realistically consider that it could end my career but I was twenty-eight and a back problem for a professional sportsman was always an alarming prospect.

Billy McNeill had seen this sort of thing before in the period when he had managed Manchester City. Alex Williams was a good goalkeeper on City's books but he had similar problems with his back that were to eventually force him to retire prematurely.

I wondered if Billy was having a déjà vu moment with me.

The post-op period is the most frustrating part. The only prescription is rest and recuperation and to me that meant one thing – Donegal.

I returned alone to my home county and, considering what was going through my mind, I was to spend one of the best weeks of my life with Toney Gallagher and Ray Ham at Toney's home up in Tullyisland.

I had been warned that I couldn't bend down, not even to pick up a pencil. When it came to sleep, I had to roll in and out of bed and when I was sitting I had to be upright in a hard chair. There's was to be absolutely no work of any kind for me.

Normally, on a trip home fishing would be high on the agenda.

I *loved* fishing but that didn't seem possible as I obviously had to be careful with my back but, as ever, Toney and Ray had the solution.

They had a large wooden carver chair that had been the property of Owney back in the day and so they cut the legs down so that it would fit neatly strapped into the bow of Toney's old white punt.

I was able to sit upright and fish to my heart's content over the side and Toney and Ray would craic away, while we travelled around the little inlets and islands picking up the odd lobster pot along the journey.

Occasionally, they would stop and craic with Paddy Rafferty, a neighbour of Toney's who had dozens of lobster pots out in the bay, and fill his head with tales of the big fishing and hefty catches they were hauling in. This was mighty stuff, I can tell you. How could anyone feel down or even think about the future when this was going on?

It did me a power of good and certainly, back at Celtic Park, Scotty would not have been able to provide *this* sort of treatment! We hit it off unbelievably with the weather into the bargain. I would defy anyone who came to the west coast of Donegal, and experienced the Mediterranean sunshine we enjoyed, to say that they would never return.

It was glorious and the sea was as calm as a millpond.

I didn't want this week to end; I knew it was special, but I also knew that it was out of character for this shoreline. It was a dangerous stretch of water and the mood of the sea could change in minutes. I thought back to the day when Denis and I were out with my dad pulling dulce and then fishing on the way home as the tide turned to fill. The wind got up, our engine broke down and we suddenly found ourselves in danger and in the most vulnerable of places. I will tell you, Denis and I pulled like Olympic scullers that afternoon.

Toney and Ray were hardened fishermen, but safety was always their mantra. They unfortunately had to witness one of the most life-changing events any fishermen could experience.

That was back in January 1975 when, on a wild night and in frightening conditions, the *Evelyn Marie* fishing trawler had foundered on the rocks of Rathlin O'Byrne Island with the loss of all six crew members on board.

I had got to know some of those lads when Denis and I would hang around Toney's house.

Ray's older brother Tom was among that group of six who perished that night. Ray was a deckhand and Toney the skipper of the *Summer Star*, the sister boat of the *Evelyn Marie*, and they were steaming into port behind them on that fateful night. They tried everything to save them but, sadly, to no avail.

In fact, that match I mentioned earlier between Celtic and Finn Harps from 1975 was to raise money for the bereaved families.

The sea was a friend to Burtonport in that it provided industry and work for the area but, equally, it could be a vile enemy on those occasions when the swell would be at its height in dreadful conditions and danger was frighteningly imminent.

The community was just about coming to terms with that tragedy when, less than two years later, on 23 November 1976, a second trawler, the *Carraig Una*, went down with the loss of all five hands.

The passing of eleven young fellas, in the prime of their lives and in such a short space of time, was a stark reminder of the dangers of the open sea and it was as chilling to recall as much as it was hard to reconcile as we sat throughout that gorgeous week of weather, floating on a still, becalmed ocean.

When I thought of the so-called 'pressures' attributed to the game of football, I considered myself lucky in that I wasn't being asked to risk my life out on the high seas trying to make a living from the wealth of produce below us in the ocean.

There is always a time to count your blessings and my ability between the goalposts, such as it was, allowed me to work and live in very privileged conditions.

Just before I had left the hospital in Glasgow, big Billy had come up to see how I was faring.

'Just lie here then get away for a week and concentrate on getting better. And don't you worry, take your time. I've just signed another goalkeeper anyway. Ian Andrews from Leicester City!'

Cheers, Billy.

HAMPDEN IN THE SUN AND
THE ROAD TO ITALY

ALLEN MCKNIGHT, WHO HAD ABLY DEPUTISED FOR ME WHEN I was previously out injured, had left Celtic for West Ham United and the chance of continuous first-team football. While Big Billy could hardly blame him for that, his departure and my operation meant that there was only one goalkeeper on the Celtic books and he was Andy Murdoch who had just turned eighteen.

For the pre-season tour of Switzerland, the club brought in the veteran former Dundee United custodian Hamish McAlpine, but, good and as well-regarded as he was, Hamish was forty and the need to go out and sign another keeper became acute.

Ian Andrews was twenty-four and in his youth at Leicester had been highly rated. I have to say, first and foremost, he was an absolute gentleman. Very polite, well-mannered, a real nice guy. Perhaps, in truth, a bit *too* nice for the Celtic Park changing room.

That was an arena where you had to be thick-skinned. Where you had to be equipped to handle the comments and humour that probably occur in most locker-rooms around the world.

I tell you, nobody really understands Celtic when they first arrive and I think the unluckiest thing about Ian was that he signed for the club close to the end of the pre-season and was not match-fit when he was rushed into the team for a glamour friendly against Cruzeiro of Brazil at Celtic Park to mark the club's centenary.

He had a reasonable start in the club's colours but the world of Ian Andrews came crashing around him on 27 August 1988 when Celtic went to Ibrox on League business. The first derby in a season is always a crucial one, as is, indeed, *your* first derby as a player, and I would imagine that if you mentioned Ian's name to any Celtic supporter, they would immediately bring up this game – sadly, for the wrong reasons.

From a promising early Frank McAvennie goal, the team disintegrated and the 5–1 scoreline after ninety minutes could have been worse. Certainly Tommy Burns thought so and he went on the Sunday afternoon television show *Scotsport* the following day to apologise for Celtic's worst defeat to Rangers in twenty-eight years.

It's not just as a paid-up member of the goalkeepers' union that I would say a *team* loses 5–1 rather than one player but any confidence that Ian Andrews was taking from his early Celtic career was practically obliterated that day.

By that time, former Scotland goalkeeper Alan Rough had also joined the Celtic ranks.

Again, a bit of a veteran at thirty-seven, he was there to steady the ship a bit and provide back-up. Certainly, he was a man who could hold his own in *any* dressing room but he wasn't exactly helping Ian to restore his confidence and he tells some hilarious tales of his time at Celtic now when he's on the after-dinner circuit.

Confidence is a fragile thing and years later I would give Roughie's replacement at Hibernian, Andy Goram, a pep talk after *his* first Glasgow derby when he felt it hadn't gone well for him.

Andy would go on to break our hearts many times in Old Firm games so perhaps it wasn't my shining hour, on reflection!

I have to say, though, that I felt sorry for Ian.

That kind of result can happen to us all but the fact that it happened at the ground of our biggest rivals ensured that it was loaded with so much more meaning.

This was now a fractious time for the club. I was recuperating nicely, following all the surgeon's instructions, but to get my fitness level back was a real hard slog. I was lucky to have a full-time physio pushing me on day to day, dragging me around Strathclyde Park. It's tough enough when running in a group, but on your own? Well, that is something altogether different.

I was eventually rewarded when I came back into the team on 22 October in a 2–0 victory away to Hearts.

My recovery period had seen me work to full strength with the reserves and it was a real tonic to read Big Billy in the papers saying that he was astonished to have me back as he thought I would be unavailable until at least Christmas.

Yet, it was a different Celtic I was returning to and those changes were self-evident. Frank McAvennie was wanting to leave the club, having only joined the year before, and, just as Billy had predicted, Rangers had not sat on their hands in the close season but had spent big money to strengthen their side. In contrast, Celtic had brought in one player and even that was forced by circumstance – the unfortunate Ian Andrews.

There was a certain amount of disarray at the club with inconsistent results and performances. It was hard to believe that this was the same unit of players who had so convincingly collected the double in the first half of 1988.

For some reason, the club sanctioned a friendly match against Red Star Belgrade of Yugoslavia on Boxing Day.

It was a dreich Glasgow afternoon and perhaps a bit surprising that 21,000 souls turned up to take in the action.

As a family, we always spent the day after Christmas up at Ann's parents but, on this particular night, Mick McCarthy and his wife Fiona were throwing a party and we had been invited over.

As usual, I left a couple of tickets for Ann's dad, Tommy, at reception and from there he would head up to the Players'

Lounge. That, incidentally, was a new concept at Celtic Park at the time and far from the plush lounge with a manned bar and food available at half-time as well as a first-class view of the game that is the norm nowadays.

In fact, it was club scout John Kelman's old office so there wasn't much room to get about although Tommy and Danny McGrain's father, who had struck up a friendship during Danny's days at the club, knew where the filing cabinet was that usually held a decent bottle of Scotch. They could have a couple of nips before and after the match.

Anyway, the game being over in a 2–2 draw, I dropped Tommy back up at his Volvo on Springfield Road as the weather was atrocious and I was taking Anton Rogan home first before heading over to Tommy and Jess's house.

A few minutes later, Anton and I were sitting at the traffic lights at the foot of Springfield Road ready to turn left out towards Rutherglen. The lights changed to green and I pulled away when, out of a side street, this car shot out in front of me.

I didn't even have time to brake properly and so I ploughed right into the side of … a Volvo. Anton shouted, 'F*** it's Tommy!' as I, badly shaken, tried to manoeuvre myself out of the car. I was driving a large Mercedes at the time and there was no doubt which vehicle had come off worse in the collision.

It was indeed Ann's dad who was unconscious, slumped at the wheel of the Volvo.

Anton got out of the car and took off like a madman, haring down Springfield Road as fast as he could away from the incident as if he'd had some flashback to a childhood experience in Belfast!

Within minutes the police and an ambulance were on the scene and then the Fire Brigade were called as Tommy would have to be cut free from the wreckage.

He had, thankfully, regained consciousness but he was, of course, still badly injured.

In the days before mobile phones, I didn't get a chance to call home until we were at the hospital and it was clear that Tommy's injuries were not life-threatening.

They did, however, extend to a number of broken ribs and his liver was pushed up towards his diaphragm.

It was Tommy's habit on Boxing Day to wear a pair of Santa Claus boxer shorts and Christmas socks that played 'Rudolf the Red-Nosed Reindeer' when you pressed a button, much to the delight of wee Andrew and the other grandchildren.

And as he lay there on the hospital bed all I could see were his festive socks and shorts. It would have been surreal had one of the nurses pressed that button for Rudolf!

The first thing he said to me was, 'What the f*** were you doing? You nearly killed me!'

I was desperately trying not to burst out laughing and said 'What was I doing?! What was *I* doing?! You were the one who pulled out from a give way!'

The argument still rages to this day and Tommy has never tired of telling everybody about the Christmas when his Celtic-playing son-in-law tried to kill him!

Injuries to key players like Mick McCarthy and Frank McAvennie and the lack of investment up against a Rangers management prepared to spend big were just a couple of the reasons why, I feel, that we did not enjoy a good campaign that season.

The League was over for us but we battled our way through to the Scottish Cup Final and that was against Rangers.

The stakes could not have been higher.

The Ibrox club, having secured the League and the League Cup, were going for a treble while we were looking to halt that in its tracks as well as picking up the only piece of silverware that was still available to us.

It doesn't matter how hard you try to play down an Old Firm final; it's just not possible to do so.

Frank had already left the club. He had been given the choice of Arsenal or West Ham and opted to return to the East End club – who were promptly relegated while the Gunners won the League from under the noses of Liverpool in a thrilling finale to their season. He was a very real loss to Celtic and my admiration for him as a player has never wavered. The feeling was that the club had lost a marquee signing, the spirits were a bit low and so Billy went out of his way to bring in another big name.

And that was Maurice Johnston.

Mo had tired of life in France where he was playing for Nantes and, apparently, in a conversation with Roy Aitken while on international duty, had expressed the wish to go back to his first love, Celtic.

As club captain, Roy informed his manager and, although letting it be known he was not in the mood to be mucked around, Billy had convinced the board to sanction the signing.

It stole all the back pages and a few of the front ones as well.

As a pick-me-up for an indifferent season and a bit of a lift ahead of the Cup Final, it was perfect.

I was determined to play in the gala occasion having missed out the season before and it was strange for Celtic to be going into a major final as slight underdogs in the press.

It was a most beautiful day both weather-wise and on the field of play if you followed the Celtic as a first-half Joe Miller goal won the game for us. At last – a chance for me to parade around Hampden in blazing sunshine, under a cloudless sky, holding the Scottish Cup.

As I did so, I thought about the Celtic variation of the Harry Belafonte hit from 1957, 'Island in the Sun'. Following the club's 7–1 drubbing of Rangers in the League Cup Final that year, the support rewrote the hit as 'Oh Hampden in the sun, Celtic 7, Rangers 1'.

Well, it wasn't quite that but the cup victory was a joyous relief for us all.

However, in essence it was covering up the cracks at the club and one of those fissures had Maurice Johnston's name on it.

Immediately after the Cup Final I, like the rest of my teammates, had headed off on holiday, but, back in Glasgow, the Johnston deal was unfurling. Allegedly, he hadn't actually signed a contract and the upshot was that Maurice Johnston would not be rejoining Celtic.

That was news in itself but when he was paraded at Ibrox a few weeks later as Graeme Souness's latest signing for Rangers, there wasn't enough ink to cover it in the press.

So many reasons have been given for the about-face, and the word out on the street at the time was that Maurice was bagging a million pounds from the deal and any way you looked at it that was a lot of dough.

I also felt that, in his own mind, he lagged behind the regard and panache of both Charlie Nicholas and Frank McAvennie as a striker and this was his way of making a statement.

Certainly, for a while his was the most talked-about name in football and he wasn't exactly a guy who ever shunned the limelight.

Of course, in some ways he united both sides of the Glasgow divide but only in the way that his name was spat out like a curse from the Celtic contingent for the betrayal just as it was being abused by a section of the Rangers support who would never subscribe to a Roman Catholic playing for their club.

Even when he scored an eighty-eighth-minute winner against us at Ibrox that November, I was still certain that a part of the Rangers crowd would never take to him. I don't remember him blessing himself *that* day.

In all the clamour around his signing, though, there seemed to be one aspect that was missing. Maurice was a good player and Celtic now had to replace him once again.

Big Billy stepped up his signing activity by, first of all, bringing in English centre-half Paul Elliott from Italian side Pisa and then Polish striker Dariusz Dziekanowski. He followed that up by purchasing the Polish international captain and defender Dariusz Wdowczyk.

Mick McCarthy had left for French outfit Lyon in the summer and Paul seemed the ideal replacement. He suffered a bit, I feel, because he had been used to playing in a back three out in Italy whereas, in Scotland, he was required to make up a defensive four.

Paul was different from Mick in that he would let play develop before flying into a tackle that, in his early days at the club, saw him pick up a collection of yellow cards. Mick's style was to break up danger before it happened but, over time, Paul Elliott became an important player for us.

Dariusz Dziekanowski, rechristened by the Celtic support as 'Jacki', was, well, flamboyant. He had that required arrogance about him and I never felt he was truly a team player, more of an individual talent.

Both Paul and Jacki were on the pitch in one of the most remarkable European games that I ever played in.

In the European Cup Winners' Cup, we had been drawn against Partizan Belgrade from Yugoslavia. We had lost the first leg 2–1 in a beautiful place called Mostar, a town that would, tragically, be almost destroyed during the Balkan conflict of the early 1990s. The away goal gave us a toehold and, as ever on a European night at Celtic Park, a huge crowd rolled up to see if we could turn the tie around.

From a neutral standpoint it was an incredible game with Jacki netting four goals, but our defending was naive in the extreme and, although we won 5–4 on the night, we were out of the competition on the away-goals rule.

With the Irish international team I had seen what it took to defend. That was our first objective but, at Celtic and on a night of high expectancy, we succumbed to the classic Celtic failure of going gung-ho for a victory but not defending as a unit. It was especially galling because, with two minutes to play, we were 5–3 up and in the next round until Partizan broke up the field once more and scored.

When you look at the success in Europe that first Aberdeen and Dundee United enjoyed, and then the way Martin O'Neill would have Celtic playing en route to the UEFA Cup Final in 2003, it's clear that the foundations for that success were cemented in defence.

On the night we defended abysmally and once again were eliminated from Europe.

There was now a period of change at Celtic Park and within weeks of the Belgrade game we lost two of our most influential players when Tommy Burns and Roy Aitken left Celtic Park.

For my part, I had lost great friends in both players but, even more importantly than that, Celtic lost two great leaders. Roy was the epitome of a captain – tenacious, commanding and a leader both on and off the pitch. Tommy had that superb left foot, an abundance of talent and he *knew* it was a privilege to play for Celtic. That was a quality that he never tired of impressing upon others in the home dressing room. The departure of both men left a gaping hole at the club in terms of leadership.

I was now the most senior player at Celtic and one day Billy took me aside and spoke to me about the captaincy. He said he felt he couldn't give me the position and had to give it to Paul McStay.

I was a goalkeeper and that just didn't happen. He felt that the job should go to Paul in that respect but he also felt he owed me the courtesy of an explanation. I accepted the decision and appreciated Billy's candour but I felt at the time, as I still do today, that I could have done the job.

Did I consider that I had the necessary experience and leadership to take the team forward both on and off the pitch?

Absolutely.

I was an established international player having represented my country in the European Championship of 1988 and was, at this time, preparing to go with Ireland to our first World Cup tournament in the summer.

It is, of course, so much easier in hindsight to take the view that the captaincy of Celtic may have been a burden to Paul, especially when Rangers were flying high. It was always going to be difficult to follow in the footsteps of Roy Aitken, not to mention the template set by the likes of Danny McGrain and Billy McNeill.

Paul McStay was one of the greatest footballers ever to grace the green and white of Celtic and a pivotal player. He was a leader on the park, but with a new group of players, a young group, they needed a strong powerful leader *in the dressing room* and Paul was quite an unassuming person off the pitch.

Around this time, the home changing room at Celtic Park needed sorting.

The core of authority was gone and my feeling was that, the young, up-and-coming Celtic players had a different view of life as a) a professional footballer and b) as a Celtic player.

First and foremost in that regard was the view of Billy McNeill that was now emanating from some of the younger lads. They did not see him as *Billy McNeill* – the first British player to lift the European Cup. *Mr Celtic* who embodied everything that was good and commanding about the club and a figure of undoubted authority with his chest puffed out as a rule and brooking no argument about who was in charge.

It was clear that the prevailing view was that he was perhaps out of touch with the modern game and, crucially, the modern player, but, perhaps the truth was that *they* were out of touch with *him*.

I had come through the ranks at Celtic and been reared on the club's philosophy and the respect that Billy McNeill had earned both as a player and a manager, but the times they were a-changin' and Cesar was no longer the presence that he had been.

I didn't always like the way that Billy managed in my early days. He was very intimidating, but I totally respected him for the way he went about his business and the fact that Celtic was always at the heart of his decisions.

It was only in his second spell at Celtic that I came to grips with Billy as my manager and when retired I started to enjoy Billy as a person who always showed great regard for his ex-players and Celtic Football Club.

Rangers were still making the running in the League and they were eleven points clear of us at the top of the table when they arrived at Celtic Park on the last Sunday in February looking to eliminate us from the Scottish Cup.

Realistically, that was the only trophy left open for us to win and that may have helped us to focus and put an end to a bad run of only two victories since December.

Tommy Coyne had been signed earlier in the season. He had been a prolific goalscorer at Dundee and was the top marksman for the Premier League the season before, but he struggled to find that touch in his first few months as a Celt.

On this particular day, though, Tommy was on hand to slide the ball into the net after Chris Woods had parried a shot just before half-time and that, ultimately, was enough to see us through to the quarter-finals.

Once again, we went all the way to the final but, as I detailed at the start of the book, there was only penalty shoot-out heartache for us when we contested the Hampden showpiece with Aberdeen.

Thankfully, things were going better for me on the international stage.

I had missed out on a couple of the early matches in the qualifiers for the 1990 World Cup due to the recuperation from my back operation. Expectations were, naturally, high, following on from the success of Euro '88 but a 1–0 defeat away to Spain, sandwiched between 0–0 draws with Northern Ireland and Hungary, suggested to some of the Irish sports press pack that those expectations were possibly misplaced.

After the no-scoring draw in Budapest, on retiring to the bar after our return to the hotel I found a group of the older journalists congregating in one of the alcoves just off the main bar. I joined them, as was the norm in those days – players, media and fans in the mixed zone in the bar!

The conversation, of course, was all about the game and it alarmed but did not surprise me to hear a very negative feeling towards the team, Jack and, of course, the result. Their opinion was that we were doomed. I reminded them that they had a choice, to stick with the team, don't ruin it now, they just might be the beneficiaries if we made it to our first World Cup; we all had a responsibility.

Surprisingly, the headlines were not too bad. The beating of Spain in Dublin became a turning point and we then went on a winning run that closed out with a 3–0 destruction of Northern Ireland at Lansdowne Road, setting us up for our final qualifying game away to Malta.

With a goal difference of plus six over the Hungarians, it would have required a huge swing to deny us a place in the World Cup Finals but if we beat the Maltese and Spain lost to Hungary then we would win the group – either way, our passage was virtually guaranteed.

The Malta game was a remarkable fixture in that, such was the Irish presence packed into the stadium at Ta' Qali, that it felt like a home game.

A dense fog hung over the city, delaying the planes carrying thousands of our loyal fans. It may have curtailed the time they had to party before the game, but we all made up for it afterwards on the streets of Valletta.

John Aldridge saw us home with a brace in a 2–0 win. Spain prevailed 4–0 and topped the group but the important part was that we were on our way to our first ever World Cup tournament.

Incredibly, we were to play against the top players in the world. The dream had come true. I couldn't wait to meet those same group of elder statesmen of the press later in a hotel bar – to thank them for sticking with us! However, I never got around to it as we took to the streets to party. My Celtic team-mate Chris Morris led the sing-song with 'The Fields of Athenry' – a memorable night, only one of many that was about to unfold.

In truth, the excitement of the international scene was, in a sense, beginning to compensate for the disappointments on the domestic front with Celtic.

This was a pattern that would recur over the next few seasons and although I was bitterly disappointed to lose the Scottish Cup Final, I did, at least, have Italia '90 to look forward to along with the rest of my home country.

In addition, Ann and I were patiently waiting on the arrival of our second child, Melissa.

Around that time, I was out in Dublin with the squad as we prepared for a friendly against the Soviet Union. Big Jack had us down on the beach between Malahide and Portmarnock for our customary walk, when he sidled up to me.

He had a knack for that and it was one of his habits to use these occasions to casually wander into a conversation with any one or two of his squad. He asked me how I was doing and I explained that things were good but a wee bit fraught with Ann about to go into labour.

We walked on a bit then he replied, 'Do you know if it's a boy or a girl?'

I replied that I didn't as we wanted to enjoy the element of surprise.

He paused and then, with that trademark twinkle in his eye, said, 'Ya know, Jack's a good name for a boy.'

I laughed.

'Our first's a boy and we called him Andrew so I don't know what we'll call this one.'

He thought for a second or two and then, just before moving away on to another group of his players, said, 'Do you still want to play tonight?'

The Jack way was to take an interest in you and bring a smile to your face.

His easy nature meant that he was open to anything that made his players feel comfortable ahead of a game.

This extended to Monsignor Liam Boyle from Limerick, who was a regular on the squad's flights around the world. He became a kind of spiritual adviser to the Irish national team and often said a private Mass on the day of a game for anyone within the squad who wanted to attend. Our celebration of the sacraments almost always ended with a rousing rendition of the hymn 'Hail Glorious St Patrick', led by Mick Byrne and Charlie O'Leary, even though I'm quite certain we never played a match on the saint's feast day.

The clergy were big supporters of the Republic and it wasn't unusual for sacred items to arrive at the team's hotel or, as happened just prior to Euro '88, at Castleport House.

On that occasion, I was home when my mother handed a cigarette packet to me.

'These arrived for you, Packie,' she said, handing me the box.

It was surprising as I didn't smoke but not half as surprising as when I opened the package, took out the contents and discovered that it was a collection of tiny balls of soil.

Gartan clay is considered by some to be a holy relic, hewn from the earth of the town of Gartan in Donegal.

The instructions were clear – make sure you give one to each of the players and you're sure to beat England. This was special clay and it could only be extracted by the members of one particular family.

Typically, I forgot about the cigarette packet, but my mother made sure I was to get it and so she sent it on to Finnstown Castle Hotel in Lucan, where we were based for our preparations, before we headed away.

And there I was, a couple of hours before the game in Stuttgart, scurrying around the players tossing small balls of white holy clay into their bags and boots. They probably thought I was mad, but nobody refused it!

That was the day we beat England 1–0.

While not being especially devout, I considered myself to be a religious person. The Catholic Church was an important staple in my youth and I was reared to attend Mass regularly but my faith is more of a quiet, personal espousal for me.

I freely confess that I perhaps used spirituality and religion for my own personal means in those times of stress throughout my career. Maybe I was a bit selfish.

My mother would faithfully light a candle at home for me on a Saturday when I was playing for Celtic just as she would then light another one on a Sunday for the game in which Denis was playing in the League of Ireland.

I had a bit of that in me and there was a day, early on in my Celtic career, when we were down to play Rangers and I decided to light a candle in my house before the match. Things weren't going the best and I definitely needed a bit of spiritual intervention.

It started off in the living room but as a non-smoker I had neither match nor lighter so I did the next best thing and tore off a strip of newspaper before catching a light from the gas stove.

I raced back into the living room but the candle was taking an age to catch and, of course, the newsprint was so flammable that I suddenly had a mini-inferno at the end of my hand with the very real prospect of burning my arm. I hurriedly dropped it into a plastic bin which duly went up in flames.

In a panic, I grabbed the bin, raced through the living room, out through the kitchen door and into the back garden where I managed to subdue the flame and put out the fire.

All the while, the neighbours were sitting out next door, enjoying the sunshine and then looking at me in bemusement tearing around the garden trying to extinguish the flames.

What was I to say?

'Eh, just lighting a blessed candle before the Rangers game.'

They might have thought I was barmy.

Yet, people have a system of beliefs.

I received a letter once from a lady from Roscommon, a huge fan of the Irish team, but especially of me because I came from Donegal. She told me that everything would stop when the game was on, 'even the haymaking', and all the family would gather around her. She was also a very religious woman and, like my mother, she also lit the blessed candle and would place it on top of the television over the goal that I was defending. When half-time would come she would get up and move it over to the other side of the box so that it would be above me in the second half as well!

*

Big Jack liked Monsignor Liam. The priest paid for his own flights and hotel bills but, through time, Jack allowed him into the dining room when we were eating our meals. He became part of the entourage and very much bought into that feeling that we were 'all in it together'.

Jack treated him as an equal and had a healthy disregard for piety which extended one night to a squad game of Trivial Pursuit.

Monsignor Liam was in the chair as quizmaster as, given his calling, he seemed to be the most impartial.

'How many players are on the pitch in a Gaelic football match, Jack?' he asked.

Charlie O'Leary, being on the same team as Jack and who was an authority on all things Irish, jumped in quickly and told Jack the answer.

Jubilantly, Big Jack said with relish, 'Fifteen!'

Monsignor Liam smiled before answering, 'You're wrong.'

Jack was disgusted. 'What do you mean I'm wrong?! Ask Charlie!'

Liam didn't balk. 'Then, Charlie's wrong. It's thirty.'

Charlie and Jack had obviously thought he meant players in one team and argued the point vociferously without fear or favour.

'It's fookin' fifteen, Liam! How am I fookin' wrong?! How can you have thirty players in one side?!'

The good father wasn't for standing down and he raged away with Jack in a manner possibly not quite becoming of a man of the cloth but the intent was as clear as it was hilarious – Liam was now one of the boys. Once again, we were all in this together.

The day before the England match in 1990, he said Mass outside our Sardinian hotel in the open air which was an unforgettable experience for any one of us who attended, and that was quite a considerable number of players and backroom staff.

To be honest, that hotel wasn't the greatest. Big Jack had a dislike for the more plush establishments. I don't know whether he felt that too much comfort would soften the players up or if he booked three-star jobs when he went on holiday, but for whatever reason Gerry Peyton and myself found ourselves sharing a small room with an equally small balcony. Our 'air-conditioning', if it could be called that, was a massive fan and was so noisy that putting it on at night ruined your sleep.

It was also our custom to wash some of our own specialised kit and gloves and, at least, the balcony offered somewhere to lay out the gear to let it dry.

I got up one morning and nipped out to the balcony to check my gloves. It was utterly sweltering both inside and outside the room so, frankly, I didn't bother with the luxury of clothes. As I was out there, in true comic fashion, the maid knocked then entered the room. The sudden draught caused the doors out to the balcony to slam shut and the glass to shatter into smithereens with me trapped, naked and vulnerable, on the outside. The maid screamed and I'm not sure that was just because of the broken glass and suddenly, no doubt on hearing the commotion, a few people rushed into our room. I had to act quickly which was why, when they all beheld me, I was protecting the maid's blushes and my own dignity by grabbing one of my Umbro goalie gloves and placing it discreetly over ... well, you work it out!

As I mentioned earlier, I wouldn't define Jack Charlton as a practical coach. He was more the traditional manager and had a great eye for the finer details. There is one memory that always stays with me and that happened during the build-up to the England game.

Jack had done his homework and it was the little things that he noticed about players that could make the difference. He told us that Terry Butcher was heavily left-sided and, whenever he had the ball, he would knock it slightly with the outside of his left foot as a way of setting it up to be clipped forward down the line or up to the dangerous Gary Lineker.

John Aldridge was told that he was to back off Terry but, as soon as he saw that flick to the side, he was to charge him down, forcing the England centre-half to panic a little and potentially misplace his through ball.

Des Walker was Terry's partner in defence. Big Jack told us that Walker was quick but, in his opinion, only comfortable when he had space and time to play. If you were running with him, he would like you to commit to the ball and, when you did, he would show a turn of pace, just getting to the ball first, and then turn away into space with it, making himself look good.

Jack's advice, again to John Aldridge, was to run with Walker but then deliberately slow up and let him get to the ball first … 'and then close him down and we'll see how good a player he is'.

Those were the little nuggets that we would take into a game, giving us confidence and making the difference. All of that came to the fore as we prepared for Ireland's official entry into the rarefied atmosphere of World Cup football.

OLE OLE!

As in 1988, our opening game against England at Italia '90 would be the one that caught the imagination of the public back home in Ireland who could never a resist a tilt against the former 'colonial power'.

Out on the pitch there was the contrast of myself and Chris Morris as Celtic players up against the aforementioned Terry Butcher and Gary Stevens of Rangers. Equally, Steve Staunton and Ray Houghton, tireless workers both, would be pitting themselves against Liverpool team-mates John Barnes and Peter Beardsley – all four of them in that squad that had just won the English First Division. John Aldridge would also have been hungry for the contest having left Liverpool for Real Sociedad and, of course, there was an Evertonian 'toffee' in our line-up as well with Kevin Sheedy looking to win a personal Merseyside battle.

The English had been roundly criticised in the aftermath of our victory against them in 1988 and would surely see this as an opportunity to right that particular wrong. Add that to the fact that both countries had Geordie managers in Big Jack and Bobby Robson and you could see why the media were building up the fixture.

Once again, I felt that surge of pride as I stood with my team-mates out on the pitch of the Stadio Sant'Elia in Cagliari on 11 June 1990. We were at the World Cup in Italy, the first Republic of Ireland squad to qualify, and representing our country in front of millions watching all over the world.

The Irish diaspora is marked and widespread and it wasn't too far-fetched to imagine that from Dublin to Dhaka, from Monaghan to Melbourne, from Ballybofey to Boston, there would be Irish men and women, boys and girls sitting around their television sets at home or, more than likely, in bars, saloons and clubs taking in the moment that Ireland deservedly took its place on the world football stage.

We had earned the right to be here and now we had to earn the points that could take us on through the tournament.

The first five minutes I spent trying to get my gloves sorted out. The rain was pelting down, unlike what we had been training in for the last three to four weeks, and the ball was like glass. I had an older trusted pair in my goalie bag that was just right.

As early as the eighth minute, though, we looked to be in jeopardy when we were caught out at the back by a superbly flighted cross from Chris Waddle out on our left flank. It sailed into that dangerous area between Mick McCarthy and Chris Morris on the edge of the box and, as I came out to narrow the angle, Gary Lineker got in front of us to chest the ball almost beyond me before following up and putting it in the net.

I'm sure Gary never looked on it as a classic goal but being in the right place at the right time is the hallmark of a great striker and the top scorer from the Mexico World Cup of 1986 was off the mark.

Once again, resilience was to be our hallmark although it took us until the seventy-second minute to get the reward that I felt our play merited. I had launched a clearance from my eighteen-yard line that was knocked down into the path of Kevin Sheedy twenty-five yards from goal. The Evertonian's first touch was intercepted by Liverpool's Steve McMahon, who had come on as a substitute, but he wanted too much time to play out so Sheeds nipped in, took the ball from him and then rifled a beautiful low drive beyond Peter Shilton.

Well, if you're going to score Ireland's first ever goal in the World Cup Finals then you should make it a belter!

There was a sizeable running track around the Stadio Sant'Elia but I could virtually feel the hot breath of thousands of my compatriots as they let out an explosion of joy from behind my goal that wafted across the pitch. It wasn't the best of nights in Cagliari, wet as we were from bouts of heavy rainfall, but for the first time in a World Cup Finals tournament the sun had come out and shone on the Irish.

There were to be no further goals in the game and we could be proud of the fact that we had matched the English. A point in the bank, honours even and, probably best of all back home, no English defeat of the Irish. We had that bond of togetherness again and the feeling was that everybody was caught up in the moment.

There was an incident just before our next game, which was against Egypt, when we were based in Terrasini, that I felt caught the mood of the Irish people and was another example of Jack Charlton's ability to communicate with ordinary supporters, indeed, ordinary people.

We were heading out of our hotel one morning en route to training when we saw a young couple standing close to our bus. They asked if they could have an autograph or two from the squad and, in the age before 'selfies', the lads obliged. In particular, they waited for Big Jack and his backroom staff to emerge and when they did so Jack posed for a photograph and signed their books as well. Jack being Jack got into a conversation with them and I guess in a moment of pure spontaneity, he suddenly asked the couple if they fancied coming to watch the squad go through their training.

This was beyond their wildest dreams and I can only speculate as to what they were thinking when, minutes later, there they were, sitting on the Irish team bus and heading out to the training ground. Once there, they watched us go through our paces before thanking all of us and in particular, Big Jack, then heading off with a story that probably nobody would believe until they saw the photographs that they had taken. I have often wondered what happened to them. In truth, I don't even know for sure that they were a couple but, if they were, did they stay together ... did they ever forget their hours spent with the Irish squad in Sardinia and, indeed, is one of them perhaps reading this book and recalling a special moment, made possible by the common touch that Jack Charlton possessed in spades?

The magic wasn't just happening across Ireland; there was a fair bit of it in Italy for us as well.

Again, I repeat, we should have beaten Egypt in the next game. Certainly, former player-turned-pundit Eamon Dunphy thought so as he berated our performance on live television.

We had the chances against an Egyptian side which showed the metal of their wares early on by putting eleven men behind the ball to defend. It was a tactic that had seen them draw 1–1 with Holland in their opening game and they weren't going to change their spots against us. Ray Houghton had our best opportunity by being put through by Sheeds; however, Egyptian goalkeeper Ahmed Shobair raced out of his goal to make a superb save from Ray's hurried strike and the chance was gone.

That 0–0 draw, coupled with England and Holland finishing goal-less, meant it was all to play for when we faced the Dutch.

As ever, preparation was key, although there was the odd, hilarious hiccup the night before the game.

Big Jack wasn't really a fan of watching match videos but someone had been kind enough to send a tape of the Dutch from one of their games to the hotel and, as it was a key match in the group, he got his assistant, Maurice Setters, to pick up the tape and organise a screening in our Palermo hotel after dinner.

We all trooped in and there was the big television set resting on top of the video recorder.

Jack issued the orders.

'Right, Maurice. Stick the tape in and start her up. The rest of you – pay attention!'

It started with the usual preamble of the national anthems, the camera was going along the line-ups and then panned out to show a small ground half empty. I sat up in the front row alongside Gerry Peyton, but we could hear some of the lads muttering in the background. Then there were a few bursts of laughter, and you could see Jack getting a bit restless.

'Pay bloody attention,' he barked.

Suddenly, a voice from the back piped up …

'Jack?'

'Aye, what is it?'

There was a pause and then …

'Jack – I don't think that's their senior team.'

And he was right. We were about to sit through an Under-21 match!

The big man was merciless with Maurice.

'Bloody 'ell, Maurice. I give you one … bloody … job … to do and you can't even get that right! One bloody job!'

Naturally, we were all in stitches as poor Maurice sat and listened to Big Jack railing at him.

Best of it was, after he'd finished with his assistant, he stood up and said, 'Ach, just watch it. They play the same bloody way anyway!'

We would find out if that was true the following night.

The match against Holland was the toughest one in the group as far as I was concerned. The first twenty minutes saw the front four of Gullit, van Basten, Wim Kieft and Hans Gillhaus of Aberdeen, changing positions, trying to pull our defenders all over the place to create openings. However, the pass never came as our lads up front closed down Ronald Koeman and Frank Rijkaard, forcing the ball to be played backwards. The movement stopped; no way could they keep that up if they didn't have the ball. We felt we were in control even if Gullit did grab that goal I described in Chapter One.

We were not without our own qualities and even Niall Quinn's equaliser has a story attached to it.

Big Jack had a way of playing out from his goalkeeper.

He was not a man for putting the ball at risk across the back four so I had two options. I either played the ball out to our full-backs Chris Morris or Steve Staunton, but only if they could progress across the halfway line, or I was simply to play it long out of my hands up to the strikers so that we could play in the Dutch's defensive third.

On one key point he was absolutely explicit.

I was not, under *any* circumstances, to roll the ball out to either of our two centre-halves, Mick McCarthy and Kevin Moran. According to Jack, *they couldn't play*, which wasn't to denigrate them. In his eyes, centre-backs were for heading, tackling and getting the ball away from danger. They weren't meant to be playing football so deep in a crucial area.

However, the heat was so sapping that day in Sicily that Mick, in particular, kept dropping back and demanding that I play the ball out to him and each time he did so I refused.

It was starting to get a bit heated between us but, to be sure, I'd rather get into an argument with Mick McCarthy than Big Jack Charlton!

Eventually, I had the ball in my hands and there, once again was Mick, a few yards away from me shouting and gesticulating at me.

I cracked.

How else can I explain the mad expression I pulled as I told him to 'Get the f*** up the pitch'? My adrenalin was flowing and I launched one of the longest kicks in my life up the park, which in turn had the Dutch defence backtracking to the degree that one of their players, Berry van Aerle, miskicked the ball on the volley back to Hans van Breukelen in the Holland goal.

He made a real meal of collecting it and Niall Quinn nipped in sharply to poke the ball into the back of the net.

I hadn't realised that my *mad face* had been caught on camera and that, even to this day, people still think it was just my motivational desire to spur the lads on.

At a recent charity event for spina bifida one young girl even told me she had a picture of that face on her wall from the match, God help her!

I mentioned to her that there was a lot more to it than met the eye!

Anyway, the 1–1 draw saw us qualify along with Holland and England who topped the group and so it was off to Genoa for the Romania match.

Sean Walsh, of course, was out in Italy, green sweater and all. He joined my family up in the stand when we were playing Holland. All the players' friends and relatives were there, including Tony Cascarino's mother who was sitting right in front of Sean. She and Tony's wife had spent the entire first half shouting at Jack, in her broad Cockney accent to 'GET TON-EEE ONNNN!' as Cas hadn't started the game.

Sean nipped away to get a bit of respite and fetch some Cornetto ice creams at half-time and was back in his position when the second half kicked off. Cas was still on the bench, his mother still shouting at the top of her lungs when we missed an early chance and everybody jumped to their feet, including Sean. As he did so, the top of his Cornetto flew off and dropped down the back of Tony's mum's dress – and she wasn't the slimmest. She let out a scream as the cold ice splatted on to her back but before Sean's cone was lost forever, he quickly rammed his hand down the back of her dress, picked up the remains of his ice cream then placed it back onto his cornet. When 'Mama Cas' turned around there was the shy Sean licking away at his cone with a look of innocence on his face. I'm not sure she completely bought his act!

By now, we had grown into the tournament and I was always struck by how much the Italian public bought into the World Cup. There was a palpable pride in the fact that they were hosting the competition and it was a complete televisual feast with a constant diet of football, including training preparations and player interviews. RTÉ were broadcasting every single day and from that coverage we were able to see how our progress was being regarded back home in Ireland.

Part of that reportage came in the form of a diary that the famous Irish writer Nell McCafferty was writing. Her daily reports were being gobbled up by a country desperate for any news on the day-to-day goings-on in the Irish camp.

Our base for the Romania game was in Rapallo, actually, at the same hotel that Scotland had used for their group matches. The Scots had been knocked out and so we managed to book into their rooms. Big Jack certainly hadn't scouted this place: it was total luxury. Massive, air-conditioned rooms and excellent dining were just a few of the items that saw us upgrade from Terrasini and Sardinia.

At the time, a couple of the Scots' players, I think Maurice Johnston and Jim Bett, were taken to task by the media back in Scotland for being seen outside their hotel, in a pub, and enjoying a little bit of hospitality. It was viewed in a poor light but, I have to tell you, that we were encouraged, occasionally, to go down to the bars and meet the Irish supporters. As a couple of us walked down, we recognised a few of the lads in one of the many bars, so we stopped and went in for a chat. Nell was there, listening, taking it all in, looking us up and down – what *was* she going to report the next morning? Not to worry, she was in the right spirit! So here we were getting praise for being down in the village, chatting to the fans albeit in a bar, while the Scots' boys were getting hauled across the coals. I don't think that would happen now.

Perhaps the difference was that we had advanced in the tournament but I still think it was symptomatic of that feeling of us all being in it together – supporters, players and media alike.

The coverage reached a peak after the Romania game. Rarely a day goes by without me at some point reliving the feeling that I had after the penalty save from Daniel Timofte and David O'Leary's subsequent strike to take us through to the quarter-finals of the competition.

It strikes me that even now as I write, a quarter of a century after the event, most people can recall where they were, who they were with and, above all, how they felt when Ireland reached the last eight of the 1990 World Cup.

An unremarkable game in itself that could have gone either way concluded with one of the most remarkable finishes in modern Irish football history. I sometimes characterise it as the moment that Ireland really 'got' football. There is no greater sporting drama to me than the penalty shoot-out.

Is it unfair? Possibly.

Is it a test of skill? Yes, but, more importantly, a test of nerve although no player should ever have his career judged on a moment that can take seconds but for which the ramifications last for years.

All I can safely say is that it was the shortest and longest half-hour I ever had out on a football pitch and, if I close my eyes, I can still feel the surge of elation, joy and pride that I felt on 25 June 1990 when I realised that we had achieved something that was way beyond anyone's expectations of us before the tournament. I have never felt more Irish than I did at that point as I truly believed the entire nation was with us inside the Luigi Ferraris Stadium in Genoa. In so many ways, they were!

*

Mick Byrne had always said to Jack as we prepared for the World Cup that he should take us all to have an audience with the Pope – as you do!

Big Jack had gone along with this because he thought that the only way we would be in Rome was if we made it to the final itself and, with the best will in the world, that was an outside bet.

'Aye, Mick. Of course I'll take you all to see the Pope.'

When he realised we were scheduled to play in Rome after Romania, Mick stepped up his campaign along with Charlie O'Leary and another member of the backroom boys, Eddie Cochran, our liaison officer. They started in on Jack again.

'Ah, come on, Jack. You promised us! You promised us!'

As soon as Jack gave the green light, Eddie, with the help of Monsignor Liam, took a hand in events. Liam was in touch with Bishop Anthony Farquhar of Belfast and Father Seán Brady who would become the Primate of All-Ireland a few years later.

'Bishop Tony', as he was known, was a keen football supporter whose club allegiance centred on Dundee United, funnily enough. Anyway, it would appear that, between the four of them, an audience was set up with the Holy Father.

A private papal audience usually accommodates about 2000 of a congregation and some of the rooms we were taken into in the Vatican as a group were incredible as well with huge Michelangelo paintings hanging on the walls. We felt that we were getting into areas of the building that very few people ever got to see.

Eventually, we were shown into a vast room where the rest of the audience were and we took our seats expectantly.

The Pope doesn't arrive immediately, of course, and so for about an hour and a half we sat and waited.

Every once in a while someone (not from *our* group) would get up and sing a psalm or recite a prayer before a choir got to their feet and launched into a hymn and that all contributed to a very serene, contented atmosphere.

Big Jack had a major worry, though, and that was the presence of the media. He instructed Mick Byrne, who would be sitting beside him, 'Don't let me fall asleep!'

Then, without much pomp and circumstance, the Pope suddenly shuffled into the room and started to address the crowd.

It was mostly in Italian but when he got to the bit concerning us, he broke into English, talking about the Irish national football team and then giving a nod of approval to our progress during the World Cup.

Then the bishops or cardinals repeated his sermon in different languages and the Pope would bless the audience after each one finished. This went on a while and Jack tells the story of him nodding off during some of the sermons, only to be woken up as the Pope would be giving his blessing.

Thinking that the Holy Father was waving at him, he would wave back!

Well, it was good manners.

At the conclusion of the public spectacle, we were called up to meet the Pope. Mick, Jack and Charlie presented him with an Irish jersey and a football and, once again, His Holiness nodded his approval.

And then came the moment that will live with me forever.

I was pushed towards the front of the group and was introduced to the Holy Father.

Remarkably, he placed his hand on my shoulder, leant in and in broken English told me that he too had been a *'bramkarz'*, *'portier'*, a goalkeeper, back in his youth.

Pope John Paul II knew who I was, how I earned my living and what had happened against Romania! The moment lasted only seconds but what a moment it was and I was transfixed by his presence.

The TV cameras and media were obviously all over it and a picture with me and the Pope appeared in just about every Irish newspaper in the country the following day.

As a group, we were all elated and I remember that David O'Leary was quite animated about the whole thing.

We all knew that something quite special had just occurred.

For me, a practising Catholic, reared in the bosom of the Church and nurtured by a faith that sustained me throughout those times of insecurity and fear that we all experience, it was an emotional and uplifting event.

Pope John Paul II was a famously charismatic individual who broke with tradition to travel the world and spread the gospel. I remember the excitement of the papal visits to both Ireland in 1979 and then Britain in 1982 but I could never have envisaged an occurrence that would end up with me standing smiling at His Holiness, the Pope, as he reminded me that before the priesthood there was football and there's him with his hand, a hand with the assured grip of a former aspiring goalkeeper, holding fast to Packie Bonner's shoulder!

It was another reminder to me, if one was required, that the game has afforded me some fantastic privileges both on and off the field of play.

There was a papal connection to our preparations for the quarter-final match against Italy as well.

The hotel we stayed in was outside Rome at Castel Gandolfo – famously where the Pope has his summer retreat.

On arrival, we all checked in and were handed our keys. Gerry Peyton and I trekked all the way up to our room and, when we opened the door, were shocked to see that 'the suite' consisted of two single beds – and that was pretty much that!

We literally could not get our bags into the room and were forced to leave them outside.

The Irish national team was preparing for the biggest ninety minutes in its history and we were having to sleep in billets no bigger than a cupboard.

Gerry and I weren't the only ones who went back down to reception to demand better accommodation. At the very least, a room that could fit both ourselves and our luggage. Oh, and a place to have a shave and a shower would also be appreciated.

The lads were all there as well and that's when we found out that there were bigger and better suites in the establishment but they were all currently being occupied by ... senior officials within the Football Association of Ireland! The blazers were being given the best rooms in the house as they had arrived ahead of the party. In fairness, once they realised that this was the case, the said officials immediately checked out and went to the Sheraton in Rome.

Gerry and I lodged in the room of the honorary treasurer Joe Delaney and his wife Joan and it would be fair to say it was spacious and palatial. I always got on well with Joe and Joan and enjoyed their company and they completely understood that the needs of the team were paramount.

As did FAI president Fran Fields who opted to stay on with the team as he felt that was his duty as the head man of the organisation.

It was good to see a face from home although it was a long way from Finn Park and the Harps.

After that, we settled down to prepare for the match and a couple of days before it Jack looked out of his window to see a large lorry arrive in the courtyard.

'What's that for, Mick?' he shouted over to Mick Byrne.

'That's the Guinness for the party after the match, Jack,' said Mick.

And, surely, there were barrels of the stuff.

Big Jack was unequivocal.

'Right! Get the lads down now and we'll all have a pint each.'

Which was fair play as we were all pretty much gagging for a pint. It was another example of Jack Charlton's understanding of the team ethic and togetherness being a vital part of the overall plan.

A pint wasn't going to harm any one of us; it might even have the opposite effect.

To be fair to the Association, they did agree to invite all of the wives or partners out to Rome to share in the big World Cup quarter-final occasion. It was also a couple of days for Ann to get a break away from looking after our new baby girl, Melissa. She must be the only baby, just six weeks old, to attend the World Cup in Italy. She didn't quite make any of the games, though!

Gerry Peyton's wife at the time was six feet tall and a real head-turner. She had been at all the games up till now, something she had done for almost all of the fixtures over the last number of years. It got to the stage that Gerry could never get *any time* after the matches to join the lads for a few beers.

So, after the Romania game, Gerry had said goodbye to her as she was going back home to England. Dare I say it, but the bold Gerry was relieved. We eventually got into our room in the hotel in Rome and no sooner had we turned the key but the phone went and Gerry answered it. I could see the relaxed expression turning to something of dismay: '... you're where?! Eh?! You're in Rome?!' He put the phone down shaking his head, 'That's another couple of grand gone,' he added wearily. Instead of going home, she had gone to Rome and was now booked into a separate hotel from the rest of the wives. It was to turn into a real issue for Gerry!

The big day arrived and as per usual after our lunch we went to our rooms for a lie-down and to contemplate what was ahead of us. Gerry and I talked through the scenarios that might come up and eventually I told him to turn off the light so I could try and close my eyes, not that I expected to sleep. It was always my way of trying to use positive mental imagery when I was resting before games – making the big save, coming to get the cross as players bounced off me.

Five minutes later the phone rang, with Gerry grappling for it in the dark. It was the wife. I could hear him whispering at first, then he got louder before finally telling her exactly what she should do with her electric hair curlers before adding, 'Do you know that we are trying to prepare for the biggest game of our lives here?'

I turned the light on and burst out laughing. For the next week we laughed at the thought of her trying to walk through Rome with those hot curlers. Her big problem was she had to get from her hotel to the other hotel where the rest of the wives were staying and she needed the electric curlers to fix her hair before she left for the game. She didn't know where she would leave the heated curlers when she was finished with them!

Let me tell you – *this* is why Jack hated wives to be around the players.

Over 73,000 people were squeezed into the Stadio Olimpico in Rome for our World Cup quarter-final against Italy.

The vast majority, of course, were for the host nation but I reckon a good 20 per cent were Irish.

Undoubtedly, it was the toughest draw we could have had as the Italians were the favourites to win the trophy on their own patch.

We had an early header from Niall Quinn that forced my

opposite number, Walter Zenga, into a reflex save but, apart from that, Italy came at us in force.

The boys had managed to more or less restrict the Italians to headers, but in the thirty-eighth minute, after we gave the ball away at the edge of their box, they counter-attacked. Roberto Donadoni picked the ball up about forty yards from our goal and strode forward, eventually hitting a shot from all of twenty-five yards. The shot was going to my right and, as I was moving in that direction to cover it, the ball swerved to my left. All I could do was to drag it with me as I fell outside the goalpost. The ball landed at the feet of Salvatore 'Totò' Schillaci, who was rapidly becoming the Italian hero of the finals. He was perfectly positioned to roll the ball into the unguarded net even as Paul McGrath attempted to make a last-second block.

Despite a typically spirited performance from the lads in the second half, it turned out to be the only goal of the game and we were eliminated from the competition.

Again, not a disgrace, but we were left disappointed and frustrated, as we would have been playing Argentina in the semi-final had we got through. Jack really felt, with the way they played a short passing game from the back, through the middle to the front, that we would have a real chance to beat them by playing our high-pressure game.

However, it was our first World Cup tournament, we had surpassed our expectations and, above all, represented our country in a manner that pitched a flag on the map for Irish football.

We had a sense that, back home in Ireland, people were responding to our achievements especially when the Taoiseach (Irish prime minister) Charles Haughey rolled into the dressing room after the match to offer his congratulations. He also managed to persuade Big Jack to go back out and around the pitch carrying an Irish tricolour, and that takes some powers of persuasion.

Like any politician, Haughey was a shrewd operator but it was still an honour for us, in particular the Irish-born players, to know that he had flown all the way from Dublin just to thank us for our efforts.

You could hear the murmurs from some of the lads, especially Mick Byrne who was a real Haughey supporter.

'Christ, it's the Taoiseach.'

'Lads, it's the Taoiseach – be quiet!'

As the Taoiseach launched into a grandiose speech ... 'Gentlemen, you have put Ireland on the map ...' Andy Townsend and Tony Cascarino decided they weren't so impressed.

'Who's this f****n' geezer then, Andy?' asked Cockney Tony.

'Don't know, mate ...' replied Andy, '... but I think he owns a tea-shop.'

Many years later I was to hear Andy recount a tale about myself from that day.

As I dejectedly made my way into the showers after Schillaci had put us out with that goal, Jack was leaning against the shower-room door, drawing on a cigarette while chatting to his captain. As I passed by, out of the corner of his mouth, he was reputed to have said, 'Aye, the Pope would have saved *that* one.'

Well, you had to laugh.

The tournament was over for Ireland, but, for many of us and certainly myself, life had turned more than a few degrees away from what it had been before and, just like a boat on the ocean, when that happens a new direction is charted out.

HOMEWARD BOUND AND CHANGING TIMES

THE RETURN TO IRELAND WAS ASTONISHING.

As I have previously mentioned, we got a little taster of this back in 1988 but the World Cup put everything up on to a completely different level entirely.

It is worthy of repetition that the pilot of our flight back from Italy flew a little bit lower over Dublin so that we could see for ourselves the huge masses of people who had taken to the streets of the capital to welcome us home.

I honestly think if Jack Charlton had announced, coming off the plane, that he quite fancied being the new president, at that moment he would have been elected, so big was the support for him. It is no exaggeration. I went into many houses and met people of all ages, and even though the majority never met Jack they all loved him. Whatever he had, I would have loved to bottle it up – total gold dust!

The plane, incidentally, belonged to Aer Lingus and had the words 'St Jack' painted just below the side cockpit window on the outer shell of the aircraft.

I doubt I will ever experience again that overwhelming tide of joy and gratitude that continued to pour over us as we made our way in from the airport to the centre of the city in a cavalcade of open-top buses.

And it was extremely humbling.

Five hundred thousand people, from all walks of life and the counties of the Republic of Ireland, had found their route into Dublin to join in the biggest possible party. They thronged the streets, hung out of office windows and climbed lamp posts and traffic lights to get a better view of the parade.

They wanted to talk about the nation grinding to a halt to watch the five matches we had played – the penalty shoot-out drama and, of course, as it was Ireland, the papal audience.

To this day it continues to amaze me that people still remember those weeks with so much clarity, still recalling every detail as if it was yesterday. It shows that when you are emotionally attached to something it remains rooted forever.

The Irish nation had realised that we were punching above our weight in the competition but, with every successive match, the momentum had been building and although we hadn't actually won anything, those few weeks in June 1990 had entirely entranced the country as well as changing the lives of all of us who took part in the adventure – not least of all me.

As much as I was enjoying the experience, I urgently wanted to get back to Glasgow to see Ann, Andrew and Melissa (now a little over two months old, having been born on 30 April), so I caught a flight to Glasgow the very next day.

All three had been in Italy along with Jess, Denis, Connell and Sean but they had returned to Scotland and Ann's dad, Tommy, who had enjoyed the tournament from the comfort of his own home.

No sooner was I back than we made plans to return to Donegal and a much-needed break ahead of Celtic's pre-season preparations.

We booked a flight from Glasgow to Carrickfinn and, as always, there was that warm sense of being home as the plane touched down on the Irish tarmac and taxied towards the terminal building.

I had been tipped off that there would be a bit of a reception waiting for us but was absolutely flabbergasted when I disembarked the tiny aircraft with Melissa nestling in my arms for her first visit to my home country.

There were thousands of people waiting for us to come off the plane.

As we did so, we were swamped with well-wishers. Some of the faces I recognised but so many of them would have been strangers to me and all of them had turned out en masse to offer congratulations.

Once again, I was home among my own people and they, in their turn, had gone out of their way to welcome back one of their own.

It was completely overwhelming and one of the most emotional moments of my life.

David Alcorn, local organiser and the one who nearly led the ol' fella astray all those years ago when Celtic came to Dundalk, had orchestrated a welcoming committee and then transport to ferry us back to Burtonport.

Our first stop, of course, was Central Park, home of Keadue Rovers. There were speeches from our Donegal TDs (MPs) Pat 'The Cope' Gallagher and Dinny McGinley but Manus McCole was also there, brimming with pride and, most importantly, the lads who had played with me back in the day.

This wasn't just my celebration – it was very much theirs as well and it was only right and fitting that I should stand, once again, on the turf where it had all started for me.

As I looked out from the man-made stage across the pitch to the goalmouths that I had defended as a raw apprentice scrambling my way along in the game, I thought back to this vital place in my journey.

I remembered the boy in the duffel coat clinging to his bag on Doherty's Coaches fighting back the tears as he left his home for a new adventure.

That night before Christmas in 1978 when I had returned home gratefully to spend an emotional Christmas with my family.

Those many nights when I had lain between the sheets of my bed in my aunt and uncle's Glasgow home, sobbing quietly and wondering if it was all worth it.

And, of course, I thought of my father – the ol' fella.

What would he have made of this?

He had travelled everywhere with Denis and I when we were at Keadue and now I was back at Keadue, having achieved dreams that in my wildest imagination would not have seemed possible when I was that gangly youth defending the home or away goal for the Rovers.

None of what I had achieved up until this point or, indeed, what I would go on to achieve, would have been possible without all of these people, players and family in my life.

Next stop was Dungloe for more of the same and it was absolutely mobbed.

It reminded me of the 'Mary of Dungloe' festival when I was a young fella. I could picture the marquee where Denis, Sean, Connell and myself had gone in the hope of getting a dance with a young girl.

Back in the day, there were three questions – What's your name? Where do you live? Can I walk you home? Sean was a shy fella, apt to panic a bit under pressure, and so, with the last dance of the evening and the event going into injury time, he popped the questions to a young lady.

'What's your name?' – 'Bernadette.'

'Where do you live?' – 'New York.'

'Can I walk you home?' – 'Ehhhhhhhhhhh.'

Memories so strong I could almost reach out and touch them.

We finally reached Burtonport, my own place, where there was a marching band waiting to lead us down the road and on into the village and again, loads of people just out to say 'Well done.'

Bonfires, bunting, cheering people and cars tooting their horns. It was all quite overwhelming and the only possible emotional equivalent to these events were the births of my two children.

I knew that, on this day and in this place, that my life would never be the same again.

One day, not that long after getting home, I was strimming the grass for my mother outside Castleport House. Casual wasn't quite the word for my clothing.

Denim shorts, hobnailed boots, an old T-shirt and a pair of goggles made up my uniform and I was covered head to toe in grass.

From out of nowhere, a group of Italian tourists arrived tentatively just beyond our front garden. One of them reached over to me and asked if this was the road where the Irish goalkeeper had a house.

I could have stripped off the goggles, smoothed my hair down a bit and swept away the grass on my arms and legs and said, 'Well, actually …' but, more than a bit embarrassed about how I looked, I told them that I thought he stayed a little bit further down the road apiece.

By the time they came back up the hill, I looked a bit more like my old self and I passed a pleasant half-hour with them talking football.

I'm quite sure that Walter Zenga or even the great Dino Zoff never strimmed their own grass!

My family handled this pressure with immense dignity.

It wasn't unusual for my mother to welcome complete strangers into the house for a cup of tea as they had just shown up because it was the home of that Irish goalkeeper.

My sister Mamie even wandered downstairs one morning in her dressing gown to find a tourist in our porch filming with a video camera.

Mamie had regularly taken time off from her job in Letterkenny Hospital to follow the Irish team but told me once that she only watched the end of the pitch that we were attacking as she would cover her eyes when the play approached my goalmouth.

God alone knows what she made of the Romanian penalty shoot-out!

One of the best stories from this time took place on the day of the Romania game.

Toney Gallagher always liked to have a project on the go up at Tullyisland. He looked after a number of small boats including the ol' fella's white punt. Now he had a new project, an old half-decker, about thirty feet in length and on its last legs. He and Ray, with the help of a few more, decided that they would spend that winter getting it back into shape, make it seaworthy and have it ready for the summer. We all bought a share in it, Denis, Toney, Ray and myself.

Toney was a bit like the ol' fella in that respect – once he had a project, neither kith nor kin would stop him from completing it.

Ray and Toney grafted away throughout the winter months stripping the timbers, renewing the decks and whatnot in the hope that the boat would be ready in time, as planned.

Of course, the work would come to a halt on the days that Ireland were playing at Italia '90 as that would be the time that Toney, Ray and that great friend from next door, Paddy Rafferty, would meet up in the Gallagher house and watch the matches together.

They actually finished the boat on the day of the Romania game and settled down to see if we could make it into the quarter-finals of the tournament at the first time of asking.

The bottles of Powers and Jameson whiskeys were their best companions on those days and, given that we went to extra-time and penalties with the Romanians, it would be fair comment to say that the boys had enjoyed Toney's hospitality.

Anyway, just as they were celebrating and no doubt toasting our success, one of them pipes up, 'Jesus – what are we gonna call that boat of ours?'

At that precise moment, up on the television screen comes the name of the boy whose penalty I had saved.

And that's how our thirty-foot half-decker had the name *Timofte* proudly painted on its bows by the time I got back to Tullyisland later that summer.

One famous individual whom Toney took out on *Timofte* was the fashion designer John Rocha. He was visiting a friend in the same business who had a holiday home beside Toney's place. The two of them hit it off immediately and promptly went out and caught a few fish. That evening they ate them fresh, washing the meal down with a bottle of wine and, of course, a few whiskeys for Toney. By the end of the night he reckoned that John Rocha wanted to buy any house he could get his hands on in the area and move Naomi Campbell in as his housekeeper!

I have to say that, after Toney passed away suddenly in 2009, the famous boat fared worse than her namesake. I spoke to Daniel Timofte in recent times and he was in good form while our old half-decker had to be scuttled and now lies some hundreds of feet down upon the seabed in the bay off Tullyisland.

Incidentally, Daniel also told me that he had a bar called The Penalty. Seriously! He said that if anybody came in and gave him stick he would throw them out before barring them from his establishment. After that story, I just had to tell him about the boat!

When Toney died, the whole environment that he had created passed along with him. Gone now is the open door, the craic, the sanctuary for depressed men to come and get the cure for their ills. It's amazing how the loss of one person can change everything forever, even if that person was as remarkable as Toney Gallagher.

Back in 1990, though, a lot was happening and the bulk of it was being generated by the fact that, after the World Cup, I was getting a lot of what they call in the trade 'profile'.

I am not a political animal, never have been, but I have a third cousin, Anton Carroll, who was an active member of Fianna Fáil. This was the party of then Taoiseach Charlie Haughey who had so memorably turned up in our dressing room just after the Italian defeat.

Anton and his wife Mary were to become great friends of mine and he invited me up to the Dáil for a private tour not long after the World Cup. In addition, I was summoned to Charlie Haughey's office. On arrival, I was met by Donagh Morgan who, at that time was the Taoiseach's private secretary, and invited in.

It was a singular honour, of course, and his state office was hugely impressive. Mr Haughey arrived and shook my hand. I had a chat with him about the football although he was not renowned as a sportsman and then, lo and behold, a photographer emerged.

And I mean 'emerged'.

I never saw the fella enter the room as – and I hope this is not treasonable – apparently there is a hidden door camouflaged into the wall of the office.

Anyway, as we stood side by side for the obligatory photograph, I became aware of Charlie's height and there was quite a disparity between us that I hadn't really noticed in Italy.

Seasoned political operator that he was, Charlie Haughey also clocked the discrepancy and he wasn't going to allow a photograph of himself looking a decent foot shorter than the Republic of Ireland goalkeeper into the public domain.

'Bend your f****n' knees,' he whispered as we closed in for the photographer.

I laughed but when I looked at his face I realised he wasn't joking and so I lowered myself down some four or five inches to make us look much closer in height!

He certainly was a shrewd operator, Charlie Haughey.

One of the offshoots of this newly found profile was that I was approached to do a number of commercial deals and, as Drury Communications had been handling the players' deals leading up to and during the World Cup, it made sense that they would handle things for me after Italia '90.

I felt I could trust Fintan Drury and Billy Murphy and they asked Liam Brady to get involved with the company. One of the first things they offered was for Liam to negotiate my upcoming contract renewal at Celtic.

I think I can say with more than a reasonable amount of certainty that, for most of the games that I played in the World Cup, and especially against England, Holland, Romania and Italy, I would have been the least-well-paid player, in terms of basic salary, out on the pitch and that included my Irish team-mates.

I had never been difficult to deal with when it came to contractual matters. I enjoyed playing for one of the biggest clubs in the world with a generous support and a history of success.

However, I was now thirty, a husband as well as a father of two children and, even though there is a perception that goalkeepers, like claret, improve with age, I was now entering a stage where I would have to contemplate my life beyond football.

Every contract negotiation would now be crucial. My view was, and will always be, that when your contract is up for renewal then that is the time to get the best deal possible. Once signed, it is time to get on with the job in hand. Of course, things have changed and sadly this is not the case any more. Agents, financial considerations and money have taken over.

I had no idea what Liam Brady said to Big Billy or any of the financial directors but he secured a three-year deal for me that increased my basic wage five times over. It was a phenomenal piece of business and allowed me a certain security as well.

Around this period, I also took a course at Caledonian University in Glasgow along with a number of other football players. It had been set up by the Scottish Professional Footballers' Association as a way of helping former players into business in that transitional time when they leave the game.

I had always been conscious of qualifications and threw myself into the course.

Even though my business acumen was limited I partnered up with Pierce O'Leary for a few years along with two other fellas in a cleaning firm called Safe Hands.

Can you see what we did there?

It did okay for a while but I started to find that it was demanding more of my time in a physical capacity than I could afford, and at key times of the week when my strict preparations for the weekend's match could not be distracted, so I sold out to Pierce.

It had given me a taste, though, of what might lie ahead.

Back at Celtic Park, the impetus was to stop Rangers winning their third title in a row as well as restore ourselves as the champions of Scotland.

Billy had gone to the transfer market again and made three key signings. Charlie Nicholas was brought back home from Aberdeen. This was the autumnal Charlie. A little bit older, a little bit wiser and with the experience that a hitherto ten-year career in the professional game could give you.

The marquee purchase was one of the hottest properties in the Scottish game and required Celtic to make their first million-pound signing if they wanted to lure midfielder John Collins from Hibernian.

Once again, a statement of intent had been made although there were as many supporters worrying if the middle of the park could accommodate Paul McStay *and* John as there were those salivating at the prospect of the two of them pairing up.

The final signing has been the subject of much rumour in the Celtic story and remains so to this day.

Martin Hayes was also a midfielder and he had been at Arsenal for about seven years when the club decided to accept bids for his services. As I heard the story, apparently a lower division club were about to come in with £70,000 for him until Big Billy got wind of his availability.

It's possible that Martin remained in Billy's mind as the guy who scored two goals against us on the night we lost a friendly 5–1 to Arsenal just after his return to Celtic in 1987 but, whatever the reason, he offered a fee of £625,000 and George Graham at Arsenal couldn't get the Highbury piggy-bank open quick enough.

Martin went on to play just ten games for Celtic in eighteen months at the club and his unfortunate spell was best summed up on the day he got locked in one of the other players' cars up at Barrowfield, couldn't get out and went to sleep on the back seat.

When the rest of us returned to the car park, covered in mud and breathing heavily from a tough session, there was Martin lying in the back of the motor, dozing with his football kit in pristine condition.

The worst indictment was that he wasn't really missed at training!

It all seemed to be a signpost of the way things were at Celtic during this time.

The League was, once again, retained by Rangers and it took a combination of our last-day victory away to St Johnstone and a Dunfermline win over Dundee United even to see us squeeze into a UEFA Cup spot for the following season.

We could have automatically qualified for that back in October had we won the League Cup Final against Rangers but we lost 2–1, once again, in extra-time.

The Scottish Cup was our only hope of silverware and, having knocked Rangers out for the second year in a row, we felt that we were in with a fair chance of lifting the trophy.

What a game that was with Peter Grant being sent off for a second yellow card as well as three Rangers players getting their marching orders into the bargain. In a strong display, we won 2–0 and were in the semi-finals.

The date was 17 March 1991 – St Patrick's Day and the twelfth anniversary of my Celtic debut. How much had changed in those years with me, the only name from that team of 1979 still playing for the Hoops.

In marking those twelve years – strictly speaking thirteen in all on Celtic's books – I had been granted a testimonial, effectively a present, for the end of the season.

A committee of local businessmen, like Richard Fitzpatrick and Tony McGuinness, undertook to organise a number of events as well as a top-table dinner and, of course, a match between Celtic and the Republic of Ireland.

The game took place on 12 May and I was profoundly grateful that a crowd of over 38,000 turned up at Celtic Park that Sunday, to take in a fairly competitive match between my club side and my international team.

It was a real Irish celebration with kids carrying flags of each of the twenty-six counties of my homeland and Tony had managed to get the famous Artane Boys' Band over to provide pre-match entertainment.

The band were a Dublin institution steeped in a history of helping orphans, teaching them musical skills that helped them onwards in life. I grew up watching the junior Artane Boys' Band lead around both teams in Croke Park on All-Ireland Day for the GAA Final and now some of these guys were playing in Celtic Park on my own big day.

Big Jack had kindly agreed to my committee's request to

provide the opposition and, as an added bonus, my brother Denis started on the bench for the Republic before joining the action as well.

It was a fantastically emotional moment to be playing on the same pitch for the first time in years and took me back to all those memories of Denis and I smashing a ball towards each other out on the grass at the front of Castleport House.

Of course, this time I didn't have to clean his boots to make him come outside and play with me!

I had always been slightly envious of Denis's career in the League of Ireland which encompassed two short spells at Finn Harps as well as great years with Galway United and Sligo Rovers.

I don't know why I felt that way. Maybe it was the fact that he was building up his own network of friends and I wasn't part of it and perhaps he felt the same way about me. We have never spoken personally about it.

I have been invited to some of their golf days and I have witnessed the camaraderie of this group of ex-players under the leadership of the great Joe Hanley, their ex-chairman. All having the craic and recounting their own personal memories of playing for Galway in the League of Ireland.

I have got to say this should also be a key objective of my great club Celtic. Former players, whether they played one game or 600, made welcome, coming together on a match day or events and enjoying their remaining years together in an exclusive group – players who wore the jersey for Celtic. A jersey that, in the words of Jock Stein, 'did not shrink to fit inferior players'. Please don't tell me that this is not possible.

Denis narrowly missed out on winning the FAI Cup in 1985, losing 1–0 to Shamrock Rovers in the final. A Galway victory would have cemented a Bonner family 'cup double' that year as we had beaten Dundee United in the Scottish Cup Final. It wasn't to be but I was in Galway recently to do one of my talks and this lady came up to me with a smile on her face to introduce herself, and in doing so she opened with 'You're Denis Bonner's brother, aren't you? Oh, Denis is our big hero in these parts, you know.'

That made me laugh. The tables were turned!

Denis's son, Patrick, named after me, came out on to the pitch after the match that day with his big cousin, six-year-old Andrew, for company as I was allowed the privilege of walking around Celtic Park and showing my appreciation to that phenomenon known as the Celtic support who had been so instrumental in helping my career by their mere presence during a match.

I had planned to make a presentation of a gift to both teams at my testimonial dinner. Many of the lads had travelled to Glasgow and given their time freely for the match.

Big Jack had told me he was happy with a box of Scotch whisky and that was easy enough but, in addition, I wanted to get something a wee bit different from the norm.

In today's world of modern technology the gift now seems rather inappropriate but, at the time, CD Discmans were the newfangled toy on the market. They were the compact disc equivalent of the Walkman – a portable way of listing to an album while you were on the move.

Although not inaccessible, they weren't the easiest items to come across but eventually I had managed to get an order for them and I even had the names of everyone embossed on the front.

On the night of the dinner, having spoken a few words of thanks, I asked the guys to come up one by one, led by Jack Charlton. As Big Jack approached the podium, I had the contraption out of the box to show it off a bit. He stopped and looked at it and I could see the puzzlement in his face.

'What the fook is that?' he asked, staring at the state-of-the-art sound machine and before I could explain he said, in a loud voice, 'What the fook am I gonna do with a toaster?!'

It brought the house down.

I think he was happy with the Scotch but he spent the rest of the evening being wound up about his gift by the rest of the lads at the table, especially when he found out the average price of a compact disc was about fifteen quid. That was the point when he started trying to sell his Discman on to any takers.

It would have been nice to go into my testimonial game with the Scottish Cup Final to also look forward to but a 4–2 replay semi-final defeat to Motherwell in April on an atrocious night for playing football had put paid to any hopes we had for silverware.

Another trophy-less season. Our second in a row and, by now, the pressure was firmly on the shoulders of Big Billy.

Liam Brady had spoken at my testimonial dinner.

Like me, back in the day he knew about the club but not much beyond Jock Stein and the Lisbon Lions, yet he spoke eloquently about both myself and the rich heritage of Celtic.

He had been blown away by Celtic Park, the club and the atmosphere during the game. Afterwards, as we sat in the bar, enjoying a quiet drink and reflecting on the day's events, he leant close into me and mentioned, in a casual fashion …

'You know, if the manager's job ever comes up here I would be very interested.'

And that was it. More than a passing remark, certainly, but not quite an application for the job although it lodged in my mind.

It would not have been an easy option for the board to relieve Billy McNeill of the Celtic job in 1991 but Big Billy would have known that two years without a trophy at the club would have been deemed unacceptable.

Celtic now had a new chief executive, Terry Cassidy, who had come into the job on the back of a career in the newspaper industry and he had a reputation for blunt speaking as well as an ability to make the tough decisions.

The upshot was that Billy McNeill was sacked.

His second stint at the club had started in the most amazing fashion with the centenary double but the deterioration in performances coupled with, as I mentioned, two trophy-less seasons, brought an end to a professional association with the club that dated back to 1958 and with whom the name Billy McNeill was synonymous.

It is sad, in this game of ours, that careers and jobs can end in a negative way and that is even more so today than it was back then.

And so the club were on a lookout for a new manager.

I was in at the ground one day when I bumped into Brian Dempsey, one of the club's directors. I mentioned the conversation that I had had with Liam in the wake of my testimonial.

It was a casual mention, no more than that, so I would not claim, with justification, to having a hand in the employment of Liam Brady as Celtic's seventh full-time manager in the summer of 1991 but he was an interesting choice.

For a kick-off, he was the first Celtic manager in their 103-year history who had not played for the club but these were changing times again and that fact, without being a prerequisite for the job, was now something that inevitably had to change as well.

I was looking forward to working with Liam, however, as I imagined that he would bring an interesting, possibly continental, dimension to the club having spent so many years in Italy soaking up their football culture, tactics and methods.

They say first impressions are lasting and when Liam Brady walked into the Celtic dressing room for the very first time to address the players, he possibly confirmed that theory.

Here was a group of players, none of whom could have laced his boots out on the pitch but would now be judging him as a manager – a first-time manager since Liam had no previous experience of running a club.

I cannot recall what he said.

I cannot even remember what he wore but what I do remember

was that the piece of paper he was holding, probably containing his notes, rattled as his hand shook.

You could hardly blame him for that, but it is amazing that what you say can be the first thing forgotten. I think there is a lesson in this for all of us.

This was a huge transition for Liam and I wondered how he would cope.

Management is all about communication and I once asked him how he had handled the pressure, the language, the culture and all of that when he left Arsenal to go to Juventus in Italy.

He told me that you have to be a loner, comfortable in your own skin and happy to keep your own counsel.

That's not possible as a football manager.

You have to be all-encompassing and have the ability to deal with groups of players as well as individuals.

Of course, most managers are judged on their signings and Liam moved quickly into the market. Paul Elliott had gone, leaving a huge gap in the middle of the defence. Gary Gillespie joined us from Liverpool. Gary was a cultured player who had excelled on Merseyside but he was subject to injury problems and that would become a factor in his Celtic career.

Tony Mowbray would later come up from Middlesbrough. On Wearside, he was club captain and certainly carried a presence. Rugged and austere on the park, he was anything but that off the pitch. Tony was one of the nicest guys you could ever meet and very softly spoken.

The big signing was my fellow Irish international Tony Cascarino who moved from Aston Villa for a fee of £1.1 million on the proviso that he could turn our attacks into goals and he was followed by a player who would have more of an impact on my position.

Goalkeeper Gordon Marshall moved from Scottish First Division champions Falkirk to Celtic Park. Gordon was only about four years younger than me but he represented a real challenge for the position. I started off the season as first choice but around November Liam dropped me and Gordon was in.

The team had been on a poor run and this perhaps reached its lowest point when we went out to Switzerland for a second round UEFA Cup match against Neuchâtel Xamax in October.

The 5–1 defeat was the worst result in Celtic's proud European history up to that point and was one of those scorelines that come back to haunt a manager.

Clearly, on the night we were awful, with our defensive frailties all too evident. Liam was highly critical of the players long after the match, even in the hotel where we were staying, and I did not escape his wrath.

There was now a different dynamic to my relationship with a Celtic manager.

Billy McNeill and David Hay had both been personally and professionally unknown to me when I worked under them but Liam and I had played together, socialised to an extent with the Irish squad and, of course, he had represented me the year before in my contract negotiations.

He had to be objective – in truth we *both* had to be – and his decision to drop me from the team was perhaps the right one – but it was a bitter disappointment to me.

Mick Martin was Liam's assistant and former Manchester City and England goalkeeper Joe Corrigan had been brought in as the first ever Celtic goalkeeping coach.

Frank Connor, of course, had been that to me back in the early days but Joe was the first coach brought into the club who was there specifically to work with myself and the other keepers.

It was both different and difficult for me. I felt as if I was being examined, checked on. I had to prove myself all over again, and with my mind playing tricks my confidence was down.

Was I hungry enough?

Did I still have the ability and agility to remain in the position?

Gordon Marshall became the first-choice goalkeeper in the winter of 1991, pretty much through to the end of the season.

There was a hegemony in the home dressing room at Celtic Park.

For a start, it was where the first team changed for training as well as on a match day.

The reserves were billeted next door in the away dressing room so that the very first thing a Celtic player would aspire to was to be in that home room as a permanent fixture.

On match day the number-one goalkeeper jersey was one of the first things you saw when you entered the room. It stared out at you – literally a marker for the man who was the regular last line of defence for Celtic Football Club.

It was a different colour from the rest of the strips, of course, and even that made it more distinctive.

For the first couple of years, this area belonged to Peter Latchford. This is where he stripped during the week and on match day, when I moved in from next door, I changed in a different part of the room. As I recall, close to the window where I could hear the supporters arriving outside.

When I broke into the team at the start of season 1980–81, it was still a few months before I would move into the usual area reserved for the Celtic goalkeeper.

There was a transitional period wherein I established myself and taking my berth at the first position gradually became the norm. Peter now had to move. Seasoned pro that he was, he had no complaints, but I wondered what he was thinking.

It was a changing of the guard.

I had held that position, by and large, for eleven years when I found myself, once again, playing regular reserve football. It was now for Gordon to establish himself and to earn the right, as I had done, to stand and change in that area of the dressing room. You may consider that a trifling thing but, psychologically, which is a massive feature of a professional sportsman, it was loaded with significance.

Not that I would give up without a fight.

Resilient, you see.

I may have been thirty-two but I wasn't prepared to walk away from the home dressing room just yet.

The season finished poorly for the lads and Liam: third in the League, ten points adrift of champions, Rangers, and, it has to be said, unlucky to lose out to the Ibrox side in the Scottish Cup semi-final.

On the final day of the season and after a dispiriting 2–1 defeat at home to Hibernian, Paul McStay ran over to the Jungle at Celtic Park, lifted off his green and white hooped jersey and threw it into the crowd. There had been speculation that he would leave the club and this appeared to be the proof.

I wasn't there that day as I was away with the reserves but it was all the talk the length and breadth of the country.

Paul was our talisman but the burden of carrying Celtic through these lean times with a group of players not really up to the standards that he had set a few years previously seemed to indicate that he had simply had enough.

Tommy Craig always raved about Paul, particularly in the centenary season. He would rail to the rest of the lads to 'Give the ball to Paul!' in pretty much any attack, even if he was surrounded, as he usually was, by a posse of defenders.

Great vision, a superb passer with equally fine ball-holding skills and a Celtic man through and through, he would have been a loss to the club but I honestly felt that he should leave that summer of 1992.

He was twenty-eight years old, in his prime, and it is my belief that, had he gone to the right club in England or even abroad, then he would have been classed in the same bracket as Paul Gascoigne.

Crucially, a big club south of the border or on the Continent would have broadened his horizons and given him that natural arrogance so necessary in the best, to believe in himself as a major talent.

For whatever reason, though, he was still a Celt when the players returned for pre-season training in mid-July and at the commencement of the campaign Gordon was still the first-choice goalkeeper.

By September, however, I had reclaimed the position.

That month is now historic in Donegal folklore as the senior GAA side had reached the All-Ireland Final for the first time in the club's history which was to be played on Sunday the 20th.

As I say, I was back in the Celtic first team and we had a League Cup semi-final coming up on the Wednesday against Aberdeen but absolutely nothing was going to stand in the way of myself and Ann getting over to Croke Park, Dublin, and cheering the lads on.

I still followed GAA. Even though I'd been in Scotland for well over a decade, I still kept an eye out for the Gaelic football results from back home. In my early days at Celtic, there was a Father Mick Lyne, a Kerry man who was parish priest at St Michael's, a goal-kick away from Celtic Park. Mick had been given permission to nip into the ground early in the morning and take a wee jog around the pitch and, as I was always one of the first into training, we bumped into each other a lot.

Mick also loved his Gaelic football and this was a period when Kerry won four All-Ireland Championships in a row (1978–81). They had a rivalry with Dublin, defeating them twice for that four-in-a-row but the 'Dubs' had done for them in 1975 as well as taking their own Sam Maguire Cups in 1976 and 1977 with Kevin Moran, later of Manchester United and a colleague of mine in the Republic of Ireland ranks. Another one of the 'Dubs' players, who actually won four All-Ireland medals and nine Leinster championship medals, was a man who would go on to become a great friend of mine as well as a substantial influence on me, Brian Mullins. Brian loved all sport and together with Anton Carroll, whom I mentioned earlier, the three of us would have passionate discussions about how to advance sport right across Ireland.

Anyway, I always had a bit of craic with Father Mick, winding him up about the 'Dubs', but he always came back at me like any good Kerry man. He told me once that at the end of the football season, instead of throwing away their strips and training gear, Celtic would hand a couple of bags over to Mick and he, in turn, would take them back home to Ireland and dispense them among the young Kerry lads.

One of the beneficiaries was his nephew Pat Spillane, who went on to win a record eight All-Ireland medals. These were the kits worn by the Lisbon Lions. How much would they be worth today, and is it any wonder that Kerry dominated the sport when they had the magic gold dust of the likes of Bobby Murdoch, Bertie Auld and Jimmy Johnstone on their backs? In later years, I would tease Brian Mullins that, just as Jock Stein's Celtic held sway over Rangers, Kerry did likewise with the 'Dubs'. Certainly, Father Mick always maintained it was the reason Kerry were rampant in the Sam Maguire Cup for such a long time!

So there you have it, one of the greatest teams in Gaelic football did their training in the gear of one of the greatest teams in Association football! I relayed the story one night to Mick O'Dwyer, the legendary manager of that Kerry side, and he said to me, 'Ah sure, I had the lads playing a wee bit of soccer during training as well. Course, couldn't tell anyone we played THAT game so we just called it "ground football".'

To be fair, in Kerry during those days that would have been the ultimate in heresy!

In 1992, there was great excitement about Donegal reaching the All-Ireland Final.

My former teacher Naul McCole was then chairman of the County Donegal GAA board and he had come down to pick my brains when I was on one of my visits home to Cloughglass. He wanted to know how the Republic of Ireland squad prepared for the big matches at Lansdowne Road.

Jack Charlton was adept at creating an atmosphere within the camp and the ultimate manifestation of this was when we travelled to the stadium on the team bus. There was a tape with a variety of songs that would be played, including 'Sean South of Garryowen', which Big Jack absolutely loved. He wasn't all that clear on the sentiment but it reminded him of a song that he would hear as a lad around Newcastle.

The main man under pressure was Charlie O'Leary as he was in charge of the tape and he had to time it to perfection, so that it would be belting out of our speakers as we pulled up to the stadium.

A sing-song was very much a part of what we were about back in those days and even Big Jack was known to get up and give us a sample of 'The Blaydon Races' – which ran to six verses with the same number of choruses so you had to stay awake when the big man was in full pelt.

Nowadays, you see young fellas disembarking from the team bus, tracksuits on, clutching a Louis Vuitton toilet bag and a set of Dr Dre Beats Headphones clamped on to their skull as they try to get 'in the zone'. For us, it was a tape-cassette player at the front of the bus and a volume control slid up to maximum so that nobody could say they couldn't hear the music. With this and Mick Byrne dancing down the aisle, it certainly got the emotions stirred.

This was the information that I gave to Naul and I don't know if he passed it on but the Donegal boys went into this game against Dublin as heavy underdogs so I guess any little snippet that could provide an edge would be welcome.

As I looked on to the pitch from high up in the Cusack Stand at Croke, I could see the 'Dubs" best player, Charlie Redmond, warming up and, over to the other side of the pitch, there was our very own Tony Boyle whose father, Anthony, had owned that stretch of land known as the block yard where Denis, myself and a host of our friends would play football for hours.

Donegal had another star man and he was called Declan Bonner.

Declan was a gifted player in both GAA and soccer and, in truth, could have, some would say *should* have, had a career at Celtic. He arrived in Glasgow towards the end of the 1982–3 season when he was only seventeen but had impressed with his ability and hunger for the game.

He was from Doochary, a couple of miles outside Dungloe, and went to my local high school, now Rosses Community School. He stayed in my house for his trial period, with a friend, Timmy McBride, who was sent over by the school team manager Paddy Murray to keep Declan company and I was given the strictest instructions to look after them.

Naturally, I had taken a particular interest in his development with the squad and had even gone as far as to ask chief scout John Kelman if Celtic would be following up their interest. John told me that the club would definitely be signing Declan and had even gone as far as to tell Declan himself, who returned home to Donegal waiting for the phone call that would make him a Celtic player.

It never came.

Billy McNeill's abrupt departure for Manchester City ensured that Celtic never followed up on the deal.

Again, it takes me back to those fine margins of luck that can make all the difference.

Jock Stein had signed me just *before* he left the job but, as Declan was waiting to put pen to paper, Billy was gone and so was his opportunity to play for the club.

When he scored the final point that day at Croke Park to seal the victory for Donegal and his manager, Brian McEniff, I'm not ashamed to tell you that there were tears in my eye. To quantify this in football terms, it was the equivalent of, say, Stranraer taking on Celtic in the Scottish Cup Final, outplaying them and winning the trophy.

It seemed like the whole of Donegal was in Dublin that day and I'm told that future Republic of Ireland goalkeeper Shay Given, himself a Donegal man from Lifford, but then only sixteen years old, had raced on to the park along with the rest of the support.

It was clear to me that the county would be, quite rightly, celebrating into the small hours of Monday morning.

That left me out a bit as I had to get back to Glasgow and prepare for the game against Aberdeen which we lost 1–0.

Another narrow semi-final defeat just like the previous season in the Scottish Cup against Rangers.

It wasn't just Declan Bonner's margins that I was thinking about that week, it was Liam's as well.

In the close season he had brought in Stuart Slater from West Ham United. Liam had played with him for the Hammers late in his career and remembered him as a player he could develop. The trouble was that, at this point, developing players were not the instant cure for Celtic's ills.

Up against a rampant Rangers we needed the finished article and it was perhaps a further sign of our desperation that Frank McAvennie was brought back from West Ham in January 1993. I have already put on record my admiration for Frank as a player but he was thirty-three when he came back to the club and for a striker that's a difficult barrier to clear. No one could ever fault his effort but as Rangers swept up the domestic treble I couldn't help but wonder what kind of a side we could have built if we had managed to persuade Frank to stay with us the first time around.

Just like his predecessor, Liam had now gone two years without a trophy. He had even tried changing his backroom staff by bringing in former Leeds, Manchester United and AC Milan player Joe Jordan as his assistant manager.

This was a huge decision involving, as it did, the removal of Mick Martin from that position.

Mick was Liam's friend. A confidant who bunked with him during their international careers and the man who 'had his back' at Celtic when doubters were expressing their opinions both in and out of the dressing room.

Joe Jordan was an immense personality to have about the place. He was forty-two when he arrived and thirteen years older than the Joe Jordan who had so spectacularly clattered into me in the opening minutes of Danny McGrain's testimonial back in 1980, but he was as fit as anyone on the first-team list and that's not an indictment of those players.

You would see him jog around the track at Celtic Park before and after training, doing his stomach crunches, and he brought a wee bit more of the Italian thinking to the club.

However, it was all too late as, following on from a 2–1 defeat away to St Johnstone in October 1993, Liam Brady resigned as Celtic manager.

I was saddened, yet, in a sense, relieved. His tenure had been extremely difficult.

When Liam first came to the club, we played golf together with Mick Martin and Tony Cascarino and I asked him how he was getting on and how he was settling in. The response was quite short and muted. I felt he didn't really want to confide in me and I wasn't going to push him on it.

That is a manager's privilege, of course, and he must stand on his own two feet but I felt that it was a lost opportunity.

I had been elated when he got the Celtic job for so many reasons but there was something like a ten-month period in his reign when we barely spoke apart from one notable occasion.

I was out of the team and I suppose I was being a little bit petulant about it and he took me out to dinner at L'Ariosto in Glasgow. That was one tough meal, I can tell you, and not because of the quality of the food, which was superb as always, but our conversation was awkward and stilted and, ultimately, nothing came of it.

In conclusion, Liam's time at Celtic was a huge disappointment for me and I am sure for him as well.

The speculation was that Joe Jordan would take over and that would have been a decision that would have delighted me, but he was rejected for a player from the club's past and I was now entering the most turbulent period of my Celtic career.

HAVE A NICE DAY? – USA '94

IF THERE WAS ONE EPISODE THAT, TO MY MIND, SUMMED UP Lou Macari's time as Celtic manager then it occurred approximately halfway through the eight months that he was in charge.

Out of the running for the League and out of the Scottish Cup, the club accepted an invitation to play a number of friendlies, including a match with Sligo Rovers, over in Ireland on 6 March 1994. I welcomed any opportunity to return home and, as I was out of the first team, I played in the match at the Showgrounds where a Rudi Vata goal brought us a 1–0 victory.

After the game, Paul McStay approached me and a few other senior players with a look on his face that suggested he was about to be hanged.

'I need to talk to you guys. I'm really uncomfortable with what Lou has just asked me to do.'

We were intrigued as Paul explained that Lou and his backroom staff had taken off for Limerick in the south of the country and just before leaving he had told Paul to go up and get the money from a Sligo administrator.

Come again?

Paul was club captain and it was up to him to go up and get the money owed to the club for fulfilling the fixture. It was an absurd situation, without question not 'the Celtic way' to my mind, and, to compound Paul's embarrassment, his brother Willie was, in that period, the Rovers's manager.

In all my time at Celtic I had never, ever heard of this practice of the team captain going into the opponent's office and asking for money owed to the club.

It was like we were a wedding band having just finished the gig and looking to get paid.

When we returned to Celtic Park the issue of the money was again raised and after a discussion between ourselves and Paul we advised him to relay exactly what had happened to someone higher up the chain – which he did.

Let me be clear: I am not saying that there was any impropriety involved here but it was another example, I feel, of the different approach that Lou Macari seemed to adopt in managing the club from what I had experienced in the past.

There was also the erroneous suggestion in the press at the time that some of the senior players had deliberately sought to undermine Lou's position in a manner that would lead to his sacking, but I can tell you categorically that was not the case.

Certainly, when he arrived in October 1993 we were all a bit wary of him. Frank McAvennie had absolutely no time for him as, to put it mildly, they had not seen eye to eye when both were at West Ham United and Lou was the manager but I always believed that a Celtic manager should be given the respect that the position holds.

Ironically, almost ten years to the month, we were, once again, up against Sporting Lisbon in the UEFA Cup.

Frank Connor had been temporarily in charge for the first leg and his oratory had inspired us to a decent 1–0 win over the Portuguese, who were managed by Bobby Robson, at Celtic Park. It was a slender lead and by the time we got to Lisbon, Lou was the new Celtic manager. The night before the game, we went out to the stadium as we always did for a training session to get used to the surface.

As I mentioned earlier, I always considered this to be a vital piece of our preparation as I could take in the surroundings, look at the position of the floodlights and check my studs with the pitch – which was a quagmire, incidentally.

For some reason, Lou decided to take me for a personal training session down at one of the goals. In his day, he had been a player of undoubted ability and his shooting was powerful and accurate. For almost forty minutes he repeatedly whacked balls in at me from all angles. They were hard, fast and aimed at every area of the goal. Top corner, bottom corner, middle, low to the left, high to the right, Lou just kept the shots raining down on me with virtually no let-up.

The mud was thick, the pitch sticky but I threw myself at everything he blasted my way and soon it became a personal contest. There were times when I could barely get up quickly enough from saving a shot low in one corner as he was firing in a shot to the top corner in the opposite side. He said nothing throughout this bizarre session. It was as if he was trying to break me like a wild stallion in the corral.

I have no idea how Jock Stein treated his goalkeepers but this seemed to be a throwback to how the keepers worked out in the 1960s and 1970s.

Never, in all my years as a goalkeeper, from the front garden of Castleport House through Keadue Rovers, Celtic and the Republic of Ireland, had I taken part in such a singular training session.

Had Lou been a player or even a coach of first-team standing, I would have told him where to go in no uncertain terms but this was my manager, my *new* manager, and I had to obey the instructions.

The following day I was absolutely shattered. I mean *seriously* tired like that stallion that had been ridden hard and put away wet.

And this was my preparation for a vital second-leg UEFA Cup tie.

We lost 2–0 and a guy called Jorge Cadete did the damage with a brace.

Now, I'm not saying that I was affected by the intensity of the night before but, with all good reason, there seemed to me to be no logic whatsoever in flogging your last line of defence until he is close to exhaustion twenty-four hours prior to a match.

Calling Lou 'unpredictable' was like saying the weather was a bit changeable.

He was the epitome of unpredictability.

You just never knew where you were with him.

He had brought in a backroom team of Chic Bates, Peter Henderson and Ashley Grimes. Ashley barely spoke to me even though I had played with him in the Irish international team and I mean a simple response to 'Good morning'. I was not sure what Peter's actual role at the club was and Chic seemed to be in as much of a quandary as we were about what Lou was doing.

My match-day preparations were sacrosanct to me and long-established.

At 1.45, there was the team talk which lasted until 2pm, at which time you would get changed before running out to the pitch to do the warm-up.

This was what I had always been used to and it was a vital part of my pre-match habits.

Under Lou, there were times when there was no team talk whatsoever. Jesus, sometimes you never saw him at all and then at 2.10pm the hapless Chic would wander in and slap the match-day programme down on to the bench in the middle of the changing room.

'Team is that which is listed in the programme,' he would say and wander out again as we all gathered around to see whose name had been ticked off on the list of players.

I guess we just had to work out the formations for ourselves.

One time, prior to a match against Partick Thistle at Firhill, I had organised my defence based on the formation from the pre-vious game. Mike Galloway had a pivotal role in the defensive wall for any free-kicks we conceded. Mike was a midfielder and I preferred to have midfielders in the wall so that the defenders could, well, defend.

Minutes before kick-off, as we're sorting ourselves out in the tiny away dressing room, Lou suddenly tells Mike to play as a sweeper for this game. To my knowledge, this was not a role he had ever played before and certainly not at Celtic.

I was trying to communicate some changes which would be necessary but now that Mick was playing at the back that was a waste of time. In my view this was complete madness.

The truth is, we were all over the place that day and conceded the only goal of the game when George Shaw nipped into the box, unmarked and on an untracked run, to poke in a cross ... from a free-kick!

Lou seemed to be testing us all the time with this sort of rhetoric.

Seemingly, he fancied neither myself nor Gordon for the goal-keeping duties so he brought up a lad who had played for him at Stoke City, Carl Muggleton. Carl was a likeable lad and, as it turned out, a good goalkeeper. One of the remarkable things about him was that he didn't really warm up before matches which I found strange. Forty-five minutes before kick-off he would be sitting casually with his legs crossed, fully kitted to play.

I said to him, 'Are you not going out for a warm-up, Carl?' but he would just look over to me and shake his head, saying, 'Ah, no. Not really. I'm fine.'

Admittedly, Lou's hands were tied with the internal strife at the club leading to a lack of funds so he had to bring in players on a shoestring such as thirty-three-year-old striker Wayne Biggins, who, and with no offence to the lad, I felt just wasn't up to the job.

His biggest purchase was to spend £550,000 to bring Andy Walker, again, like Frank McAvennie, a hero of the centenary season, back from Bolton Wanderers.

It seemed that, as a club, Celtic were bringing in some players who should not have been allowed to leave in the first place whereas Rangers were signing the likes of Danish midfielder Brian Laudrup, who was, quite simply, world class.

These were difficult days to be around Celtic Park although a trophy, *any* trophy, might have helped to salve the wounds but the internal strife saw the club pulling itself apart and we as players could do nothing about that.

At one point there were much-vaunted plans to build a top-class stadium further down the road from the historic home of Celtic Park, siting it at Cambuslang.

I certainly felt that the ground needed a complete overhaul and welcomed any suggestion that could bring that forward. Part of Rangers's success was rooted in the fact that they had invested in their stadium years before, meaning that a significant proportion of their revenue was available for stellar signings like Laudrup.

It all came to a head in March 1994 when Scots-Canadian businessman Fergus McCann led a group of shareholders who ousted the incumbent Celtic board, much to the delight of the vast majority of the support.

It was the start of a new era for the club and, to a lesser extent, myself as well.

Throughout the turbulent times at Celtic, when I was in and out of the team, Jack Charlton had stayed faithful to me and I was still his first-choice goalkeeper when it came to international duty. The momentum of the Italian World Cup carried us through to the Euro '92 qualifiers but, despite an unbeaten run of two wins and four draws, we were squeezed out of qualification by England who were one point better off than us.

That was a sore one and acted as an incentive to get back to a World Cup Finals tournament which, in 1994, was being held in the USA.

Our group included Spain, who were always automatic qualification favourites, and Denmark, the reigning European champions from 1992, so it was clearly going to be tough to qualify.

Lithuania, Latvia and Albania were also in the group and we fancied ourselves against all of them but Northern Ireland represented an unpredictable challenge in more ways than one.

The games against the North, we suspected, would be absolutely crucial – and so they proved to be.

We had won handsomely in Dublin against them by 3–0 early on in the campaign but were scheduled to complete our programme of qualification by going to Belfast in November 1993.

There were a few permutations that would take two out of ourselves, Spain and Denmark through to the finals. The Danes were in Madrid looking for a result while we needed to, at the very least, avoid defeat and hope that Spain would win at home.

Big Jack had taken us out of Dublin as our traditional base for preparation and so we checked into the Nuremore Hotel in County Monaghan, close to the border. It was a beautiful retreat affording us privacy to relax, prepare and it even had an area for Jack to indulge his passion for fishing.

We had been there before on a number of occasions and trained at the local junior football club's ground. After Italia '90 there were crowds of about 4000 people watching us – seriously!

Jack loved having us out in the country and felt that the interaction between the Irish squad and the ordinary supporters was an integral part of the overall success of the team.

Of course, we hadn't won anything, but we were putting Irish football on the map.

In addition, as I have made clear, Big Jack liked people and they absolutely adored him.

Schoolkids would come down after class and watch us go through our paces. When we jogged up the side of the pitch, people would clap, and when they eventually got tired of that, for a bit of a craic, one of the lads would start the applause again and everybody else joined in.

It was a special time and afterwards, for around an hour, we would hang back and sign autographs. Regrettably, so much has changed in the modern game with 'security' being the watch-word now and thus that side of mixing with the fans has been neutered. Understandable, perhaps, what with the age of mobile phones and Snapchat, Instagram and so on that allow images to go viral in seconds but, nonetheless, I do feel the game is all the poorer for it.

The fixture between ourselves and the North had the potential to spiral into a political football and that was the last thing anyone wanted but, this time, it was deadly serious – total concentration was required. For our part, we were focusing on getting a result but, given the sensitivities involved, FIFA offered a dispensation from their rule that the away team had to be in the country of the hosts twenty-four hours prior to kick-off and both sides agreed to it.

Thus it was that we set off from Nuremore Hotel on our team bus and travelled the couple of hours across the border and into Belfast.

The tension around the stadium was thicker than a heat wave.

This was, after all, a Republic of Ireland team playing at Windsor Park, Belfast, and on the verge of qualifying for another World Cup Finals.

Northern Ireland manager, Billy Bingham, was under pressure himself to get a result and potentially derail our progress to the USA, and as he strode up towards the dugout that night he set about stoking up the home support, waving his hands in the air and encouraging uproar from the crowd.

Even I, who had played once before in a friendly for Celtic in Belfast on a night when there was far more riding on the outcome than a football result and when the battle for some kind of supremacy was taking place on the terraces all around me, could feel a higher pitch of tension than I had ever experienced in a football stadium.

It filled the air and you could almost taste the foreboding element of it all.

Windsor Park exploded when the home side took the lead seventeen minutes from the end. Jimmy Quinn hit a screamer from outside the box. I felt I had the measure of it, only to see it dip in the glare of the floodlights and then the ball was in the back of the net.

Billy Bingham turned to the home support and punched the air.

While he was doing that, Big Jack was making a substitution, bringing Portsmouth midfielder Alan McLoughlin on to the pitch. His impact was virtually instant as he fastened on to a ball from about twenty yards and fired a volley low into Northern Ireland goalkeeper Tommy Wright's bottom right-hand corner.

Alan would represent us forty-two times and score a couple of goals but this one was by far the most important strike of his career as it brought us level, a position we maintained until full-time.

We remained on the pitch when the final whistle was blown and waited for what seemed to be a lifetime to hear the news from Madrid. It was a cold November night and the first thing to do should have been to get back in and take a hot shower but none of us wanted to go in until we knew the score.

A roar went up when we realised that Spain had won 1–0.

We were on identical points with the Danes and on an equal goal difference but our goals-for tally was nineteen and theirs was four less: an incredible statistic considering that we were heavily criticised during our time under Jack for not scoring enough goals.

As I mentioned earlier, my international career was, in a sense, compensating for the lack of success at club level with Celtic and the fact that we had qualified for another World Cup tournament was cause for great excitement back home in Ireland.

Towards the end of season 1993–4, I had, once again, regained my place in goal for Celtic and on the final day of the campaign we travelled to Aberdeen for a game against the Dons, the result of which was academic.

We were a distant fourth in the table and, although the changes at Celtic Park in the boardroom promised much for those supporters who dared to hope, it had been a miserable season all round for the club.

We drew 1–1 against Aberdeen and then returned to Glasgow.

Back in the day, the trip to Pittodrie was one of the longest you could make for a fixture and it was a terrible return journey if you came back empty-handed. I just wanted to get home, see my family and then look forward to a night out that had been arranged in the chapel hall for our local school. A sort of parent/ teacher affair designed to raise funds and I knew that Charlie Nicholas and Tommy Burns would be there with their wives. We could unwind from the season and escape the game for a while in the company of friends.

When we got back to the ground, I was getting off the bus when Lou Macari intercepted me.

'Got a minute?' he asked, casually.

'Of course,' I replied and followed him into his office.

Once in, he cut to the chase.

'I'm releasing you.'

And that was it.

No explanation.

No regrets.

No discussion.

A curt 'goodbye'.

It wasn't the biggest shock if I'm going to be completely honest.

In truth, if he was going to build his own side then he had to look at both myself and the likes of Charlie, who told me later that night that he had also been released, and move us on.

Of course, it's one thing to think these moments through and speculate about the possibilities but it's quite another when the reality hits home and the brevity of the message was a bit on the cold side – as was the messenger.

It was 14 May 1994. Sixteen years to the day, possibly even the hour, Jock Stein had sat in the Ballyraine Hotel in Letterkenny and offered me a contract that made me his last signing for Celtic Football Club – and now it was over.

I left through the front door of the ground, got into my car and drove back to the house mulling over what I would tell Ann. As ever, her support was invaluable and there wasn't really much time to brood about the situation as we had a night out with good friends – the best kind of tonic.

Tommy, Charlie and I were now ex-Celtic players and it was a night to share the good times, reminisce about some of the outright mental times and toast what we had all achieved during the playing times.

Tommy Burns was still involved in the game as manager of Kilmarnock. Along with assistant Billy Stark, they had got the Ayrshire side promoted to the Scottish Premier League the season before and, possibly more important than that, had consolidated their position in the League by finishing in a respectable eighth position out of twelve.

A few days after our night out, Tommy approached me.

Did I fancy coming down to Kilmarnock?

I was concentrating on going to the World Cup. I didn't want to be potentially the only player there without a club and it was, of course, a chance to link up again with Tommy and Billy, so

I thought the very least I could do was go down and discuss the situation.

Tommy made it clear that this was not about sentiment. He wanted an experienced pro who could make an impact. Tommy had done the same the year before with George McCluskey and that had worked out very well indeed.

The upshot was that I met with both Tommy and Billy as well as Bob Fleeting, the chairman at Kilmarnock. In addition, I met Jim Moffat, the real financial man behind the club, and we shook hands on a deal.

I now had something to look forward to after the World Cup and I was struck by the ambition of the Ayrshire club; but, more importantly, it would be great to work again with two men who had real passion and ambition to be successful.

However, my preparations for the tournament itself were not as meticulous as I wanted and, without realising it, the pressure was building up, creating anxieties that would affect my performance.

There was the training for a start.

Big Jack had taken us down to Orlando in Florida as our base camp before we travelled up to New York for our opening fixture against Italy.

The heat was an instant problem but that was the point. We would be up against Mexico in our second game and that was in Orlando. The temperature would not have been a factor for the Mexicans but for us it would be a considerable drawback.

The actual walk from the pavilion to the training pitches was a couple of minutes and when we arrived we were absolutely drenched because of the humidity. The sessions could only last twenty minutes because anything beyond that was exhausting. My preparations for a match normally involved at least an hour of training.

In addition, Orlando had a surreal quality about it. Frankly, you felt as if you were in Disney World, which, in a marketing sense, we were.

What I really loved about Italia '90 was that the Italians ate, drank and slept their football. They were steeped in it and took every opportunity to watch it, talk about it and play it.

Nobody in Florida knew what the World Cup *was* let alone that their country was hosting it.

We would wander into a mall with the squad and people would see us in our tracksuits and ask us who we were and what we were doing there. When you mentioned the tournament, they looked blankly at you and then got confused because they perhaps thought that Ireland had a baseball team in the World Series.

I now look back and realise that I was having a major crisis of confidence and the Italian game, up in New York, was on the horizon.

There are no excuses but by now you will have gathered that preparation has been the cornerstone of my life and any number of things can affect that; and when that happens, it gets inside your mind.

I had a contract with German sports company Reusch who supplied me with gloves that bore my name. FIFA had rules about logo sizes etc. so I had left my own gloves at home and was to rely on new ones that were sent to the team hotel in Orlando. This was a big mistake.

I noticed right away that the foam was slightly different in the palms. Apparently, the factory that supplied the original foam had gone bust. They just didn't feel right and that started to concern me.

Big Jack had also spoken to me about a tactic that he wanted me to carry out in the first game against Italy. He told me to roll the ball out from my eighteen-yard box and launch it up the field. David Seaman of Arsenal had introduced this to great effect that season. That, along with the new back-pass rule that had been introduced in 1993 to counteract the amount of time-wasting that had gone on at Italia '90, was also playing on my mind.

The lack of proper training, the gloves, new tactics, new rules – all these things in isolation were manageable but together they combined to drip-feed the pressure that I was feeling.

When Ann arrived at our hotel the night before the Italy game to pick up the tickets, I could barely speak to her. In a sense, she would have thought that I was just getting 'in the zone' for the game ahead but the truth is that I was beyond nervous.

I reasoned with myself.

I was thirty-four, an experienced pro with more than 600 appearances for one of the biggest clubs in the world. I had performed on the international stage many times and yet. And yet.

I remembered once, in my early first-team days at Celtic and ahead of a game against Rangers, admitting to Danny McGrain that I was extremely nervous.

Danny had calmed me down. He told me that nerves were a good thing, the most natural thing in the world, but it was when the nerves control you that you have a problem. It drains your energy.

There was a story prevalent around that time about a former Celtic goalkeeper, Alistair Hunter. He had arrived from Kilmarnock and for a period was a sensation, helping the club to a title and then playing an outstanding game against England at Wembley when breaking into the Scotland set-up.

Ally looked set for a great career in the game but in a crucial winner-take-all 1974 World Cup qualifier against Czechoslovakia, he lost a bad goal. The kind of goal that people always remember a goalkeeper for and, although Scotland prevailed 2–1 on the night and went to the tournament in West Germany, Ally Hunter did not make the squad.

It was said that he had never really recovered from losing the goal. I'm not so sure that was the case as Ally fought his way back into the first-team going on to win a League Cup medal in a 6–3 final against Hibs a year later but I used the story as a motivational aid vowing from an early age that I would not let my confidence be shattered by any eventuality out on the field of play.

In 1994, on the eve of the game against one of the favourites for the tournament, I needed a psychologist or, at the very least, a goalkeeping coach.

I have never forgotten that feeling and it has stayed with me right through to the work I now do for UEFA assisting professional goalkeeper coaches to achieve their first ever UEFA diploma. At this level, the psychological element probably makes the difference in whether a goalkeeper can really fulfil his potential.

On the day of the match, I tried to stay focused.

The pressure was intense. The heroics of 1990 in Italy had raised the bar of expectation from everybody back home. Apparently, one of the first things that Jock Stein said after his Celtic side had won the European Cup in 1967, making that the final trophy of five in a season when the club literally won every competition that they had entered, was: 'What will they expect of us next year?'

Success breeds success and one of the things that I was conscious of, and, indeed, I suspect my fellow squad members were as well, was that for all the triumphs of 1990 we would now have to at least emulate that – there was this overwhelming feeling of having to do it all again.

I had, as I explained, always used religion, my faith, as part of my make-up but my confidence even in that had waned.

The dressing rooms in the stadium where American-sized and they don't do average. We could have parked the team bus in there and still have room for a three-point turn.

When substitute goalkeeper Alan Kelly came out on to the pitch to help me with my warm-up routine, I made the mistake of wearing a short-sleeved shirt to stay cool in the soaring temperature. Alan was pinging balls at me but I'm not sure if it was his adrenalin or perhaps his own nerves but his delivery of shots was just not on the money. Then again, was it *me*?

They would either be too fiercely struck or slightly off target and the ball would skid off my bare arms as I attempted to catch it. My mind was playing tricks.

At least the pitch was good. I had played in Boston a couple of years before for the Republic – in fact, it was the only time I was ever sent off in a match for a challenge in the box that I couldn't pull out of – and I remember the grass being very broad-bladed and apt to slow down the game. The Giants Stadium grounds-people had returfed the playing surface and it felt all the better for it.

There was a certain tension in the dressing room beforehand. Jack had given us the game plan and that was to concentrate on stopping the Italians from getting their fluidity going – knock them off their stride, harry them at every opportunity.

At last, the moment came for us to take to the pitch and we were summoned from the changing area. Now was the time to be strong. The long walk would end with us standing side by side with our opponents, the imperious Italians, naturally installed as one of the favourites for the tournament, and they would be like film stars, immaculately groomed, boots gleaming and with that air of relaxed superiority. This was what we would have to face down. When you play a team like Italy the game can be lost in the tunnel. We needed to stand tall and remind them that we had been in their backyard only four years before and lost narrowly despite giving them a real game to remember.

And so, we filed our way down the corridors, the echo of our boots clacking off the walls, our kit of dazzling white shirts and emerald green shorts dancing with the light, the roar of the crowd muffled yet audible above us.

With every step, we knew that we would soon be face to face with our opponents, both teams knowing full well the importance of a good start in the competition, and so we rounded a corner and there they were – the Italian World Cup side of 1994, the best in Italy with arguably the best player in the game in Roberto Baggio, and they were, as we had anticipated, immaculate.

Unfortunately, they were also wearing immaculately white shirts! Someone had got the team colours mixed up and the referee, Mario van der Ende from Holland, was not happy.

We all looked at each other in disbelief. There were pre-match meetings for this sort of thing where team kits were analysed and approved and yet, somehow, some way, someone had made a mistake. With little over ten minutes to kick-off in a match that would have millions of Irish and Italians all over the world eagerly awaiting their first glimpse of their own players, both teams were wearing the same colour jersey!

I still don't know who took the decision – maybe it was the fact that we had another hamper in our dressing room with green shirts in it – but we all had to race back to get changed and a delay in the match was inevitable.

Kitman Charlie O'Leary was under severe pressure as he practically threw himself into the hamper where, miraculously, he had placed a change of strip and that is how, when we emerged from the tunnel, the Irish boys were wearing the classic combination of green shirts, white shorts and green socks.

I'm still not sure if the Italians thought it was all some big trick to keep them waiting but it wasn't – a mistake had been made although I know from my time in the game that there is nothing worse than being held back from taking to the pitch. Tunnel time is torture. You're so close to the atmosphere and the pitch that you can almost smell the grass and taste the ambience and all you want to do, all you *have* to do, is get into the arena, get the national anthems out of the way and get on with the game.

The Italians were being denied this and there is perhaps an argument that they had yet to hit their collective stride when we took the lead in the eleventh minute.

Ray Houghton scored the goal – a fantastic self-manufactured volley from outside the box that soared over the head of Italian keeper Gianluca Pagliuca. Thirty-two-year old Ray Houghton, a man whom some felt was too old to be active for us in a prestigious tournament, had opened the scoring for Ireland just as he had back in 1988 against England. That Irish magic was back and in his celebrations he ran towards the part of the stadium where our families were situated, did a roly-poly and ended up feet away from Ann and young Andrew who were going off their heads. There is actually a picture!

It had surprised me a bit to see how dominant the Irish contingent were in the Giants Stadium. I had imagined New Jersey, in particular, to be a very Italian-American city but perhaps I had seen too many films, although it was a unique sight for us all, when our coach crossed through the car park before the match, that there were hundreds of people, displaying Irish insignia and badges, enjoying their barbecues.

Now, *that* was very American.

Strangely enough, I had a quiet match and, apart from one blocking save, had very little to do. Paul McGrath playing alongside Phil Babb was immense. It was probably his finest game in an Irish jersey in my opinion.

You could also perhaps say that about Tommy Coyne. My former Celtic colleague was now plying his trade at Motherwell and he had been tasked by Jack to play as the lone striker in the Italy match. Tommy ran the leather from his boots and was instrumental in the knockdown that teed up Ray for the goal. After the match, he was asked to provide a sample for drug doping and such was his dehydration from the shift that he had put in that he couldn't come up with the goods. He was plied with copious amounts of water and was eventually able to fulfil the requirement but the dangerous side effect to this was that he was seriously ill on the flight back from New York to Florida.

There was a real concern that Tommy could be gravely affected and I remember looking on anxiously as Mick Byrne stretched him out across a couple of seats and massaged his head all the way to Orlando. It was uncomfortable to watch and it was with a great deal of relief that Tommy came through an ordeal that, at one point certainly in my mind, looked as if his head was about to explode.

The victory over Italy, a first in Irish international football, was the perfect start and back home in Ireland the celebrations were rapturous. Here was a side that would go on to contest the final, losing to Brazil on penalties, which meant that the only team to beat Italy over ninety minutes was the Republic of Ireland. How the Irish celebrated that! Right on the final whistle, I recall a couple of our supporters racing on to the pitch only to be ejected swiftly and with little nonsense by some US Marines but you would have required the entire armed forces of America to hold back the wave of euphoria that swept all the way from New Jersey across the Atlantic Ocean and into every house back in the old country.

It was a special moment – a memory from the world stage – and we were all delighted that the country could again have a huge party. But for us it was time to move on and focus on our second group match.

Next up for us, then, were Mexico.

They were a real slippery side, difficult to mark and very much at home in the melting temperatures. Big Jack was supremely conscious of the sun and his mantra was that we should stay out of it at all costs. Personally, I thought it was a bit like being on holiday; you built up your stamina to it over three or four days rather than avoid it.

Prior to the Mexico game, he had some of the lads wear white baseball hats during the preliminaries, line-ups, national anthems etc. Quite wise when you consider that a monitor beside the pitch was clocking a temperature of 130°F.

Jack had worked out that this formal part of the proceedings could have you standing for a good ten minutes in unforgiv ing, direct sunlight and with some of the fair-skinned guys like Tommy Coyne and Steve Staunton it would be best to take precautions. In particular, with Tommy, given what he had endured post-match against Italy.

There was also FIFA's ludicrous ban on taking water during the match. In this sort of heat that was potentially fatal. I always carried a bottle into the goalmouth with me anyway but our backroom staff tried to get over the problem by filling small plastic bags with water and throwing them to the players on the pitch, with varying degrees of success.

Mexico were a decent team but, in this heat, they looked like world-beaters. They handed us our first ever group defeat in a World Cup tournament by two goals to one – and didn't even look as if they were perspiring.

Luis García of Atlético Madrid scored both the goals. We had Denis Irwin at right-back and I tell you, on his day, he was one of the best I ever played with but he couldn't get near García.

From a neutral perspective, the game is possibly best remembered for John Aldridge's substitution after the Mexicans went 2–0 up in sixty-five minutes.

Aldo had been trying to get on the pitch for at least five minutes but the over-officious FIFA representative wouldn't let him even though Tommy Coyne had left the field and we were temporarily playing with ten men.

The fact that Aldo brought us back into it with a header seven minutes from time makes a case for saying that, had he been allowed to come on at the time that Big Jack wanted, he could have made a difference.

The bust-up on the touchline was spectacular with Aldo's thoughts on officialdom clearly being broadcast all over the world and Jack Charlton wasn't far behind him in condemnation.

The heat, the micro-training sessions, the result, the touchline mayhem – I was beginning to hate Orlando.

A friend of mine, Willie Callaghan, was at the Mexico match with his family and he told me that the seats in the section they were in were made of metal and when he sat down in his shorts he burned himself quite badly.

I couldn't wait to get back to New York!

The final group game was against Norway.

We reckoned that they would play a 'British' game – plenty of cross balls for a big striker to latch on to at the back post – and consequently we worked endlessly on this in training.

As it turned out, they barely crossed the halfway line.

Big Jack's lambasting of officialdom in the Mexico game saw him receive a touchline ban so he watched the game from up in the press box. It was a match we dominated and perhaps should have won but the 0–0 draw was enough to see us through to the next round of the competition for the second time in a row.

The advantage of Jack being in the press box was that he knew right away that we would be going through as the media lads kept him up to date. Mexico, ourselves and Italy were tied on four points at the end of the group stage and we all qualified.

Our 1–0 victory over the Italians put us in second place, below the Mexicans, and meant that we would play, somewhat inevitably, the Dutch.

They seemed to have a habit now of playing us in the big competitions.

The game itself was one to look forward to – but the venue?

We were off to the tropical heat of Disney World again – have a nice day!

Looking back, the Holland match was a bridge too far for the team in a sense. Our game was to pressure high up the pitch, especially against the Dutch, but the conditions would not allow us to do so.

We had some real young talent coming through in the shape of Gary Kelly, Phil Babb and Jason McAteer and, of course, Roy Keane was developing into a world-class player, but personally I felt that Paul McGrath was still the master. He made the world sit up and take notice.

Yet, the Dutch had time to play the ball about and they punished us with barely ten minutes on the clock.

Marc Overmars took advantage of a bit of hesitancy and broke through our defence; nobody could catch him and he played it across the goal where, telepathically, he knew Dennis Bergkamp would be and we were 1–0 down.

If we could hold it to that up to half-time there was a chance but then came a moment, five minutes from the interval, when the sky collapsed on us – and I was at the centre of it.

A ball was played to Dutch midfielder Wim Jonk well outside the box. He took a couple of touches before firing a shot towards goal.

It curled up towards my left side but was not overwhelmingly powerful.

I cannot, in any way, shape or form, explain what happened next.

As I moved to clutch the ball, it swerved from my grasp and trundled towards the net.

It wasn't the heat.

It wasn't the gloves.

It wasn't the pressure.

As clichéd as it sounds – it was just one of those things.

onegal return after Italia '90. Back among my own people.

Where it all began – Keadue Rovers and a return after the 1990 World Cup with a lot of the lads whom I played with back in the day.

Myself, my mum and Castleport House – home of the Bonners.

With my award from the FAI for reaching 25 caps. Little did I know that I would go on to amass 80 – to date a record for a Celtic player.

Rivals for the jersey but Gerry Peyton was a friend and mentor who helped me immensely. We always worked the hardest under big Jack! (Inpho Photography)

The one about the Irishman, the Englishman and the Scottish football team. Myself and Rangers' goalkeeper Chris Woods in more formal times.

Saipan 2002: The famous photograph that went around the world but the camera is deceptive. Roy wasn't happy but he wasn't throwing the bottle at me! (Inpho Photography)

Myself with Mick's Republic of Ireland backroom staff. *Left to Right:* Mick Byrne, Mick McCarthy, PB and Charlie O'Leary.

oney Gallagher and award-winning fashion designer John Rocha out on 'Timofte' –
ut no Naomi Campbell! (Magella Sharman)

oney always found time to take me out on the boat when I came home to Donegal.

Back Row, Left to Right: PB, Margaret, Ann, Bridget Mary, Denis. *Front Row Left to Right:* Mamie, Mum, Cathy.

Feeling as proud as anything I ever achieved in my own career. With my son Andrew and his youth caps for the Republic of Ireland.

Melissa Bonner

78

78

78

Oireachtas Rince na hÉireann 2009

Melissa was also a champion – a world champion at Irish dancing.

It's a privilege to be involved with a worthwhile charity like Spina Bifida Hydrocephalus, Ireland. (collinsphoto.com)

The Bonner family now with the addition of grandson Alan. *Left to Right:* Michelle, Andrew, Ann, Alan, PB, Paul, Melissa. (Grant Parfery Photography))

Perhaps my mind had moved that stage ahead of itself wherein I had clutched the ball successfully and had already initiated the move that set up our counter-attack.

In all honesty, I cannot say what caused that goal to happen – it just did and I was wounded by it. That expression about the ground opening up and swallowing you whole seemed most appropriate. I had always thought it a cliché but, in that moment ...

This was a horrendous mistake at a vital time and I felt it killed the game for us: 2–0 down against a side comfortable with seeing out an advantage meant that we were up against it to get back into the game.

It never happened and we were out of the competition.

I was in complete shock in the dressing room afterwards and the tears flowed. In my seventy-seventh international appearance and by a distance, one of the most experienced Irish internationals on the park, I felt that I had, without equivocation, let my country down.

It was an inescapable place of despair to be and the lads, perhaps quite wisely, left me to my own counsel.

I had to give myself a shake.

There were post-match duties to perform and I had agreed to an interview so I got myself showered and headed down to the press room to fulfil my obligations.

Two things of startling polarity occurred, one in the television studio and another back at my hotel.

Before the first interview I sat for five minutes on one side of the room, Liam Brady on the other. He had been analysing the game for one of the Irish channels and even though I stood, wounded by the experience of my mistake, and, frankly, in need of some succour, perhaps the friendly gesture of a man with experience of disappointment out on the pitch in full view of a country, a man who could empathise with me and tell me that everything would be okay – Liam just sat, stuck to his chair and not a word was exchanged between us.

I returned to the hotel and wanted to be on my own.

This, of course, wasn't possible.

Denis and Mamie were there and Ann was bringing up the rear.

They came up to the room.

I remember that Denis and I sat discussing the match and that moment. A few tears were shared and it occurred to me that we had shared so many things in life. His opinion, his support, mattered to me. It was the calming support of a brother in a time of need. There is none better and along with Ann and my family it helped to soothe my pain.

Eventually, it was decided that we should all get out of the room and down to the rest of the lads. We headed out of the room, looking for the lifts.

Coming out of the lift (the Americans called it an 'elevator'), I bumped into Eamon Dunphy – the scourge of the Irish sporting media. A man who would forensically examine an Éire performance and give his opinion without fear or favour.

A man who had the power to wield his views like the Ten Commandments and bend the narrative towards his point of view on the most obscure moments in a match that had affected the outcome even if you had not realised it at the time.

My mistake, the one that had effectively knocked us out of the competition, was meat and drink for his analysis and yet, as I emerged from the lift, he came up to me without uttering a word, reached up to me and planted a kiss on my cheek!

Now, to many that may have had connotations of a biblical betrayal, it might have Jesus/Judas connotations and I did not know quite how to read it, but I do know that when it came to writing up his report of the match, Eamon Dunphy took the long view rather than the easy one which was to blame Packie Bonner.

Still, I confess … it took me a long time to get over the events of USA '94. It was the lowest point in my professional career.

The people of Ireland were fantastic, though, and once again we returned to the proverbial heroes' welcome.

This time it was a bit more organised, maybe *too* organised, with a reception in Phoenix Park, but, in all honesty, my heart just wasn't in it and I felt as if I was just going through the motions. Yet, we owed it to the fans to be there.

It was the end of an era in so many ways.

Things would be different now and not just because new players and perhaps a new manager would come in. That was only to be expected but there was another feeling in the air.

Ireland was a different place. The so-called 'Celtic Tiger' was driving the economy, wages, housing prices, and there was an affluence in the country – even in Donegal where everybody seemed to be building the house of their dreams.

This was new in the Irish experience and that confidence could manifest itself on the field of sport.

Given what we had achieved over the last decade, there would now be a certain level of expectation every time a Republic of Ireland side took to the pitch. There certainly was in 1994 at the USA World Cup.

That, in a sense, was progress and in later years I would be invited to drive our football programmes towards new goals with a structure and a plan – but that was for another day.

CELTIC – THE FINAL YEARS

WHILE I WAS COMPETING IN THE WORLD CUP, CHANGES WERE once again taking place at Celtic Park.

Fergus McCann had dispensed with Lou Macari's services and was on the lookout for a new manager. I had taken a call from Tommy Craig one night asking me if I would consider returning to the club. I think he had the impression that he was in the frame for the job but, when the next Celtic manager was announced, it was another Tommy who was charged with taking the club forward in the Fergus McCann era – Tommy Burns.

I was delighted for my friend. Along with Billy Stark as his assistant, he was back where he belonged.

It did, however, leave me in an awkward position.

I had agreed to join Kilmarnock under both Tommy and Billy and now they were gone.

Bob Fleeting still wanted me to come to Ayrshire but, before I could make a decision, I took a call from Tommy at Celtic. He still wanted me to work with him but this time it would be in Glasgow. In all probability, I would be second-choice to Gordon Marshall for the number-one position but I would be expected to coach as well.

It was a conundrum as the fresh challenge down in Ayrshire had a real appeal to it. I would meet new people, new challenges, maybe new opportunities in the future and get away from the goldfish bowl that is the world of Celtic and Rangers.

But – it was Tommy.

How could I say 'no' to Tommy Burns?

And so I decided to accept the contract at Celtic.

Looking back – and in no way is this a reflection on either Tommy or Billy – I feel I made the wrong choice and for the solid reasons that I previously listed.

However, no regrets.

Every decision we make in life has repercussions and I will never know how it would have worked for me at Kilmarnock. In addition, the Ayrshire club became involved in a protracted compensation case with Celtic in the wake of Tommy and Billy leaving and that could have been awkward for me and my friends as well.

Besides, Tommy would need the grass-roots support of a long-standing pal as he took on the biggest challenge of his fledgling managerial career.

Fergus McCann and Tommy Burns – two men with a real desire to make change happen at Celtic, but two men with differing views of the way ahead.

Fergus had come in with a far-reaching plan that involved a complete transformation of Celtic Football Club from the summit to the base: a new all-seater stadium funded by a share-issue scheme, a high season-ticket threshold and a successful business model to take into the twenty-first century.

Tommy's thinking was much simpler – he had to stop Rangers equalling Celtic's nine-in-a-row record of League title wins and he had two seasons to do so. There was no other plan to focus on as far as he was concerned.

Two divergent opinions that were bound to clash at some point in the relationship. Business was Fergus's issue and, allegedly, he asked a lot of questions when he found out about the structure of a deal that Tommy had sanctioned with Motherwell to pay £1.75 million up front for talented midfielder Phil O'Donnell. The chief executive questioned Phil's injury record in relation to the fee which the club paid outright rather than in instalments based on appearances.

Tommy was unrepentant but if he hadn't realised that every deal he made would be scrutinised to the last dime then he did after Phil moved to Celtic Park.

The first season was always going to be difficult in that, effectively, a new team had to be built while offering a realistic challenge to Rangers's domestic dominance.

The support were crying out for a trophy and a real opportunity presented itself in November when Tommy and Billy took the team to the League Cup Final. The bulldozers had already moved into Celtic Park so the team were playing their home games at Hampden, which wasn't ideal and obviously would give Celtic a possible advantage in the event of a national final.

The League Cup was therefore moved to Ibrox for the occasion and the opposition were Raith Rovers from the First Division.

Celtic have a chequered history with the competition, and even under Jock Stein there was a run of lost finals in the early 1970s, but the 1994 final had a great deal riding on it.

The first trophy in five years – a successful start to Tommy's era as manager – a platform from which to mount a League title challenge.

All of these were important in themselves but Fergus was also launching the Celtic share-issue campaign the day after the final and the 'feelgood' factor could be important in raising the value of the stock when it came on the market in January 1995.

Charlie Nicholas had also been invited back to Celtic by Tommy and the move appeared to be justified when he put us 2–1 in front with six minutes left to play.

It seemed now that Tommy would have his first trophy but the euphoria lasted less than two minutes when a shot from outside our box, through a ruck of players, could only be parried by Gordon Marshall up into the air and Gordon Dalziel headed home.

The game went to penalty kicks and the psychological pendulum swung the way of the Fifers. Sadly, Paul McStay's strike was saved by the Raith goalkeeper and the search for the club's first trophy in more than five years continued.

It was a strange experience for me to be sitting in the dugout for a final involving Celtic but the pain of defeat was just as raw.

The League Cup had been hastily built into Fergus's plan but perhaps the sting of the loss acted as a rallying cry as the share issue became one of the most successful and oversubscribed in football financial history.

I bought shares and I know that some of the lads, including Tommy Burns and Billy Stark, did as well. Of course, like a good many Celtic supporters, these were shares that were never to be sold.

Out on the pitch, things were difficult to say the least with the team going eleven League games without a win between the end of September and the last Saturday of the year.

I had been concentrating on my coaching and other new duties but, of course, had stayed reasonably fit which was just as well since I was reinstated in the first team on Boxing Day.

A 0–0 draw was followed up by a 2–0 victory over Falkirk but, even by the turn of the year, it was clear that we were not going to win the League.

By and large, I remained Tommy's first pick until the end of the season but he was keen to make changes up front as well and so Dutch striker Pierre van Hooijdonk arrived from Holland and from day one with a debut goal against Hearts he looked the real deal.

The title race was well over by the time I played my final game against Rangers in May. They were the champions but we did bring some joy to the support with a spirited 3–0 victory. It was a strange season in that our record against Rangers was our best since 1988 with two wins, a draw and one defeat. Tommy Burns had even won his first Glasgow derby as a manager back in August with a 2–0 victory at Ibrox and, as you know, I always consider that to be important.

These were just potential shoots of growth, though, while the biggest sign of a stride or two forward would be that elusive trophy and we had the Scottish Cup Final of 1995 to look forward to against Airdrie from the First Division.

Of course, Raith Rovers had shown us that lower League status meant nothing in a one-off, winner-take-all game.

In all my years at Celtic, I have never felt pressure of the kind we were under to win that cup. I was thirty-five and felt, with some degree of certainty, that it would be my last competitive game for Celtic.

Obviously, I wanted to go out as a winner but there were far greater items on the agenda and Tommy Burns and Billy Stark were leaving nothing to chance in their preparation.

The feeling was that we should get away from it all and not just to Seamill as usual. Tommy wanted us out of the country and out of the reach of the press but when he put it to Fergus, the offer was to send us to Jersey in the Channel Islands, which was more offshore than off-limits.

Fergus stressed the core of Celtic support that there was on the islands but Tommy and Billy felt, quite rightly, that that was the last thing we needed at that point. Eventually he told Tommy that there was a budget of £5000 maximum and if he could get us somewhere for that, then so be it.

We ended up in Italy, on the shores of Lake Maggiore.

It wasn't sumptuous but it certainly got us away from it all and allowed us to focus on the task ahead.

Then it transpired that there would be an extra charge for the use of the nearest football facilities and, of course, the total budget had been blown on flights and accommodation.

Eventually, somebody spotted a decent stretch of grass that lay between two busy main roads and that mini-island became our Italian 'Barrowfield'.

Gordon Marshall and I discovered a garden area behind the hotel, similar to Seamill, and we based ourselves there for our workouts.

And so, as Celtic prepared for their first Scottish Cup Final in five years, the game that could end our 1990s trophy famine, the first team were being put through their paces on a parcel of land surrounded by Fiats, Alfa Romeos and articulated lorries on the move and Gordon and I were playing 'shots' in somebody's back garden. The parallels between myself and Denis doing the same outside Castleport House as teenagers were, once again, irresistible.

Just to complete the picture, kitman Jim McCaffrey was out on the lake, in a rowing boat, where his job was to fetch any misplaced balls that ended up in the drink!

It was like *National Lampoon's European Vacation*.

Throughout it all, though, Tommy and Billy kept our minds firmly fixed on the enormity of the job ahead of us – we *had* to win that trophy.

Walking out on to the Hampden pitch on 27 May, I couldn't help but think of the differing Scottish Cup Finals that I had played at the national stadium. I had seen every angle of the story from the heartache of extra-time and penalty shoot-out defeats to the ecstasy of lifting the old trophy after a hard-fought victory.

There was also, of course, the agony of that injury that kept me from participating in 1988 and, at thirty-five, I considered myself lucky that I was possibly getting one last chance to perform in one of the high points of the Scottish football calendar.

The game itself won't live long in the memory and it was certainly among the poorest of the Cup Finals that I had played in if you valued entertainment and flowing football.

Airdrie sought to contain us and, hopefully, get something on the break; apart from an early save that I had to be smart to make, I had little to do in the game.

Our full-backs were always important in the way Celtic played. Tosh McKinlay had come to the club late in his career, but was right out of the mould and, with that sweet left foot, he played the perfect cross into the box for Pierre van Hooijdonk to head past John Martin in the Airdrie goal. We were one up.

The First Division side huffed and puffed but Peter Grant, rightly named man of the match, was in superb form in midfield. Supporters still talk about the pairing of Paul McStay and John Collins who played that day but, for me, Peter Grant was a vital cog in the Celtic engine room.

It's all about balance and, as much as I admired John as a player, I felt that on occasion he would play the ball into feet just to get the return for a shot at goal. He was terrifically fit, pressing the first player, then the second and sometimes even the third. We learned to press as a team, all doing it together. The structure and roles were very clear and in my opinion it was much more effective.

With McStay and Grant you had the artistry with the industry, the greatness with the grit, and both worked tirelessly for the team, yet most of the time Peter's contribution in particular went unnoticed.

However, when I reflect on John Collins's career, I do now feel that the powerful self-belief and individual focus that he had were vital components in the success he enjoyed in that career. After all, we are talking about a player who played at the highest level in the UEFA Champions League with Monaco, in the English Premiership with Everton and Fulham and, of course, with the eyes of billions watching, he stepped up to score a penalty against Brazil in the opening match of the 1998 World Cup Finals.

Arguably, if Paul had been given that personality trait that John had in abundance, he would certainly have made his mark anywhere in Europe, but I will never forget his contribution to the team in the centenary season. We could not have achieved what we did without playing *as* a team – and both Peter and Paul, flanked by Tommy Burns and Billy Stark, were immense as a unit.

The feeling of release when the final whistle went in 1995 was mighty powerful.

Paul McStay let out the roar of a winning captain for the first time as Tommy Burns and Peter Grant ran to embrace each other and their skipper. I still don't really know where Tommy placed this victory in his career but, whatever he achieved as a player and a manager, nobody would forget that he was the man who reversed the slide for Celtic. After six long years without a trophy, Tommy Burns had delivered in his first season.

I made sure that I was able to stand back from it a little as I wanted to savour the occasion. It was appearance number 641 in my Celtic career.

I had been a one-club man throughout my professional playing career, playing for teams that won four League titles, a Scottish League Cup and three Scottish Cups. (I didn't play in 1988 so I couldn't count that one.) I had played in better teams than the 1994–5 vintage but, in terms of importance, that Scottish Cup victory is right up there with the sweetest of moments.

The following season we were all back at Celtic Park – the *new* Celtic Park. There were still sections to complete but Fergus McCann had been true to his word and the stadium was developing into a magnificent arena for the team to play their football.

Tommy had gone into the transfer market again and brought centre-half John Hughes from Hibernian and German striker Andreas Thom from Bayer Leverkusen. This would be the ago-nising campaign when the boys would lose one League match all season, against Rangers at home in September, but finish runners-up in the title race by virtue of too many drawn matches.

For my part, as much as I enjoyed working with Tommy and Billy, I was a little uneasy as there was no definition to my job. Tommy's view was that there was lots to do and that I had a roving brief to do it, but I always preferred to have a designated task, a project to which I could devote myself.

The difficulty with this situation was to present itself one day when I went to assist Willie McStay, Paul's brother and my ex-team-mate, with a training session for the youths who assembled during their school holidays. Near the end of the session Willie had to go home urgently as his son had suffered an accident. I offered to keep things going until the workout ended. When all was over I called the staff together and enquired if everything was organised for the next day.

That came back to haunt me the following day when Willie came into the office and accused me of trying to take over the team and to remind me who was in charge. Clearly one of Willie's loyal lieutenants had reported back and possibly misrepresented the facts.

I thought this was a little petty but I wasn't about to stand around and take this accusation on the chin. In no time at all, Willie and I were arguing the toss – loudly. Tommy came into the room as he had heard the raised voices and wanted to pour some water over the fire.

Suddenly, Willie was cool with the whole situation, which was a complete reversal from what he'd been telling me for the last five minutes.

It left me with a poorer opinion of Willie in terms of his outlook on my contribution and, I have to say, in many ways it was also Tommy's fault as he had not allotted me a position. I'm not interested in titles per se but it's difficult to mount a defence of your work when you have no clear nomination for what you do.

I was always happy to help and get involved and not just on the training ground as well.

I was asked one day if I would fly over to Belfast and represent the club at a charity occasion after Paul McStay had cried off. Fergus McCann had launched a couple of initiatives, including Celtic Charity and his 'Bhoys Against Bigotry' campaign, both of which attracted a lot of media attention, inevitably not all of it favourable.

It was a one-day affair.

The club were involved in a project that saw kids from both Catholic and Protestant backgrounds being taken away from their schools and out to joint ventures, holiday trips and the likes.

I arrived at the Europa Hotel in Belfast where the launch was being held, spoke to a few people and had my photograph taken with the kids for the newspapers before taking a flight back to Glasgow.

It was one of those things that you did as a Celtic player in those times. Get involved with the community, represent the club, that sort of thing, and to be honest I thought no more about it until a wee bit further down the line.

I had a telephone call one night from a fellow in Northern Ireland, a big Celtic supporter and a guy I knew well but, even so, his call was a bit random. We batted it about for a minute or two about the team, new players etc., and then he got to the rub when he asked me if I had been in Belfast in the last few months?

It had been a while since the school trip and such a small event that I struggled to remember it but when he reminded me of the day, it all came back to me.

Anyway, it transpired that my photograph had appeared in the newspaper, which, of course, was the whole point of the exercise, but I was now being told that there were a few people who weren't too happy about that occurrence for one simple reason. It had appeared under a headline that filled out the story by saying that a part of the trip was being funded by one of the British Army battalions, obviously as a public relations exercise.

Two things should have been clear here – the first was that I was representing Celtic Football Club and the second was that I had no say as to where the picture appeared or how the story was written.

I felt that was enough but now I was being told that the whole episode had displeased some people. In itself, this was quite chilling and out of my control, but, given that the greater percentage of my family still lived in Ireland, I felt I had to address the situation.

I approached Fergus McCann to ask if he could offer any help but was told in no uncertain manner that both he and the club would not be associated with this potentially political situation.

I was on my own and, frankly, a little bit disgusted by the way I was being treated by Fergus. I had gone out to do a job for the club for which I was now in an awkward situation, and I was being told that this had nothing to do with Celtic. There was nothing for it but to meet up with the people who were displeased and state my case, and so a meeting was brokered in Glasgow by my original phone caller.

It was difficult and at the end of it I came away wondering if I had done the right thing but, throughout the entire episode, my first thought was always to be crystal-clear on the facts of the situation.

People often asked me if my childhood and early adulthood were ever affected by 'the Troubles' in Northern Ireland but the truth of it was that we were brought up with very little mention of it.

The ol' fella was not naive about what was happening but, as a family, we were raised never to judge people by anything other than their character.

It was an inclusive upbringing and the fact that we lived on the very edge of the Atlantic, with some of the finest beaches in

Ireland, it was inevitable that the area was a holiday spot for people of all backgrounds. They would arrive in their caravans and pitch up for a couple of weeks and occasionally we, as kids, would play with the holidaymakers' kids.

One time that meant we palled about with the children of James Chichester-Clark, the Ulster Unionist MP who would go on to be Prime Minister of Northern Ireland although we had no idea who he was at the time.

In 1969, when the Troubles broke out, Castleport House became a retreat for a group of young Catholic children from the North, who were getting a welcome and much-needed break from the trauma that was unfolding on their streets on a daily basis. These were the children of previous guests and were familiar as to what respite could be offered in the peace and tranquillity of Burtonport.

It was a mixed bag of people who would come out to the area and their only recourse to what was happening across the border would be in the nightly news reports on our television set.

There they would gather, Catholic and Protestant, and digest the bulletins as their very presence became testimony to the fact that they were in a house that was apolitical.

My sister Cathy reminded me recently about the story of the Reverend Derek Poots. A lovely man, he would bring his family up to Burtonport every summer but, on the first occasion he did so, he was sitting one night with the ol' fella watching the news. The Reverend Poots hadn't let on what he did for a living, booking under the name Dr Poots, but at the conclusion of the news, as he stretched back and started to empty his pipe, the ol' fella looked over at him and said …

'So where's your parish?'

The good reverend started in amazement.

'Sure, how did you know I was a minister?' he asked.

The ol' fella didn't miss a beat.

'I've never seen anyone come into this house with as shiny a pair o' shoes as those and not be in the Church!'

Both men laughed heartily and a friendship was formed.

As I say, the Reverend Poots returned to Castleport in his caravan for many a summer while his family grew up.

My sister Cathy told me that he hadn't been up at the house for years but turned up unexpectedly in 2013 for a visit. An older man and not in the best of health, he explained that he wanted to see Donegal again and Castleport House with its unchallenged view of the Atlantic and miles of sand.

He passed away a few scant months later but we all like to think that his time in Burtonport seared his memory with wonderful thoughts, and the fact that his faith was never an issue was a testament to the values of my parents who firmly believed that when you entered Castleport House you left your politics and your creed firmly outside the door.

*

Jack Charlton once told me that you should only really manage a team for four years so it was a surprise to myself that he chose to stay on in the Ireland job after the 1994 World Cup.

By that time, he'd doubled the period of management that he subscribed to but obviously felt he still had something to offer the team.

Perhaps it was the lure of leading an Irish team through the European Championship of 1996 as they were taking place in England. There was an outside possibility that he could walk out with an Irish side at Wembley on the ground where he had enjoyed his greatest moment as a player thirty years earlier when England won the World Cup.

Whatever the reason, it sadly didn't work out as we failed to qualify for the tournament although we did take the campaign to a play-off at Anfield against ... Holland. Well, who else?

We lost 2–0 and roughly ten years after he had taken the job, Jack Charlton bowed out as the manager of the Republic of Ireland. It had been a remarkable decade, unparalleled in Irish international football, full of wonderful moments, and the Irish public had taken this plain-speaking, lovable Geordie, an Englishman to his very core, into their hearts.

Possibly, Jack had been a little too loyal to some of the players who had served him so well over the years and I include myself in that number as it was clearly time for change in the squad.

A new man was required to take the team forward and that man was my former club and country team-mate, Mick McCarthy.

This was an undoubted gamble.

Mick was relatively young, at thirty-seven, and had only been in management at Millwall for four years but I knew how strong an individual he was and in my estimation he could do the job properly.

Having played my final game for Celtic in the 1995 Scottish Cup Final, I was now also winding down my international career as well.

Alan Kelly Jr played in virtually all of the Euro qualifiers although I did have the distinction of captaining my country in one of the early matches in the campaign – a 4–0 win over Liechtenstein in Dublin.

That was an unforgettable moment.

The boy from Donegal who had dreamed of playing professional football since the minute he had tried on Packy Joe's battered old boots as a child was now leading his country out on to the pitch at Lansdowne Road, Dublin. I still consider it one of the highest honours of my career.

So now Mick was in charge and I was flattered when he called me up and asked if I would be interested in taking on the role as goalkeeper coach for the national side.

It was on a game-to-game basis but I was delighted to be asked and agreed immediately as the squad prepared for a clutch of friendlies ahead of the 1998 World Cup qualifiers.

Alan Kelly looked to be the main goalkeeper but there was another young man who was starting to impress and his name was Shay Given. Like me, Shay was, as I have said, a Donegal boy, and I remembered him from his youth days at Celtic. Our paths first crossed when he was fourteen and I was over in his hometown of Letterkenny running a goalkeeper summer camp. He was good but not in a way that singled him out to me.

Liam Brady signed him for Celtic and he developed quickly at youth level, having an outstanding season around the time of Lou Macari's tenure as manager. I had spoken to Shay one day and he told me that there was a possibility that he would be offered a professional contract.

His situation was that he earned £80 a week plus his digs money but when Lou put the deal to him it was a rise to £120 per week *without* the digs money.

Any way you did the arithmetic, Shay would have been worse off with the contract.

As Lou put it, 'If I push the boat out for you, son, then it's not going to keep me at the club.'

Shay was out the door.

This was round about the time that I was leaving Celtic to go to Kilmarnock and so I told Tommy Burns that Shay was also being released and that he should snap him up for the Ayrshire side. I also told him that I would work with him, coach him and look after him. Tommy agreed that this was a good idea.

There were shades of my early days at Celtic Park and what I would have given to have had someone from Donegal who could coach me and, in a sense, help me with the transition not just to first-team football but in adjusting to life away from home.

When Tommy took on the Celtic job, he was just as keen to sign Shay so, on a pre-season tour of Ireland, we arranged to meet up with him at the Burlington Hotel in Dublin.

When we got there, Shay had his father with him. I have to say it reminded me a little bit of 1978 and my parents and I waiting for Jock Stein in the Ballyraine Hotel. That memory became even more vivid when I saw who else was with Shay and his dad – the bold Fran Fields was there!

The sense of déjà vu was powerful and I couldn't help but wonder if we managed to sign Shay, would a game against Finn Harps be five years down the line!

I guess Fran was advising Shay but the matter proved academic when the young fella from Letterkenny told us that Blackburn Rovers had made him an offer of a professional contract – on £500 a week.

No worries about the digs money now, then.

To be fair to Tommy, he acknowledged that Celtic could not come anywhere near that wage for a youth player but we shook hands with Shay and wished him all the best in his career. And to think we could have had him a few months before for a few extra bob. I was left to wonder how Celtic could ever really compete at even youth level for a player, on that kind of money.

There are no guarantees in this game but it's fair to say that Shay's development and subsequent career has been a marker of his quality.

He was twenty when I started working with him in the international set-up and what he had was the ability to look you square in the eye and really *listen* to what you were telling him. That and his capacity for hard work marked him out as someone who would go far in the game.

As he was starting out on his international career, I was bringing mine to an end and that happened out in New York in the summer of 1996. I'm not entirely sure why Alan Kelly wasn't there, possibly an injury, but I was back-up goalkeeper and I played my final full match in a 2–2 draw against Mexico before then coming on as a substitute against Bolivia in a game we won 3–0.

It was a bit strange for me as I didn't know which camp to be in. Should I be with the players or the coaching staff? It all goes back to that clarity of position and, to be honest, I was happy to get the matches out of the way and concentrate on my coaching.

Mick was finding his feet in the job and had some big decisions to make, especially in terms of his squad. Now he was in the position of telling lads with whom he had played, such as Paul McGrath and John Aldridge, for example, that they would not be in his squad.

He also had to make changes to Ireland's style of play and I actually feel that he tried to introduce a more creative style of football, reminiscent of the sort of thing Tommy was trying to do at Celtic.

Each had pressure on them (that comes with the territory) and for Tommy Burns that pressure was racked up for season 1996–7 as he tried to halt Rangers's bid to equal Celtic's nine-in-a-row League-title record.

Again, signings were made.

Portuguese striker Jorge Cadete had arrived at the club as well as centre-half Alan Stubbs but if there was one signing that fired the Celtic imagination it was the Italian Paolo Di Canio.

Here was a guy, loaded with talent and hard to dislike. His work-rate was phenomenal, even out on the training ground, and he became an immediate hit with the Celtic support who always reserved a special fondness for flair with a little streak of temperament thrown into the equation.

Fergus McCann wasn't a fan of Di Canio and the feeling seemed to be mutual. Tommy would occasionally nip round to Paolo's house with a bunch of flowers for his wife in an attempt to pour oil on the troubled waters of another flare-up between one of his stars and the man at the top.

Tommy's job was to handle the mixed bag of foreign players now at his disposal as well as the domestic players. We were all a bit surprised one day to hear that Paolo had organised a meeting as he wanted to address the players. With everyone in the room he stated his case which was basically that he wasn't getting enough of the ball and certain players were not passing to him. He named Andreas Thom and Pierre van Hooijdonk. It soon became a war of words between the passionate Latin players, i.e. Paolo and Jorge Cadete, and the cooler talents of both Andreas and Pierre who were schooled in the efficiency of Dutch and German football.

Word reached the press, of course, but there was a hilarious way of defusing the situation and so Paolo landed up at training, with his head swathed in white strapping and bandages. That little episode was instigated by Peter Grant – problem sorted!

This was a period when Celtic were playing some of their best football in years but, once again, it was not enough to stop Rangers winning the title. In fact, the lads lost all of the Glasgow derbies that season in the League but knocked their old rivals out of the Scottish Cup at Celtic Park.

That officially made us favourites to take the trophy although I recalled those seasons of 1990 and 1991 when we had done the same thing and not gone on to win the cup.

And so it proved to be as another atrociously wet night for playing football saw Falkirk, from the First Division, knock Celtic out of the cup in a replayed semi-final match. That was Tommy Burns's last game as manager of Celtic. There had been speculation about his position for weeks but with Rangers homing in on the title and another trophy-less season to endure, Fergus decided that Tommy's time was at an end.

If I recall correctly, he was encouraged to leave by the back door but Tommy Burns insisted, having come through the front entrance as manager, he would leave that way as well – head held high. My friend had visibly aged in the job and the pressure had been enormous. He was devastated to leave, though; Celtic were a huge part of his life.

Paolo Di Canio was equally as devastated. He loved Tommy Burns and saw his dismissal as the final straw in his Celtic career although he was still under contract as a player. He retreated to Italy.

It was a strange period to be at the club and I needed to clarify my own situation.

Before that, though, there was a benefit game for me out in Dublin. This was not an unusual thing and most Irish players who attained a certain number of caps were offered such a match.

Remembering how great it had been back in 1991, Celtic were asked if they would provide the opposition for the game. A committee had been formed and they dealt with the negotiations for the deal which amounted to £52,000 plus expenses. Apparently no discount was on offer from Fergus – even for a player who had accumulated more than 600 appearances for the club!

Paolo was still out in Italy and as he had allegedly written an article having a go at Fergus, Billy Stark, who was in interim charge of the team, was told to get him back and out to Dublin. This he did, only to then be told that under no circumstances was Paolo Di Canio to play in the match which was a pity as a lot of people would have been looking forward to seeing him out on the pitch.

In the event, it was a great day but when I think about it now, perhaps it should have been more of a game between Ireland and an international select side. It had been a long, hard season at Celtic Park.

I wasn't sure how the wind was blowing and in the close season I was, as usual, back home in Donegal when Wim Jansen was appointed Celtic manager.

The club were out in Dublin in the pre-season and David Hay, who had stayed on after Tommy and Billy left, had organised the trip. I travelled to the capital and joined the squad, continuing to take the goalkeepers as my contract was not up until the end of July. I didn't really speak to Wim as I felt if he wanted me to stay around he would come to me.

After a training session at Celtic Park, when we returned to Glasgow, the first time I was to see a young Henrik Larsson in action incidentally (and little did I realise the impact that *he* was to have), I decided that I would go and see Celtic's new general manager Jock Brown, to find out their plans for my future.

Jock was also a lawyer so I imagined he knew a thing or two about negotiations.

I can still see him to this day. As I entered he was sitting back in a chair casually, with his long legs stretched on top of his desk, which I found a bit unusual. He got quickly to the point. I was to be offered another contract as the goalkeeper coach for the club. It was a full-time position and the salary was ... £18,000 a year.

I have to say I laughed and told him that I could earn more than that crossing back and forth to Ireland at speaking engagements, not to mention working with the international squad.

He wasn't impressed and it was very much a take-it-or-leave-it proposal. It was, in actual fact, a marker that I was not wanted at the club as I am absolutely certain that Jock knew I would not accept the position for such little pay. This was a full-time job we were talking about and I had a living to earn.

Jock's attitude was 'so be it' and my time at Celtic was now, officially, at an end.

I took the opportunity to mention that Peter Latchford might be interested in doing the job, that I was sure the money issue would not be a major concern for him. I remember Peter telling me when he was out of the game and his business went under that he was in that lonely place. He had seen his kids off to school and when they returned he was still sitting in the same armchair having barely moved.

As it turned out he was offered the job and took it. The yield the following season was great: Celtic finally won the League title for the first time since our centenary season and one of the star performers was the goalkeeper, Jonathan Gould.

I have no idea what Peter's deal was but I was delighted that, in a sense, I was able to give something back at the end of my Celtic days to a man who had been a great help to me at the start of them.

The only question now for me was – what next?

DESTINATION JAPAN

MICK MCCARTHY TOOK THE REPUBLIC OF IRELAND TO A PLAY-OFF for the 1998 World Cup Finals and, I felt, was unlucky to lose by the odd goal in five over two legs against the Belgians.

It has to be understood that Mick was trying to take the team through a transitional phase up against the expectations that had come from Jack Charlton's three major tournaments in a decade.

I sometimes wondered if that fact, or indeed Mick himself, was ever appreciated.

I recall a time around that period when he and I were sitting in the reception area of the Dublin Airport Hotel having a coffee after a training session with the squad. A couple of older ladies were looking over at him for quite a while as though they were trying to recognise him.

Eventually one came over.

'Ah, now – I know your face.'

Mick just smiled as I started to laugh but she persisted.

'Ah, I definitely know you. Are you on the TV?'

But still Mick never responded with his name so she went away, only to return moments later with a large smile on her face.

'Ah, I DO know you. You're the football manager. The new Irish manager …'

This time Mick nodded only for her to say …

'You're JACK McCARTHY, aren't you?'

By now I was convulsed and, fair play to Mick, he saw the funny side as well.

I was enjoying my time with the international team, apart from the obvious disappointment of non-qualification, but the desire to get involved at club level was a burning one. I remember one day when Tommy Burns and I were having our usual chat over a cup of tea. I was telling him how frustrated I was getting and he said not to worry. *We* would be back in the game soon, so 'enjoy the break'.

True to his word, when he took over at Reading in March 1998, he invited me to join him as assistant manager. Tommy joined the club a couple of days before the transfer deadline closed. He was desperate to make an impact and signed a number of players but unfortunately, in League terms, Reading were too far adrift. The players were psychologically finished and the club was relegated.

The big focus now was to cut the wage bill, but try to compete for at least a play-off place the following season. Fulham, under Kevin Keegan, and Manchester City, under Joe Royle, were also in the same division!

I could still maintain my work with Ireland, so I jumped at the chance and joined the club at the start of the pre-season. It was an exciting time in that Reading were also about to make the switch from their old stadium, Elm Park, into the new Madejski Stadium.

We were there for close to eighteen months and all along the way Tommy maintained to me that we were '... here to learn'.

And we certainly did that! From living with him for an initial six months I learned first hand that the rumours about Tommy Burns were true. Legend had it that his wife, Rosemary, would be up a ladder changing light bulbs as Tommy would be sitting devouring a football match on the television. *Man About the House* he wasn't!

I soon realised that I was cook, cleaner, washer-upper and general DIY guy to my friend. It reminded me of the first six months when Ann and I were married and Connell, who had moved back to Glasgow from England looking for work, had lived with us up until around Christmas.

He had that Tommyesque quality around the house as well and the mixture of one small bathroom, Connell's penchant for taking lengthy showers and Ann's morning sickness from being a few months' pregnant was potent enough for me to tell him, in the nicest possible way, that he had to sling his hook!

Eventually, Ann's dad, Tommy, got him a position in East Kilbride where he went on to be a considerable success. I still don't know if he's any use about the house but he could not have been any worse than Tommy Burns.

We had some laughs, though, as Tommy always maintained his humour. There was a guy we signed from Croatian side Hajduk Split, Mass Sarr Jr. He was Liberian and apparently best friends with George Weah, former FIFA World Player of the Year, something he reminded us about – continually!

Mass had one of those fantastic debuts for the club where, I kid you not, he played like Pelé. After the match, when the players had all departed, it was the custom of Tommy, myself and Reading coach Stevie Kean who was also a former team-mate at Celtic, to stretch out in the individual baths in the dressing room and shoot the breeze. That day, there was only one subject.

Tommy started it. 'What about Mass Sarr? Whose idea was it to sign him? Me?'

Stevie and I disagreed.

'No, it was me, Tommy,' I asserted just ahead of Stevie who was adamant that *he* had spotted Mass's potential when he went to Croatia to see him play and we, all three of us, argued the toss over who had made the deal. Tommy had the final say – 'I am the manager so I'm responsible.'

Unfortunately, Mass's debut proved to be a false dawn and he never, ever played as well as that again for us. I wondered for a while if we had misread his CV and mistook Liberian for Librarian!

Cue the post-match bath, then, a few months later, when the three of us were once again stretched out, this time after a less-than-thrilling performance from George Weah's 'best mate'.

Tommy started it again.

'Right – who the f**k was responsible for signing Mass Sarr again? It certainly wasn't ME!'

And, yes, you guessed it, Stevie and I put up an equal fight like Simon Peter before the cock crowed!

But Tommy was right – we were there to learn and I had my first taste of running a team when he was off sick for a couple of games and I was in charge. Although I had discussed team line-ups and tactics with Tommy, and had worked with Stevie on the training pitch, the matches themselves were my brief and it started well with a 4–0 win over Luton Town.

I told Tommy not to rush back after *that* one but next up was a visit to The Den – home of Millwall.

That was a hell of a place to go and I reckon I did more shouting from the sidelines than I ever did as a player that night. At half-time we were at 0–0 which wasn't bad and I sat the lads down and started speaking to them. We had a lad called Darren Caskey, who had once been at Spurs, and Tommy had taken it upon himself to get Darren fit and make him a player, which he did. However, on the night in question, Darren stood up to me, in front of the rest of the group, saying that I more or less hadn't been watching the game if these were my opinions.

It was a testing moment. I had been challenged by one of my own players and I had to justify myself to him and the group. I think I just talked over him and I'm not sure if that was the right or the wrong thing to do. Nowadays, I would have taken him aside afterwards and told him never, never to address me like that in front of the players again but, in real time, back in that dressing room, I dealt with it by just keeping going with what I had to say.

I saw myself more as a coach and with so much to learn about the management side of the game. I remember challenging Tommy one day at Reading when I thought he was wrong. He just paused and said simply, 'NOW you're an assistant manager.' Which I loved.

By the early part of season 1999–2000, the team were struggling again and it was no real surprise when Tommy and I were called into chairman John Madejski's office and told that our services were no longer required.

It had been a quick eighteen months and, as Tommy constantly reminded me, 'a learning experience'.

I was disappointed, of course. Ann, the kids and I had made the move down south for this new phase in my career but, thankfully, we had only rented out our Glasgow home and within a short space of time we were back up north.

By now, I had convinced the FAI of the need for a more concentrated approach to goalkeeping courses and that, alongside my duties as goalie coach for the Republic, amounted to a part-time contract.

Mick was still not having the best of luck on the tournament front, missing out, once again narrowly, on qualification for Euro 2000. The lads had finished a point behind the former Yugoslavia and one ahead of Croatia. No mean feat, given that the Croats had been semi-finalists in the 1998 World Cup, losing out to eventual winners, France.

The reward was a play-off against Turkey and, after a 1–1 draw at Lansdowne Road, we headed off to Bursa for the second leg. It was a dreadful trip involving a precarious boat journey once we had landed in the country and concluded in a disappointing 0–0 draw. We were out on the away-goals rule.

The pressure was now on Mick to go all the way to the 2002 World Cup that was being held in South Korea and Japan – the first ever Asian venue for the tournament. We were drawn in a qualifying group that included Portugal and Holland so it was never going to be easy but the lads had a superb campaign from start to finish with seven wins, three draws and no defeats.

The upshot was that we finished second to Portugal on goal difference, knocking out the Dutch and advancing to play Iran in the play-offs.

This was Roy Keane's time and he had been absolutely superb throughout the campaign, justifying his selection with great performances as well as playing a real captain's role for his country.

His crowning game was against Holland in Dublin when he completely dominated the midfield, negating the pacey threat of Marc Overmars with a crunching tackle early on. A Jason McAteer goal in a 1–0 victory got the headlines but it was Roy Keane who was, beyond a shadow of a doubt, the man of the match.

A young Louis van Gaal was the Dutch manager and strangely everything about their way of playing went out the door when he threw on all his big forwards in the last fifteen minutes. They reverted to playing high balls into our penalty box looking for that elusive equaliser but we hung on and Steve Staunton, who was playing in the centre-back position, won every header.

We got our lucky break earlier in the match when Ruud van Nistelrooy broke through on goal and Shay Given brought him down; it looked like a certain penalty but the referee waved away the claims.

At times like that you need luck and I remember thinking a few years later, when Thierry Henry deliberately handled the ball in the box to set up the French winner for William Gallas that knocked Ireland out at the play-off stages for the 2010 World Cup, if it was karma for the Dutch not being given a stonewall spot-kick against us back in 2001.

And so, Roy was the main man as the lads lined up to face Iran in Dublin for the first leg of the 2002 play-offs.

There had been a bit of doubt about him playing in the game as his manager at Manchester United, Alex Ferguson, was making noises about his fitness but he turned out for us, played well and the lads won 2–0.

It was the following morning as we all boarded the bus for the airport that the news came through that Roy Keane would not be travelling with us to the Iranian capital, Tehran, for the second leg.

Even though I was a staff member I had no idea that Roy had an issue, so like the rest of the group I was in complete shock. At first, no one in our party could believe it but when the bus left without him we all knew it was true.

This was a real concern. Here we were taking a young group of players into the unknown realms of the Middle East – into a city that most of them had only heard about through war bul-letins – for a lucrative, high-stakes match and we were without our captain, our biggest influence.

And, believe me, if there was ever a player you wanted out on the pitch in such a hostile environment with a combustible atmosphere, it was Roy Keane.

Yet, he wasn't there. His place went to the industrious Matty Holland of Ipswich Town.

Access to the dressing rooms in Tehran came from a walkway under the main stand and then another walk halfway around the pitch. The stadium was nearly full and we could see hundreds of bottles of ice thrown by the incumbents in the stand.

They were still at it when we took up our position in the dugout and I have to tell you that we never left the shelter of that dugout for the entire ninety minutes! As the teams were lining up, the place went completely quiet and a chanting prayer bel-lowed out over the loudspeakers which was taken up by every single Iranian, whether in the crowd or in the squad, giving the whole occasion an eerie sensation.

The intimidation from the terraces and stands was incredible but the lads nullified the crowd until about ten minutes from the end when Iran scored. The stadium erupted in a frightening cacophony of sound and I think if that had happened in the *first* ten minutes we would have been severely under pressure.

As it was, we held on for a famous aggregate win. Mick was elated, as were we all, and the players hugged one another at the achievement.

We didn't waste much time with that, though, as the bus was waiting to take us straight back to the airport and a flight to Dublin. It had been a fascinating cultural experience but no one was in the mood to prolong it so we showered quickly and boarded our bus.

The fascinating thing was that the road from the stadium to the airport was littered with glass; literally billions of shards strewn either side of our bus. Apparently, this was the only protest open to your everyday Iranian and, as a measure of their disgust at the national side, the passengers on the buses back from the game had kicked every bloody window out of the public transport.

It was a bizarre sight – even for a man who had driven home after playing in an Old Firm match!

The aftermath of the game was all a bit strange. The Republic were back on the big stage for the first time in eight years and the man who had done the most to help that along wasn't there to enjoy the occasion with his team-mates. Later on, we heard that apparently there had been an arrangement that Roy would play in the first game but if the result was favourable then he would be returning to Manchester.

I'm not entirely sure of the veracity of the story but I do believe that in the Iranian fixture lay the seed of an episode that would very shortly become known as 'the Saipan Incident', and I was right at the heart of that one.

Preparation, as I have so often said, is the foundation for success and, given that the 2002 World Cup was being staged in Asia, then most of the European sides were looking to get out East as early as possible and start acclimatising to the conditions.

Ireland were no exception and so Mick along with former player, Irish international-turned-travel operator Ray Treacy and liaison officer Eddie Cochran set off to scout for a suitable venue for the lads to relax and counteract the effects of jet lag prior to the tournament.

They alighted upon an island in the Western Pacific, north of Guam, called Saipan. It was a good choice, relatively close to Japan and South Korea, and allowed for relaxation with light workouts.

A fairly innocuous landmark until then, Saipan was set to become the 'Watergate' of Irish football.

Two issues raised their head when we arrived on the island. Firstly, we had assurances that a training pitch would be ready for us – it wasn't. There was little grass on it and what *was* on it was being cut by the locals when we got there, but if you had been raised on the playing fields of Donegal and the likes then this was surmountable.

Then came the gear which had been sent out separately by courier company DHL with everything from training kits to balls in hampers. Somewhere between Los Angeles and Tokyo there had been some kind of customs delay. Thankfully, kitmen Joe Walsh and Johnny Fallon had some back-up hampers on our flight just in case of such an eventuality but I'm afraid it did cause more than a stir.

We had moved on from 1990 by now and there was far more media intrusion in the Irish preparations, ultimately leading to questions being asked about the professionalism of the set-up.

I have to tell you now that, in my opinion, their interpretation of events was wrong and wholly misleading. The concept of going to Saipan was excellent and England assistant Howard Wilkinson later admitted to Mick that the Irish plan of being in Asia early was a far better one than England's decision to stop off in Dubai and then fly from there to Japan.

We were there to tick over before the serious work commenced at our Japanese training base.

It was obvious, even prior to getting to Saipan, that Roy Keane was not happy. Something was bugging him from the get-go. Bertie Ahern was the Taoiseach and he had come out to our hotel in Dublin to wish us all the best in representing our country but Roy was reluctant to get involved.

When we landed in Amsterdam en route to Saipan, Roy sat away from the main group, on his own, reading a book. Nothing wrong with that; everybody has their own way of dealing with the mental fatigue and sheer boredom of foreign travel. Shay Given fired up his laptop and was playing, on a loop, an Irish radio skit of Roy that was accurate in terms of his accent and actually quite funny, but I could see that Roy wasn't party to the hilarity as he sat with his face getting redder and redder. That was perhaps understandable as nobody likes being the butt of the joke.

Saipan was formerly a part of the American Commonwealth and did have the feel of a holiday resort about it, and perhaps this grated with Roy as I would see him take off for long, solitary walks along the beautiful beach that stretched out in front of our hotel.

Although this reminded me of Donegal, and the space, sanctuary and solitude that I required in order to recharge my batteries, it did strike me as a bit odd that Roy would seek his own company at this time, as though he was wrestling with some issues.

Mick McCarthy was all for inclusion. Like me, he had played

in that era when togetherness was the key and not just with the squad, and so he hosted a barbecue in Saipan one night for the press as well as the players. Again, Roy seemed to be unhappy about this as well. There was an uneasiness about him and the feeling was that only physio Mick Byrne was able to communicate with him. Mick Byrne intimated to Mick McCarthy that Roy was now thinking about returning home and, as I understand it, there were a couple of discreet yet frank discussions between the three of them as to how to avert that situation.

Matters came to a head on one of the training days. Myself, Mick McCarthy and his assistant, Ian Evans, would go down to the pitch in the morning and set up for the session with the players following on about a half-hour later. However, the temperature and humidity reminded me of Orlando back in 1994 and, with that in mind, I mentioned to Mick that I would like to take the goalkeepers, Shay, Alan Kelly and Dean Kiely down with us to the set-up to start early and maintain their sharpness. Mick and Ian agreed and the trio of keepers were all up for the suggestion.

And so we got down early and I put the boys through their paces for a good half-hour, at which point the team bus pulled up.

The goalies and I were on a water break and I noticed that Roy and Steve Staunton were having a little bit of craic about the fact that we were down at the pitch early but I thought nothing of it.

For the next forty-five minutes we had shooting practice on a small pitch with one goal at either end. Two goalkeepers would work while the third one would walk around as recovery before relieving one of the others who would, in turn, do the same walk. It was a decent session in demanding heat and at the end of it Mick wanted to play a quick practice match, no more than a fun kick about, to conclude a light workout. That wasn't unusual but, given that the goalkeepers had been out and working for a good thirty minutes before the rest of the squad, I took it on board when Alan Kelly approached me and told me that he, Shay and Dean were knackered and wondered if they could opt out of the game?

I thought this made a great deal of sense and Mick agreed and so all three of them trotted back to a makeshift tent to get some water while I stayed out with the main group. As they did so, I could hear Roy creating a fuss out on the pitch.

'Where are the goalkeepers going?!' he shouted.

I responded that the boys had done enough in this heat and that they were knackered.

'They're supposed to be knackered!' he offered, and turned away, quite unhappy about the development.

I thought it best to ignore the comment.

The tent had a cordoned-off press area but on the day in question there was only one photographer hanging about although his name escapes me, even now. Brendan McKenna was our press officer and a veteran in the field but I remember sitting beside him on the flight out and asking if he was the only member of staff who would handle press relations. My mind went back to the mayhem that broke out when we qualified to play Italy in the quarter-finals in 1990 and how a whole posse of reporters and cameramen were on us like hawks on a field mouse looking for an angle. Any similar success this time around would be replicated and much more with press activity but Brendan was quite relaxed about it.

'Ah, sure, we'll handle things,' he replied in a moment of what would become quite shortly a massive overstatement.

The practice match had concluded and Roy was striding towards me as I picked up some loose balls.

'What's the story with the f****n' goalkeepers? What's that all about?!'

'Roy, forget it,' I replied sharply.

Roy was finishing a bottle of water and as he did so he threw it off to the side and away from me but in that very instant an alert photographer had sized up the situation and he took a picture.

They say the camera never lies and yet, to look at this snap, it would appear that Roy was actually throwing the bottle *at* me, which was not the case! I thought little of it but I know that he then went into the tent and had a go at the goalkeepers.

Alan Kelly was a big lad and not one to take a dressing down so he told Roy to behave or he would 'take him outside'.

I have been on literally hundreds of training pitches in my time and, believe me, none of this stuff is unique. It's a pressurised environment with players working hard and occasionally tempers get frayed. I didn't even think that much of it half an hour later when, prior to boarding the team bus to return to the hotel, Roy marched up and demanded to know where Mick was – again, 'words' were exchanged between the pair.

The blue touchpaper moment to all this occurred when the photographer mentioned to a young Sky Sports reporter who was hanging around that Roy and I had had a huge bust-up out on the pitch and he had a photograph to prove it. The reporter immediately sought out Brendan McKenna and asked if this was true.

'Aye, surely,' Brendan responded in all innocence. 'The two of them were going at it out there.'

And that was it. The combination of the breaking story and the photograph that alleged that Roy had thrown a bottle of water at me went viral within hours.

We weren't to know anything about this. In fact, I went to bed that night oblivious to the coming storm and it was only when I woke up in the morning to a mobile phone *bursting* with messages that I thought there was something out of the ordinary going on … and I didn't think for one minute that it was happening in Saipan.

I phoned Ann immediately in Scotland.

'What's going on with you and Roy?' she asked. 'It's all over the news here that you've had a bust-up and Roy's leaving for home and you'll be leaving as well.'

I told her that there was nothing going on that didn't happen on a thousand training grounds every day, so I dismissed it. By the time I got down to our private breakfast room, there were only two people left, ironically Roy and Alan Kelly, sitting together having the craic, the best of pals again. I got some cereal and joined them.

'Roy, do you know what's going on back home in the press?' I asked and he was *fully* aware of the situation.

He responded coolly, 'Ah, don't worry. That's just the press, you know.'

And as far as I was concerned that was the end of the matter.

A slow news day and a story that would disappear into the atmosphere as the next one came along.

Which it did.

But this time it was Roy giving an exclusive interview to Tom Humphries of the *Irish Times* where, principally, he slated some of the players in the squad. Again, I've never been sure if he had been taken out of context but it was an article in one of the leading newspapers back home and, as such, could not be ignored by Mick McCarthy.

He called myself and Ian Evans up to his room and before taking a shower showed us a fax of the article that had been sent to him in the middle of the night.

As he showered, Mick would holler out to us that he had to sort out this situation now, before we headed to Japan. If we'd had the hindsight of what was to happen we may have counselled Mick differently, but at the time I agreed with Mick's sentiment, as did Ian. Let's be frank: this sort of thing could be absolutely fatal for squad morale.

He contacted Mick Byrne and told him to keep the lads in the private dining room we had after their dinner so that he could talk to them. It was a slightly bizarre scene when we entered the room as there were a couple of guys floating around the tables, playing a guitar and an accordion as 'entertainment'.

Mick McCarthy was not in the mood for a sing-song and so he whispered to Mick Byrne to get rid of the musicians. Once they had left, he addressed the group and in the main it was about passports and baggage and making sure that they had everything good to go for the trip out to Japan the following day. He outlined the fact that we'd had a few issues in Saipan with the training pitch and facilities etc. but assured us all that this would greatly improve in Japan.

And then the mood darkened as he addressed Roy directly who, throughout the entirety of Mick's speech had sat impassively with a glass of water in front of him, staring blankly at the wall.

'Roy – I've got a fax here from an interview you gave to the *Irish Times*. Can you—'

But before he could finish his question Roy took off on a rant – and it was deeply personal – and his venom was directly aimed at Mick. He even dragged up a story from ten years earlier when they had had words on the bus after a relaxation day in Boston to the effect that Roy had told Mick what he thought of him then and that his opinion had not changed ... in a decade!

It was, frankly, astonishing and embarrassing. Now, I knew Mick McCarthy well. I was on the pitch with him at Celtic one day when he punched out a man mountain called Crawford Baptie, who played for Falkirk, before heading up the tunnel as if he had just swatted a fly. Mick McCarthy could handle himself in any company and yet, as a manager, he opted to allow Roy

Keane, the captain of his team, to throw insults at him for what seemed an eternity before responding verbally. I was surprised, I seriously thought that Mick would have been on him like a flash, but times had moved on. He was an international manager now, showing creditable restraint.

Mick brought up the incident prior to the return game with Iran and Roy's 'injury' that had ruled him out of the match. You could see the rage building in Roy's eyes.

But he had truly crossed the line as far as Mick was concerned, there was no way back. It was over.

Mick looked at his captain 'Go. Piss off.'

Roy muttered something under his breath to the effect that he was 'better out of this whole thing'. He stood up and stormed off to his room.

There was complete silence for a minute or two. Everybody was in shock. Potentially one of the greatest players in the world had decided, by his actions, that he wanted no part of Ireland's bid to advance in the greatest international tournament in the world.

For me, personally, pure conjecture: I don't know if there was something going on in Roy's life and I could not surmise what it was. When I look back at the pattern of behaviour, from the Taoiseach's meeting in Dublin; the solitary figure reading his book in Amsterdam Airport while his team-mates were having a laugh; the long, lonely walks on the beach; and, of course, the strange discourse out on the training pitch – all of these incidents pointed to a man who was not at ease with himself or his surroundings.

We could control events in Japan but what was happening back in Ireland was beyond our remit. The 'Keane Debate' dominated the radio and TV networks at home and seemed to split the country. There were demonstrations outside the FAI headquarters. Bertie Ahern, a staunch Manchester United supporter, even waded into the argument with an opinion.

Eddie Jordan, another United man, had reportedly made his personal plane available to Roy if he wanted to go back and, if I remember rightly, even one of the members of Westlife got involved in the debate.

We were loyal to Mick McCarthy and yet I felt I had to make a point to him. My feeling was that he should, at the very least, offer an olive branch to Roy in order to provide him with an opportunity to return to the squad.

This would be a huge gesture on Mick's part but if Roy was to return under his own steam then Mick would have had to resign and we would have done likewise as the only honourable thing to do.

I do know that overtures were made and the door was left open – but Roy did not come back.

In a team sport, togetherness is everything and I felt that Roy had broken that solemn, binding code with his team-mates and his manager.

Look at where the camaraderie and cohesion of a tight-knit group of players and management had taken us in the past. It had only been twelve years since Italia '90 but that felt like aeons ago.

Others, perhaps those with fond memories of Italia '90, took Mick's side of the debate, arguing that one player cannot be more important than the team.

At the time I felt sorry for Mick and anger at Roy. If he had issues with players in the squad, then they should have been addressed behind closed doors and not in such a public forum. This sort of thing could destabilise meticulous preparations.

In time, I would feel a degree of sympathy for Roy; 2002 could have been his year to stamp his name alongside some of the greats who have played on the international stage.

Equally, I sympathised with the young Irish supporters who had no memory of 1990. This was their World Cup. Their moment in the sun to take in the group matches collectively, get behind their country and make their own memories – and all of that was being hijacked by a sideshow.

In a sense, Roy would have been right to perhaps question facilities and travel arrangements. He certainly would not have put up with the FAI administrators getting priority accommodation over the team in 1990 but, then again, neither did we.

The world was a different place in 2002. Club football holds the upper hand in the financial sphere but, realistically, how can the FAI compete with Manchester United on an issue, like, for example, first-class travel everywhere? Their priority is to husband the game back in Ireland, spread the finances around and promote the grass roots in places such as Donegal, Cork and Tipperary.

Manchester United generates wealth and commerce to provide luxury for the modern-day player and I wonder if that is in the expectation that it will aid performance to a level that wins the UEFA Champions League.

I do feel that modern players are pampered beyond belief in today's game and, in some cases, the slightest deviation from their expectations can prompt outrage of nuclear proportions.

Undoubtedly, there were deep roots in the ensuing row that developed between Mick and Roy and the abruptness of the latter's departure laid bare those roots. Mick retained his own counsel with us as Roy served notice on his personal opinion of his manager once he had returned to England and spoken to a clamouring press hungry for details. In that respect, we will never know if the bridges were reparable between both men at the time although, given the level of venom directed at Mick McCarthy by his captain, it's hard to imagine that any form of recovery could be found.

I can't speak for Roy, but if Mick was struggling to deal with the fallout from this episode, then it wasn't immediately apparent.

In point of fact, as Ian Evans told me, a few years later when Mick was the manager of Wolves and Roy was in his first managerial position at Sunderland, Mick phoned the Wearside club as he was interested in a player.

When he told the girl at the end of the line who he was, there was a complete silence.

'And I'd like to speak to Roy Keane, please,' he added.

There was a pause.

'I'll need to see if he's available,' came the response.

Eventually, Roy came to the phone and both managers discussed the availability of the player whom Mick was interested in but, just before the conversation came to a conclusion, Mick observed that both clubs would be playing each other a little later on in a League fixture and in doing so noted that the press would be all over the pair of them like a rash. In that respect, both men agreed to publically shake hands when they reached their respective dugouts.

I have to say, after everything that had occurred out in Saipan, the subsequent coverage, not to forget the personal venom directed at Mick, I thought that this was a hell of a gesture on his part. Even to pick the phone up and ask Roy about one of his players must have taken some guts.

The press covered the story but no one appeared to note that this famous handshake came as a direct result of Mick McCarthy choosing to phone Roy Keane. In my eyes, it raises his profile not just as a professional but as a man.

As to the players themselves in 2002? I would argue that, if anything, they were galvanised into showing their colours.

The euphoria that greeted the goal scored by Matty Holland to earn us a 1–1 draw with Cameroon in the opening game of that World Cup was emblematic of a group of players pulling together. Matty, of course, had originally come into the team as Roy's replacement in Iran.

That was followed up by the contribution of another 'Keane', this time, Robbie, who made his name with a ninety-second-minute equaliser against Germany in the second group match for another 1–1 draw.

He followed that up with the opener against Saudi Arabia as Gary Breen and then Damien Duff gave the lads a 3–0 victory to take us into the second round and a match against Spain.

This one was a story of two penalties. The one that Ian Harte missed that could have drawn us level with Fernando Morientes's opening goal and the one that did come as our equaliser from Robbie Keane in the ninetieth minute.

This match taught me that, as one of the assistants, you have to be almost an antenna for the manager, especially when everyone is getting excited around you, and I have to put my hands up along with the rest of the backroom staff in saying that we, none of us, noticed that as the second period of extra-time started, Spain were playing with ten men. They had made all their three substitutions and when injury struck, they opted to play with a reduced number of outfield players.

It was a grave error on our part and annoying as the game went to penalty kicks.

My immediate concern was to prepare Shay Given for the shoot-out and I had done some homework on the Spanish for this eventuality so I ran to Shay hoping to get him in the zone as quickly as possible.

In actual fact, Shay was already in the zone, but not the one I had anticipated. His first words to me were 'I want to take a kick!', which I thought was unusual to say the least. More than anyone else out on that pitch, I knew what it felt like to stand up to a player and beat out his shot that carves the way open for success. Here was a moment for Shay to possibly experience that high – to relive the euphoria that I had felt in 1990 and to become a national hero. It was the moment that changed my life forever and now, twelve years later, the mantle was being passed to Shay Given and yet his mind was on *taking* a kick rather than *saving* one. It truly was a brand new world.

In the end, he never got his wish as the quality of penalties wasn't that high from either teams and Spain edged us 3–2 with a spot-kick from Gazika Mendieta.

And yet, how could this World Cup be classed as a disaster for Ireland?

Rocked by the loss of their influential captain on the eve of the tournament, they had rallied to be unbeaten over ninety minutes in all their fixtures, had racked up the highest win for an Irish side in the tournament with the Saudi match and had come within penalty kicks of a quarter-final place.

The unanswerable question was, of course, could we have achieved more with Roy Keane in our starting eleven?

I have often wondered about it but the atmosphere that I felt Roy generated – it seemed to me that everyone was walking on eggshells around him – would, in my opinion, never have been conducive to a successful campaign and it is, after all, a game of opinions.

As it was, another 'Keane' lit up the tournament for us and made himself a household name back in his own country.

GIVING SOMETHING BACK

THE 2002 WORLD CUP HAD BEEN A DRAINING EXPERIENCE FOR me and when I returned home Ann and I took off for a short holiday. As always, I needed some sanctuary. A space of my own. Time to breathe and think things through as well as recharge my batteries.

That usually meant Donegal but, that year, Ann and I took off for a walking tour of the West Highland Way in Scotland. This is a ninety-six-mile stretch of land between the outskirts of Glasgow and Fort William with numerous stops in between and, although extremely popular, still allows for acres of emptiness where you can be completely alone with your thoughts. As such, it was an ideal antidote for all the drama of Saipan and Asia.

Once again I marvelled at Ann's capacity to make sacrifices on my behalf. She has that rare quality of allowing me space and time to meditate on issues and relieve myself of all the stresses that the world of football can bring to your door.

Mile after mile we walked past the shores of Loch Lomond, across Rannoch Moor and up the Devil's Staircase and for so much of that trip I was left to my own thoughts.

We talked, of course, but Ann understood that there would be times when I just needed to walk and breathe rather than engage in conversation.

When I look back at my career, I have been blessed with a life partner who is willing to make those kinds of sacrifices in order to keep me focused on what I have to do. When I was a professional player, it became habitual for me to go up to Ann's parents' house on a Friday night and stay over so that I could have a sleep that was undisturbed by the children. This was a vital part of my preparation and nowadays leaving the family home twenty-four hours before a game for an overnight stay in a hotel is very much common practice to condition players for the match.

Back in the day, it was unusual.

There were also the endless treks that Ann would make with me to various Celtic events that the club expected me to attend. As I would be feted by the support, signing autographs and speaking to the fans, Ann would sit quietly at the table, usually beside a priest who had also been invited, and make no complaint whatsoever. She understood that engagement with the Celtic support was what helped to put food on the table and account for the lifestyle that we enjoyed.

This is an element that, alas, is sadly missing from the modern player's diary.

When I was at Celtic in the early days, it was common practice for Big Billy or David Hay to come in after training and delegate players to go to various functions on the following Saturday night and represent the club. There was nothing in our contracts about this but we accepted that it was part of our job to meet and greet the people who paid our wages and we did so willingly.

Charlie Nicholas and I once visited Shotts Prison to have a chat with the inmates, which was a salutary experience. We met a prisoner called Sammy Ralston who would, in time, make a name for himself by being party to an insurrection in Peterhead Prison that got widespread publicity. Sammy was a big Rangers man but he chatted away telling us that he was only in prison at that time because of Rangers's legend Sandy Jardine.

'How's that?' we asked.

He told us that he had taken part in the infamous pitch invasion of Hampden Park after Celtic's extra-time victory over Rangers in the 1980 Scottish Cup Final and, on seeing Sandy, went up and offered his hand.

Sandy Jardine was not impressed and made a citizen's arrest, handing Sammy over to the nearest policeman.

It seemed a little far-fetched – but Charlie and I weren't going to argue the point!

Ann didn't go to Shotts with us but she did attend her fair share of events and she was one of a number of Celtic wives who routinely made those kind of sacrifices.

And that was what I needed after the 2002 World Cup, an escape into the Scottish wilderness. What a tonic it was and at the finish of it I was ready to move on with the next stage of my career which was prescient, because, as Ann and I completed the walk by coming into Fort William, my mobile phone started ringing. It was Brendan Menton, honorary secretary of the FAI, and he wanted to know if I would be interested in coming over for an interview relating to the position of technical director.

This was interesting as I had originally applied for this job in 1997 only to lose out in the final interview stage. The feedback at the time was that I possibly did not have the required level of experience and, of course, since then I had been at Reading as well as my other coaching duties within the FAI system. Naturally, I was very interested and agreed to an interview.

The Saipan incident, in my opinion, scarred Mick McCarthy deeply and, I would argue, also did the same to Roy Keane. But Mick had more to lose. The country was divided, like never before. It was going to be hard for Mick; he would be judged on results.

Certainly the case could be made for a very credible World Cup, but the start of the Euro 2004 qualifiers did not go well for us and Mick left the Irish job in November 2002.

I think it's only now that people in Ireland have come to realise the fine job Mick did with the team. He had to take over from Jack, bring a group of talented young players up to the level of senior international football and change the way we played. He got to two play-offs and qualified for a World Cup where he had to deal with the immense pressure of his captain going home virtually on the eve of the tournament.

The Saipan incident also had another knock-on effect and it was more political. The honorary treasurer, John Delaney, had called for an independent review of the pre-World Cup situation and, as a result, a Scottish company called Genesis was appointed to carry out this review. In their report, one of the key recommendations was for organisational change.

Around the time Mick left, I had been working with Brian Kerr who was now the outgoing technical director for the FAI as well as the manager of the under-age teams. Brian had enjoyed considerable success with a unique achievement in Irish football history – his sides had won both the Under-16s and Under-18s European Championships. As part of his remit he began the process that was to lead to the Association's first technical development plan and I had been invited on to a working group that was to begin the consultation for that plan. It was a blueprint for the future of football in Ireland and we were travelling around the country attending meetings and canvassing opinions from the people involved in the game at all levels.

Brian had also enjoyed great success in the League of Ireland with St Patrick's Athletic and I was very impressed with his passion for the game in his home country.

It would be fair to say that he and Mick McCarthy did not share the best of relationships. There was a communication issue between them.

I felt it was essential that the two men at the head of the international senior and under-age set-up should have a constructive relationship but it wasn't to be in this case and, in a sense, it made life difficult for me.

I was stuck between Mick and Brian in my respective jobs and I made no comments to either one about the other, choosing to throw my commitment 100 per cent into my work with both men. I'm not entirely sure that Mick understood that and it may have irritated him a bit that I chose to stay on when he decided to leave the Irish post, but there was a crucial difference: we were not working for a club side. This was my country, Ireland, and that was a primary consideration.

It did come as something of a surprise to me when Brian became the manager of the national team a few months after Mick quit as he had never expressed interest in the position throughout the time we worked together.

Brian brought in Chris Hughton as his assistant and this gave me an opportunity to re-establish old acquaintances, having played behind Chris with the Republic and marvelled at the way he could communicate and organise things around him. I could tell even then that he would be a good coach with a potential to reach the higher echelons of the game and he has not disappointed me in that respect.

Brian also elevated Noel O'Reilly to the coaching staff. Noel had been his mucker, the man who 'had his jacket', an assistant who was part of the glory days at youth level and St Patrick's Athletic. A remarkable character with a gift for communication, Noel worked in St Joseph's School for the Blind and was taught the guitar by one of the pupils. That patience and dedication spoke volumes to me about the kind of man he was and, in addition, he was highly respected throughout Ireland as a coach.

Perhaps one of the more controversial decisions that Brian made when he took on the international job was to open up discussions with Roy Keane to see if he would come back into the squad. He was trying to make a big impact at the start, but, naturally, I was none too pleased and I made it clear to Brian during our staff meetings. I didn't think Roy should have been given the opportunity; after all, he had the chance to come back before and turned it down.

I have to be honest and say I thought seriously about walking away from the job, but in the end I came to the conclusion: why should I? I was not the one who left the squad and it was never in my make-up to consider putting myself before my country. I had a serious job to do, to help the international goalkeepers, guys who turned up without question or favour when selected and worked endlessly to achieve success for the cause.

Finally, I agreed to relent, but I made it clear that I wanted to meet Roy on his first appearance back, to clear the air, to move on. Probably similar to what Mick was thinking as Wolves manager when he had to make that phone call to Roy at Sunderland about a player.

Roy came in for his first game back but disappeared as quickly, having picked up an injury. I went to his room just before he left but he didn't want to talk, limiting himself to 'we will catch up the next time'. He played in a number of other games under Brian, but we have never had that chat!

Brian Kerr's new job speeded up the process of appointing a new technical director and, following on from my interview, I was delighted to take up the post in February 2003.

Now was a chance to really give something back to the game in my home country so I took up the baton to complete the process and to write up the development plan.

This was to be the keystone to Irish football in the future. A real focus for everyone, to grow participation, create pathways for talented players and improve the workforce.

It would not be an easy task and along with chairman Pat Duffy and Richard Fahy, whom I would make my assistant, we set about the task in hand to complete a plan that would spread throughout the country, reaching into every village, town and county that wanted to develop talent in the field of football.

The result was *Football for the Future*, a detailed document outlining main actions and responsibilities to take the game forward in Ireland.

However, I had heard stories of other FAI documents that had lain on shelves gathering dust. I was determined not to let this happen to this plan. Too much hard work had gone into the document's conception. I ensured that an implementation plan would be included in the document outlining key targets, actions and responsibilities.

We presented the final document to the affiliates in Dublin's City West Hotel and around 200 people turned up. I still wasn't happy. I needed their mandate before they left the building. As I gave my final words of thanks at the end, I spontaneously asked for a show of hands to grant permission to me to lead the implementation of this plan.

I distinctly remember that *everyone* apart from one older gentleman in the front row raised their hands. I was elated – we were off and running.

In short, if that is possible, it was a people's charter for the game in Ireland designed by the people for the people and it was our hope that the fruits of our labour would become apparent as we progressed the scale of the game throughout Ireland.

It was time-consuming work but I absolutely loved it and considered it a privilege to give something back to the game which had supported me throughout my life, as well as having an active and leading role in mapping the progress of the game in Ireland.

As I drove around the country, meeting the various individuals and clubs who were eager to participate, I often reflected on my first tentative steps in football back in Burtonport. I had succeeded despite the lack of real organisation back in the day, but if I could combine the new strategies and programmes along with the many people out there who had the passion of, say, a Manus McCole or a Richie Kelly for developing talent, then I felt that the job would be more than worthwhile.

I enjoyed this freedom to drive around Ireland and, in many cases, discover a country I had never seen before, such as passing through the crossroads at Spancil Hill in County Clare. I had always thought it was a myth in the famous Irish ballad bearing its name and now here it was, Spancil Hill, in front of my own eyes. The time spent traversing the roads of Ireland gave me time to breathe and think, to be alone. Oh, and to play a bit of Andrea Bocelli on the CD player, very loud indeed. Later on, I would have to surrender to the demands of hands-free mobile phones but to motor around the country-side blaring out the voice of the Italian tenor was a fantastic release.

Being out in the field I thought would be the biggest part of the job. I was not designed for the day-to-day running of an office. I had to learn fast and it appeared to me that there was an endless stream of meetings. In addition, it interested me that some of the people I engaged with in private, prior to the meet-ings, would, on occasion, change their persona once we were sitting around the table. It was as if they had to put on an act to survive. Clearly, control was everything.

By the time we were seeking to implement the technical devel-opment plan and look for funding, John Delaney had gone from being honorary treasurer to the interim CEO of the Football Association of Ireland.

I had known John's parents, Joe and Joan, for years and always had great respect for them. I remember meeting Joe at the Cup Final at Lansdowne Road not long after John had become CEO. His words to me were short and to the point: 'I'm glad you're getting on well with John ...' and then he turned and walked away. I wasn't too sure about this at the time. It seemed an odd remark but I have to say that I was very happy when John took our plan and ran with it completely.

Throughout this period, I had seen less and less of Tommy Burns. However, we had remained close, a friendship forged in our times at Celtic and cemented with the relationships that existed between my family and his.

Tommy was back at Celtic, helping firstly Martin O'Neill and then Gordon Strachan. In addition, he had joined forces with former opponents from both the pitch and the dugout in Ally McCoist and Walter Smith as a coach with Scotland. This was a continuation of the work he had done with the much maligned Berti Vogts when he was in charge of the Scottish national side and in any conversation I have with Berti, when I meet him on my travels, Tommy's name always comes up with a smile and a story.

Tommy loved working with Ally and Walter as well. Rosemary, Tommy's wife, has always mentioned that this period was one of the happiest of his professional career. There was no real pressure on him, but laughter all the way, and the Scottish team were having a measure of success.

He had moved on and built new relationships when he was diagnosed with skin cancer in 2006. A malignant melanoma was cut from his leg and to our mind, and I am sure his as well, the feeling was that he had caught it in time. Sadly, this was not to be the case and two years later the cancer returned and this time it was full-blown and terminal.

He had received that news on what should have been one of the greatest days of his life, the birth of his grandson and first grandchild, Cole, and it's virtually impossible to imagine the multitude of emotions that Tommy must have felt on that day.

He and Rosemary, in trying to maintain some form of normality, had headed off to Asda immediately afterwards and as Tommy sat in the car, Rosemary found the presence of mind to shop for baby clothes and then started making some phone calls. One was to Ann who, in turn, relayed the devastating news to me.

A couple of hours later, Tommy, Rosemary and their two sons, Michael and Jonathan, set off for Wishaw Maternity to see Cole for the very first time.

Even on this day of days, there was a classic 'Tommy' moment. In his haste to see his first grandchild, Tommy parked the car quickly and somehow managed to leave his headlights on.

The upshot was, of course, that when the family returned to the vehicle the battery was completely flat and as Tommy sat in the driver's seat, the two young fellas put their shoulders to the task of pushing the car towards a jump start.

For a few minutes they huffed and puffed, asking in loud voices if their dad had let off the handbrake. Tommy nodded.

Again, the lads heaved and pushed away to no avail. When they emerged from behind the car, spent and sweating, they saw Tommy convulsed at the wheel. He had kept his foot on the brake the whole time!

He never lost that humour and a bit of that was required when he arrived at my house the following Saturday evening when I had returned home from Dublin. Together, my friend and I sought out a quiet space in my conservatory to have a private moment. I knew what was coming and yet I wept anyway – we both did – as he laid out the full extent of his diagnosis. The cancer was back and it was terminal.

Tommy vowed to fight it. He wasn't beaten yet and he always had his faith. That was a bedrock for Tommy Burns. As I have mentioned, throughout my career and, indeed, my life, I have perhaps been a little selfish in using religion as a crutch, a support in those times when I was at my most vulnerable.

Tommy simply lived his faith and on occasion would almost put it before his family and his colleagues. It wasn't unusual for us to trudge down from Barrowfield after a heavy training session and then ask Billy Stark where Tommy was.

'You know where he is,' he would reply and we would nod in understanding that Tommy Burns had nipped into Mass at St Michael's church en route back to Celtic Park.

Billy fully understood Tommy's need for that outlet, that moment of inner peace in his life, and I wouldn't be honest if I didn't say that Tommy Burns could return from the Mass a much more contented person.

He would need that faith for what he had to endure and at the start of May 2008 I had a phone call from Ann while I was at a conference in Italy. I had thought that it might be about Tommy but, instead, it was news that my mother had taken a heart attack in Burtonport.

Tommy was failing but Rosemary insisted to Ann that I should go to my mother rather than come back to Glasgow, and so I headed to Ireland from Italy and was still out in Donegal with my mother who was, thankfully, on the mend when Tommy passed away at 4.10am on Thursday, 15 May. At Rosemary's behest, Ann had come out to the house the night before and had remained there until 3.30 in the morning.

I bitterly regret not being able to see my friend in those final days and hours although I might not have been permitted to do so anyway as Rosemary, perhaps wishing to preserve Tommy's dignity, actively discouraged visitors. I like to think that I would have been welcome at the end and it was an honour and a privilege to be one of the men, George McCluskey, Danny McGrain, Peter Grant, Walter and Ally among others, who was asked to bear Tommy's coffin on the final journey to his ultimate resting place.

Nobody talked about Tommy Burns without smiling. I thought that humour was his greatest gift although he was a damn fine footballer and a brilliant coach as well. His wake and funeral were awash with those memories of the man that were unforgettable, such as the time after a bruising defeat for Reading that he entered the players' lounge post-match where all our family and friends were waiting and, instead of dwelling on the loss, attempted to pull a tablecloth off without disturbing the cups, saucers and glasses that were on it – he failed and in the middle of all the debris he laughed and said that he had seen a guy on the telly do it and it had worked for him!

My favourite memory, though, dates back to our time as young players in the Celtic first team. Ann had bought me a fantastically rich, deep-blue woollen overcoat for Christmas and I had paraded it like a catwalk model when I checked into the dressing room for training that day, giving it out loud and large about the quality and the tailoring – a *big* mistake!

To this day, I am still not sure how it came about, but, later on, when I emerged from the tunnel towards the track for the running session, I was met with absolute hilarity. There wasn't a Celtic player whose eyes were not wet from crying – and the reason?

Tommy Burns had given my coat to John Hayes and Andy McCann, the groundsmen, and they had hoisted it up the flag-pole that towered above the Jungle in the North Stand. I can still see it to this day, stretched out and almost fully billowing in the wind as my team-mates fell around me in laughter. The moral was that you never flaunted your Christmas presents in front of the characters in the Celtic dressing room – especially Tommy Burns. They most certainly broke the mould the day he was born.

*

Tommy's passing marked another one of those milestones in the changing fabric of life both in a personal and professional way. He had kept his enduring interest in the game by coaching at

Celtic and Scotland whereas I had an expansive brief to organise the game right across the board in Ireland.

The Celtic Tiger was still in full vigour and a buoyant Ireland, confident perhaps in its own independent destiny for the first time, was flourishing. Football was following suit and one of the big ideas from this time was the decision to completely overhaul the Lansdowne Road Stadium where the national team played their matches.

Those matches, unfortunately, had not been going too well for Brian Kerr and, indeed, all of us. The failure to make Euro 2004 was followed up by a poor campaign in the World Cup qualifiers and once it had been determined that the Republic were not going to Germany for the 2006 tournament, Brian was relieved of his position.

Jack Charlton, of course, had always championed a minimum four-year tenure in a job and in my opinion it seemed a travesty that Brian, with all his passion for the national team and a job that he had craved all his professional life, was given just under three years to make his mark. Even more so when you consider that he was parachuted into the job when the Republic had already made a poor start to the Euro qualifiers for 2004.

And now, in November 2005, he was gone and a manager who was ahead of his time with his eye for detail and his use of video analysis in a way that is now common practice in the game was lost to the Irish cause. Nowadays, players are encouraged to analyse their own performances and it still seems ludicrous to me that he could have been criticised in some quarters for being 'over-reliant' on this technology.

As ever, a good number of names were bandied about as contenders, all of them with management experience and a legitimate case to take on the job.

I played with Steve Staunton for a good few years at international level and was a real fan of the work he did out on the pitch but, I have to say, I was stunned when he became the next manager after Brian. After all, he had come from Walsall as an assistant player-manager. Where was the necessary experience, particularly when two successive qualification failures perhaps demanded someone with a track record of lifting a squad, not to mention a country?

I tell you, I'm not a betting man but I sure wish I'd stuck a few quid on Steve becoming the manager of the Republic of Ireland in January of 2006!

Steve Staunton decided to bring in Alan Kelly as goalkeeper coach. While I was disappointed to cut my connection with the international players, I assumed that there would still be a necessity for some kind of working relationship between the senior manager and the technical director. The only connection was meeting Steve at the odd FAI function. It was clear: *my* focus now was solely within the technical department.

We were creating new and challenging programmes in the area of social and community development. Our coach education was expanding and we had introduced the emerging talent programme to assist schoolboy clubs with their elite player development. In addition, our summer camps had gone from a participation of 4000 kids up to 20,000 in a few short years – a remarkable success any way it was viewed.

Despite that, though, the executive meetings were hard to navigate and drove me crazy with frustration. They took place almost every week. Fourteen executive staff in the one room, generally being required to give a report on their activity that would take roughly fifteen minutes per report. It was three hours of my life that I knew I would never get back again.

My time now was becoming more and more precious to me and I found that I would arrive back home in Scotland completely knackered and of no use to family or foe. I was never a big one for sleeping on planes but there were times when I only woke up from a Ryanair flight when the wheels touched down on the tarmac in Glasgow.

In later years, I would start to question why I was doing this job. We had made incredible strides but there were so many other areas that required improvement. I felt I should have been using more of my time managing and communicating with my staff, now numbering almost 100 people, and measuring the outcomes of our plan as well as adapting new strategies for the future.

The building of the new stadium marked a moment in history as an alternative venue for matches would have to be found while the process of construction went on, and so it was that on 24 March 2007 that Wales arrived in Dublin to play a friendly match at Croke Park.

To any Irish person with a love for GAA football, this was a huge moment. A political gesture of the utmost significance as Croke was the home of the Gaelic game and, to some tradition-alists, the playing of Association football in this holy of holies was anathema but I felt it was a sign of the maturity of thinking in Ireland that such a game could be staged at all.

An outstanding memory is of the magnificent gesture made by the FAI in offering a ticket for the match to every single living Irish footballer who had turned out for his country whether once or a hundred times. It was a full weekend package involving a tribute dinner and a commemorative international cap.

Abiding memories for me of that weekend were watching one such player from way back, his name escapes me, coming up to another former team-mate, giving him a real bear hug and thanking him from the bottom of his heart. Apparently, this fella had come on as a substitute for his team-mate and those few minutes in an Irish jersey were the sum total of his international career – he would never forget that!

Equally, there was a fella, a goalkeeper, Jimmy O'Neill, originally from Dublin, who had played for Everton and Ireland in the 1950s and 1960s and this was clearly a major moment in his life. His wife told me that since he got the letter inviting him over, not a day went past without him asking her, 'When are we going over to Ireland?' The emotion streamed out of him, the gratitude overwhelming. To once again be reminded of his part in the Irish set-up was a humbling experience and it looked to me like one of the great nights of his life. Jimmy died a few months later and so the realisation of that dream close to the end of his days left a poignancy with me.

It was an equal delight for me to catch up with Sean Fallon. You know, of course, that he was a formative figure in my early Celtic career and just to stand and talk with the man, listening to that authentic Sligo burr, brought it all back to me as well as completing a circle.

Perhaps one of the knock-on effects of the stadium project was that the main focus was changing towards the sale of tickets which, inevitably, might have deflected from the mandate for the technical development plan and that was a concern because the timescale for that plan had come to a completion in 2008.

If I have a criticism of myself it's that I did not start working on the second plan to build on the successes of the initial phase at an earlier stage, but I have learned from that process that it is a mistake in leadership to neglect looking to the future.

My staff worked on making stringent cuts to the costs relating to their programmes, while myself and my assistant worked forensically through the budgets. It was imperative to me that the vision, values and objectives of the technical development plan continued as this was the road ahead for the future of Irish football at all levels. It still required adequate funding and the right people.

People like Pauric Nicholson who had been around football in Ireland all his life. A man who worked for nothing for years before being given the chance to get a full-time job. A man who had real passion for the game and gave every moment of his time so that young people had the chance to fulfil their dreams just like himself, when he played as a young man for Athlone Town against the mighty AC Milan at St Mel's Park. He hit the post that day and still describes it in a way that would vividly capture the imagination of anybody listening.

A sadness for me around this time was the passing of Brian Kerr's former right-hand man, Noel O'Reilly.

When he was helping Brian with the national side Noel also had a dual role within the FAI and I was delighted that he was to remain in the technical department after Brian's dismissal even though, without doubt, Noel had the habit of driving me crazy on occasions during our staff meetings.

He would often sit listening, without saying a word, and just as I was winding up the meeting he would suddenly interject by throwing a hand grenade into the proceedings. It was always in the form of a question and, as infuriating as it was, I came to learn that he was almost always right and I valued his wise counsel, as Brian Kerr clearly did throughout the years of their partnership.

He was a great guy to have around and his passing upset all of us.

On both a personal and professional level, these were difficult times and it is, of course, a matter of public record that I left my position as technical director at the FAI in the winter of 2010.

It has been well documented that I was, quite naturally, upset and sad at having to leave the job. So much had been achieved, so much that I and my staff were rightly proud of, and if I am being completely honest I did not think the position would end the way that it did. I am, however, bound by a confidentiality agreement with the Association and, although I cannot stop the speculation that was expressed in the media at the time and beyond, I have honoured that agreement and continue to do so to this day. I have worked hard to earn my reputation for fairness and transparency in all that I do. It is the only way I know how to conduct my affairs even when I have been challenged as to the nature of some of the events at that time.

I believe that I did the job to the best of my ability and when the time came for me to leave, I took a leaf from the book of my very dear friend, Tommy Burns, by departing with my head held high and through the front door.

I wanted to leave everything, all files and information, up to date and in order so that there would be a continuation of the work that we had begun.

Uppermost in my thoughts was that the FAI, like any bureaucratic organisation, needs to have consistency. Information and knowledge are key tools but controlled knowledge is useless unless it is shared.

On my final day, I collected my staff and good friends together, had a few pints and talked through the good times, of which there were plenty, and I wanted them to know that they should be proud of what we had achieved in our time together. Ann came over and we packed up the car and said goodbye to Clontarf, the house we rented in a quarter of the city. A snowfall of blizzard conditions was swirling around us as we headed back to Glasgow on 26 November. It seemed strangely appropriate.

I would like to take this opportunity to publicly thank those people who made my time at the FAI enjoyable, productive and a learning experience unlike any other.

At the time I left, I felt the best way to express my appreciation was to issue an email to the key people who represented the football family throughout Ireland, which I did. Unfortunately, the email was picked up and published by a national newspaper to which the FAI took exception as they construed this as a breach of my confidentiality agreement.

As it was a personal 'thank you' from me to those who had helped me in my tenure at the Association I was astonished at this reaction.

Among that group of email recipients would be my PA, Louise Dolan.

She left around the same time as I did but very quickly had to deal with an issue that transcended the politics of football.

Within the first week of 2011, Louise took a massive brain haemorrhage and the very first reports I received on her condition strongly suggested that she would not pull through. It was, obviously, extremely devastating news but, happily and incredibly, Louise made a remarkable recovery and at the time of my writing she has returned to being the same Louise whom we all knew and loved.

It is true what they say – sometimes to enjoy the good times you have to recall the bad – but as Mick McCarthy's assistant, Ian Evans, used to say, 'Don't let them live in your head.'

WHAT ELSE CAN ONE DO IN THIS LIFE?

IT'S NO COINCIDENCE THAT I HAVE CHOSEN TO WRITE MY autobiography in the year 2015 as it celebrates the twenty-fifth anniversary of the most remarkable moment in my professional career – the penalty shoot-out against Romania and Ireland's subsequent qualification to the quarter-finals of the 1990 World Cup.

In a sense, I look at that as the peak moment, the summit as a player, if you like, of my achievements on the field of play. Of course, when you reach a summit there is only one place to go thereafter and that is down.

Up until 1990, I had been on a crest of a wave of success, playing for a team and a club who had silverware in their DNA. There were disappointments but the trajectory of my career had been one built upon the championships that I had won as well as the cups. The experience that I had gained took me all the way to that moment when I faced off Daniel Timofte from a range of twelve yards with the hopes and dreams of two nations hanging by a thread.

It was the high point without a doubt. After that? Well, professional turmoil as I watched Celtic go through four managers in four years – standing back as the club pulled itself apart before emerging from the wreckage as a once-again force in the Scottish and, to a degree, European game.

As I mentioned earlier, the lack of continental success with

Celtic would be one of my regrets but, on the whole, I played for the club through interesting times, enjoying my fair share of medals and silverware.

People often ask me what my best save was both domestically and internationally and, for the latter, the assumption is the penalty stop from 1990; but to be honest that wasn't so much a good save as a significant one. For my best, I have to go back to Stuttgart and Euro '88. Our very first tournament – up against England, the old enemy, and leading by Ray Houghton's sixth-minute header then defending with the odd breakaway. I'd had a few saves to make and then came the closing minutes and a Glenn Hoddle free-kick from our right-back position. I had made an error in the first instance by electing to go for the cross and then pulling back at the trajectory of the ball but I got lucky. It was a typically inch-perfect flight from Hoddle and Gary Lineker was on to it in a flash with a header to the right of my goal. I reckon that even he thought it was in but, just as quickly, I moved instinctively to my right and pulled off a reflex save that was so sudden it was behind for a corner before I realised that I had made the save. It was a crucial stop at a crucial moment and I savour the memory of it to this day.

Domestically? Well, there's a fair chance a lot of people won't recall a player named Andy Ritchie who played for Greenock Morton back in the late seventies/early eighties. Andy had been on Celtic's books and a genuine tip for the top but Jock Stein traded him to Morton in the deal that brought Roy Baines to Celtic and big Andy went on to carve a name out for himself down at the tail of the bank. I think he's still the only part-time player in Scottish football history who went on be named as Player of the Year.

His speciality was the dead ball and his set-piece ability was on a par with any Brazilian's, I can tell you. On this particular day, and I'm fairly sure it was during my second season as first-choice goalkeeper, Morton were awarded a free-kick some twenty-five yards from goal. I found out only recently that the goal that I was defending was right in front of an area at Cappielow known as the 'Wee Dublin End' – how appropriate.

Anyway, Davie Provan set up the wall for me as per my instructions but Andy had a habit of crouching low down so that the goalkeeper couldn't see him as he made his move. I saw him at the very last second as he curled a ball over the wall and up to my left-hand side. The home support were on the verge of a celebration when I stretched every single sinew in my body, sprang across my goal-line, clutched the ball in the top left-hand corner and fell to the ground. Best of all, I held on to it and there weren't many goalkeepers who could say they did *that* with an Andy Ritchie free-kick.

It was a product of practice as Frank Connor used to have myself and Peter Latchford working on this technique of a full-out stretch to get to a shot. A 'TV save' he used to call it – pretty spectacular and one that the cameras loved.

My work with Frank was very much a part of my success in those early days but I held on to all of the things he taught throughout my career.

Sometimes, it's only in retrospect that you appreciate people and the contributions they have made to your life. Celtic Park was a great place to be about when I was breaking through and forming friendships that would last a lifetime. When I think of the parties we used to have, particularly down at Tommy and Rosemary Burns's house where it might be fancy dress but always, and I do mean always, ending with a sing-song. Danny McGrain, Dom Sullivan, Roddie MacDonald, Frank McGarvey and our wives just relaxing, enjoying ourselves and the camaraderie that comes from working together in training and playing on a Saturday.

A great bunch of lads, just like the Irish squads that I played with under the leadership of the ringmaster himself, Jack

Charlton. It should be clear by now that I rated Big Jack as the best manager I played under. His ability to create an environment for players to thrive in and to give of their best was second to none in my opinion.

In my own situation, the very fact that he picked me consistently throughout his time as manager of the national team instilled a huge confidence in me and contributed greatly to my development as a goalkeeper and as a person.

You should never underestimate the role of confidence in success.

I was flying back from America once when I came across an article in the newspaper *USA Today*. It had such a profound effect on me that I kept the paper and still use the points from it in the seminar work that I do now when I address groups.

The title of the article was 'Soul of a Champion' and was written in conjunction with a television programme that looked at the reasons that the very top sportsmen and women dominate their particular discipline. Each of them had talent and ability but there were also four common denominators among this collection of champions.

The first was competitiveness. That inbuilt capacity whether through nurture or nature that would make you go that extra mile when the road was long or find that extra inch in your climb just to compete.

I think of playing Big Billy McNeill at table tennis or Jack Charlton at Trivial Pursuit or Roys Aitken and Keane at *anything*! These were guys who had that zeal to play until victory was secured and, as such, they would inspire you to have the same attitude.

There is an age for that, of course, and I believe that to be early adulthood such as we were taught in the Celtic reserve side. I strongly disagree with the pressure that is put upon kids at an under-age level to win at all costs. There is, after all, a difference between competing and winning and I find that, a lot of the time, that push for victory in children's competitions comes from a coach.

The second key ingredient is that confidence I talked about. There is a fine line between that and arrogance and your confidence can be a fragile item, easily affected by managers, colleagues, the media, the supporters etc. Yet if you can keep that inner belief then there is no limit to what can be achieved.

Next up is composure – an emotional intelligence if you like that remains unaffected by the hullabaloo that is so often generated around you. The champion has a way of staying cool in the white-hot heat of a moment which tends to lead to the fourth staple for a winner – focus.

In football terms, focus on the final action, the save, the strike in a penalty shoot-out.

It can be the hardest one of all but if you can stay focused on your goal, that linear path with a dispassionate eye and a steely gaze, then once again your limits are whatever you allow them to be.

The article resonated so clearly with me as, for all my life, from understanding the art of falling in love with practice right through to devoting myself to achieving my goals, I have sought to keep those four key ingredients in my make-up. Even if, sometimes, I didn't realise that I had any of them at all.

A thorough understanding of yourself, what motivates you and how you can use that as a tool through life was brought home to me, way back in 2001, when I attended a tutoring course in Limerick.

I had been urged to go by Declan McIntyre when he was assisting me with the goalkeeping development plan.

What an experience it was! One of those rare environments that I had gone into without as much as a light going on with other students when I mentioned my name. All of that sort of stuff was left at the door and you approached the course with an open mind and a willingness to dig into your psyche.

I was to meet two remarkable gentlemen at this course. The first was Liam Moggan and, literally, within that week, he changed my view of so many things. I had to do research, work with people from unfamiliar backgrounds, make presentations, think differently, forget about being single-minded, a trait that was hugely important in the world of a professional player because, now, it was all about other people. As an introvert, I had to work hard to make this adjustment. Yes, it was difficult and yet fantastically exhilarating when I completed the task. These were life skills that I was to develop – skills that were to set me up for the future. From this base, I came to understand myself a lot better and that has led me into delivering talks at seminars and conferences on behalf of various companies and organisations.

I use the experiences I have gained out on the football pitch as a means to galvanise an audience and encourage them to reach their goals.

The second was Pat Duffy whom you may recall was invited to chair the working group for the technical development plan by Brian Kerr.

Both of these men had the ability to facilitate, inspire, listen – real qualities of leadership.

Unfortunately, Pat is no longer with us but his legacy lives on and in no less an august body as UEFA who have recently used his department at Leeds University to review the UEFA coaching convention. It was a bitter-sweet moment for me when I visited Pat and told him about UEFA's decision. This was a connection that he had been desperate to make for quite some time and when I relayed the news to him it brought a smile to his face for those final few days of his life.

Both UEFA and FIFA have become a big part of my working life since I left the FAI in 2010.

I did a great deal of soul-searching at the time of my departure but it is not in my nature to bemoan my situation. Rather, I react and try to seek the positives in life. There is no point in lying around fighting for breath when you have received a punch, even metaphorically. Although now I had no full-time job, UEFA still saw the merit in keeping me involved as a technical adviser to begin the task of leading a working group which would create the first ever UEFA Goalkeeping Coaching Diploma for those goalkeeping coaches operating in the professional game.

I have spent the last four years devoted to this work. It gives me an opportunity to work at home and abroad, to engage with people from a diverse group of cultures and really grow as a person.

Equally, the work that I have developed has allowed me to adapt and change direction to other areas of my working life outside the football arena. It has always been my passion to work with young professionals whether they are in the sports industry or teachers or perhaps businessmen/women and I have been fortunate to have the opportunity to do so.

The penalty save from 1990 was a turning point that I am grateful for but will always be a moment in my life that, in the eyes of many, has defined me. The skills, knowledge and confidence that I have acquired, aligned with my personality and accumulative experience, have allowed me to evolve into other areas of society. I like to think that I have taken that forward and, having had the opportunity to change my journey, I have appreciated what it takes to succeed in all walks of life.

The knowledge and experience I had of football and the confidence that I took from the tutoring course also led me into another strand of work and that was in the media of television and radio. It's an area that I grew to enjoy and I regularly guest with BBC Scotland and Sky Sports, but it started for me when

TV3 in Ireland asked me to present their coverage of the UEFA Champions League. I rarely perspired out on the pitch, no matter the occasion, but I have to tell you the very first time I did live television I completely soaked my shirt in sweat – and it had nothing to do with the hot lights!

In that arena, I worked with old friends like John Aldridge, Mark Lawrenson and Kevin Moran as well as Welsh great John Toshack. It was also a special treat to work with the legend that was George Best, although this humble, much-loved man was in that period when he wasn't in the best of health. I was asked one night by TV3 producer Michael Lynn to drop George back at the Westbury Hotel where he was staying with his wife.

On television, George was fine but off-camera he was struggling. It transpired that he did not have access to his medication and on the way back to the hotel he literally slumped in the front seat of my car, clearly in pain, dealing with it bravely yet not in the mood for any conversation. There were a few moments when I seriously wondered if he would make it back to the Westbury and then we stopped at a pelican crossing in the city.

There were a couple of real beauties making their way across the road, turning all the heads around them, and all of a sudden George sprang into life, sitting up straight and passing an admiring comment to me. The man was back and all it took was the appearance of a couple of pretty girls. Obviously, the stories about George Best that I had grown up on were more than just a myth!

Liam Moggan and Pat Duffy are just two of the many people whom I have been extremely fortunate to have in my life. When I look back at the list of influences who have shaped me from my earliest days – my parents, family and close friends, Manus McCole, Toney Gallagher, Brian Mullins, Sean Fallon, Frank Connor, Billy McNeill, David Hay, Tommy Burns, Billy Stark and Jack Charlton to name but a few – then I can see that those influences have been exceptionally positive and encouraging on my journey.

I have also come to appreciate the importance of the Irish heritage in the story of Celtic. The club's background with founder Brother Walfrid coming from Sligo – a sod of turf from Donegal being sewn into the earth on the first Celtic Park pitch – and, above all, the identity that the club clearly gave to those of my compatriots who came across from Ireland looking for work and sustenance. It is easy to see why Celtic has an emotional pull on anyone with an Irish connection and vice versa.

Aiden McGeady is a case in point.

I happened to be up around Glasgow Green one day many years ago when I bumped into Mick Gillespie who was in charge of Queen's Park Under-12s.

'I've got a crackin' player for you here, Packie, and his grandparents are from Gweedore,' he said as I watched the young Aiden dominate the proceedings. I kept an eye on his progress and mentioned it to Vincent Butler who looked after the Ireland Under-15s ranks. When the time was right, Aiden was invited over to Ireland on a trial basis and he naturally impressed. The die was cast and he was a part of the Irish set-up from an early age and through choice as well. The ensuing outcry, therefore, when he emerged on the senior scene picking up Player of the Year awards but electing to play for the country that had nurtured him from his teenage years was, at best, short-sighted and, at worst, mischievous in the extreme.

Having worked away from Glasgow for a while, I had lost that contact with the city, especially the intensity of the Celtic–Rangers axis, but the situation with Aiden brought it all home to me in the sharpest fashion.

That connection of heritage has also been close to the advances that I have seen in Irish football over my time in the game. When I was growing up the big names were the English clubs who featured on the television every week and although there was always a fair smattering of Irish names among them such as Pat Jennings, Liam Brady and Johnny Giles, the lack of a strong international identity for Ireland was easy to understand.

That has most definitely changed. When supporters in Ireland talk about the game now, they do so with a reference to the success of the national side. Expectations have been set.

It was my earnest hope that the implementation of the technical development plan would bear fruit for generations of Irish supporters to enjoy.

In my opinion, the business of the Football Association of Ireland is to develop the sport as a game for all the participants in the country. That is the absolute fundamental criterion of the Association because, without the players and supporters, there simply is no football.

No World Cups, European Championships, UEFA Champions League participation for Irish players – no League of Ireland development – no junior clubs like Keadue Rovers who provide the heartbeat for the part-time rank-and-file supporters and, above all, no schoolboys and girls with the passion and desire to get out on that pitch and perform to the best of their ability.

I took inspiration from a set of dusty old boots hanging on the back door of a closet that fired my imagination into believing I *could* play the game. In the twenty-first century there still has to be that inspiration, whether it comes from a television channel chronicling the Republic of Ireland as they compete on the world stage, a packed Aviva Stadium or standing behind a goal on a wet Friday night in October just so you can watch Finn Harps play Cobh Ramblers.

Sport and education are so important in Irish society. They have the ability to glue a community together, unite in a common purpose, and participation is key to that process.

It has to start at an early age, from childhood if you like, and it needs a plan – a plan for the child, for the community. Responsible leaders integrating, creating the opportunity for young people to enjoy participation and follow their dream.

When I travel around Europe and beyond, I am always struck by how sport is naturally accepted as a key ingredient in the success of a country and a people.

During the Celtic Tiger period, I felt that Ireland lost a piece of itself as my mother would have said; we had '... lost the run of ourselves' – a fabulous and accurate expression. The feel-good factor involved in international success on the sporting field right across the board through football, rugby, athletics and beyond was a crucial element in defining our nation. Of course, it's nice to sit back at a certain age of my life and dream of how it could all be for the future generations of Irish sportsmen and women.

Government will always have to take the lead and set the policy both at national and local level. But it requires imagination, innovation and the will for the real leaders in the community to come together and make it work.

If I can take a quote from the technical development plan, *Football for the Future* – 'All decision making in the future should be based on what is right for the Player.'

Not long after I left the FAI, I was approached about running for political office in Ireland. I suspected that this was on the back of the support I offered to the 'YES' campaign during the Irish EU Treaty Referendum of 2012 or the lobbying I had done with the Irish government with my FAI colleague John Byrne during my time as technical director. Now, here was man who knows a thing or two about the political landscape in Leinster House and during his time working with the FAI was a critical ally to the football clubs around the country when it came to political red tape and bureaucracy.

For a while, I met with some people and held discussions as I was intrigued as to what was involved and why they considered that I could be a suitable candidate.

Ultimately, I decided against the move. I don't really see myself as a party political animal or being fully aligned to a particular faction. Don't misunderstand me; I do maintain an absorbing passion for Irish politics, following the various twists and turns through the media, but I would not be able to give of my best in the partisan world of party politics.

I would work with anyone of any political persuasion who would advance the cause of Irish sport in general, and Irish football in particular. Indeed, I have a proven track record of doing so but the various ins and outs of daily political life is not quite for me.

Still, I admit that, for a while, I was intrigued and flattered to be considered as someone who had the capabilities to represent my people and my community back home in Donegal. After all, who wouldn't be – but perhaps that's for another day?

Despite living in Glasgow since 1978, I have continued to work back in my home country so I have had the chance to observe the changes in both societies.

The Glasgow I knew has changed beyond comparison in that time, redefining itself in a global sense just as Donegal and Ireland have in the same era. I consider myself fortunate to have both of these differing places and cultures in my life. The Glaswegians themselves never change. They still abide by their principles and good nature and, despite being the goalkeeper for one of the big two clubs in town, I can honestly say that I have never been verbally or physically abused by anyone in the city.

And in Donegal I am still welcomed with warmth by fellow Irishmen and women.

Glasgow and Ireland – two different points on the compass, open to change but still adhering to their fundamentals. The world is a smaller place now – communications are instant – but the thought of having to leave home and set down new roots can often be the barrier to success.

My hope is that a growing, healthy Irish economy can, once again, take the Irish people forward and in a sense reverse a great deal of the migration for which we are famous.

Football has given me a living and a lifestyle – has provided for my family and given me some of the most satisfactory moments and unbelievable highlights that I have been privileged to enjoy.

Playing with one of the biggest club names in European competition on a regular basis and having to travel for all home or away games for the international team, my biggest disappointment was being away from my children for long periods. Times when I should have been around to help with the football run or even the Irish dancing in Melissa's case. Even though Ann had no Irish background she started bringing Melissa to Irish dancing classes when she was four years old. She loved it and it was to be a part of both their lives until Melissa was twenty-four. I was there on each occasion when she would go on to win three gold medals in the World Irish Dancing Championships. Andrew had his international caps and Melissa her world medals, happy moments that made a father and mother extremely proud.

I used to wonder, when Andrew was a child, if he really knew what I actually did for a living. Around his first Christmas at St Cadoc's Primary I was asked if I would open the Yuletide Fete which was used to raise some much-needed funds for the school. They always liked to get somebody who lived in the area, somebody with a bit of a name, to open it, to make it a bit special for the children and indeed the parents. To give it impact they kept it a secret from the children until a week or two before it was due to happen.

On the day that it was announced at school, Ann went down to fetch Andrew. When the bell rang, he raced out of the school very excited, down the hill to the lollipop lady, across the road and started to shout: 'Mum, Mum, guess who is opening the school fete this year? It's Pat Bonner, the Celtic goalkeeper!' You can picture the disappointment on Andrew's face when *Mum* had to explain to him that this was *Dad*! He burst out crying.

The moral of the story? No matter how many penalty saves you make in World Cups or how many games you play for the mighty Celtic, in the eyes of your children you will always be silly old Dad. Your feet are firmly planted on the floor and, to be honest, I don't think I'd have it any other way.

Football has also allowed me to be useful for a cause as worthy as spina bifida. I mentioned before that, for a time, I was embarrassed whenever people brought up the 'penalty save' from 1990, but I came to realise that the significance of that moment has allowed me the privilege of making a difference to the lives of others. And in that respect I include my niece Una Bonner, daughter of Denis and Agnes, who was born with the condition. I first became involved in the charity when a share of the proceeds from my Irish benefit game in 1997 were donated to the Spina Bifida Hydrocephalus Association. The goal is simple – to help those with the condition to live a full and active life and Una surely achieves that on a daily basis. Such as the regularity with which she swims fifty lengths in a twenty-five-metre pool and, above all, by attending Letterkenny Institute of Technology, just like her brother and her father before her. She also shares Denis's personality as well as that of our dad, the ol' fella himself, which can't be a bad thing. Quite simply, she is an inspiration.

Football is nothing without romance. It is a love affair that can lift an awkward young boy out of his rural background from the Atlantic shores of west Donegal and take him to the summit of the world stage as a man.

In many ways, I'm still that boy who travelled home for his very first Christmas as a professional player seeking the comforts of home and family. Like my father and mother before me, Donegal is in my blood. It is my sanctuary and a place where I know I can always return to when I need that time to relax, think and take in the salty air as it whips off the ocean.

Nothing stays the same and gone are the days when Denis and I could look out on to the water at the vast fleets of fishing boats on their way to haul in their catch, and identify them by the names, colours and shapes of the vessels.

And yet, Burtonport will always be home and, in that respect, a certain part of Donegal will never change for me.

On my journey, I have met so many remarkable people, all of them different, some positive, some negative, but each of them with some influence on my life.

The positive ones are the easy influence but I do feel, quite strongly, that even the negative ones had something to offer. After all, who am I to say when I am right and they are wrong?

I will, however, always stick to the principles that were instilled in me by my parents, the most important of which is – there is always a correct way to do something.

I am forever being asked if I would change anything throughout my life. I guess anyone who looks back would pick out a moment, an incident, perhaps a decision, that, in retrospect, they would change but the truth is I have enjoyed my career and my personal life with a close-knit group of friends as well as my loving family and that's good enough for me.

Would I do it all over again?

Yes.

Have I learned from it?

Of course, and those experiences take me forward and into those areas of mentoring, tutoring and development that have become a passion for me.

It delighted me to see Jack Charlton as a guest of honour in 2015 when the Republic of Ireland hosted a friendly against England. It struck me, though – this colossus of a man was eighty years old. He was fifty-five when he took us to the World Cup in Italy and I thought he was old then.

As I write this book, *I* am now fifty-five! Where did those years disappear to?! God willing, I hopefully will at least see Big Jack's age and then maybe some more. There are no certainties, of course, but in the cathartic way of writing my autobiography I do know one thing – I will try and live that life to the full and not let anyone loose in my head. In other words, follow my own path.

Is there a secret to it all? It's hard to say but when I reflected on it recently the words of the late Sean Fallon sprang to mind. He little knew that he was a few days from his own passing when he was asked to sum up how to live one's life for an RTÉ documentary on his own life.

And if there has to be a 'last line' in *The Last Line* then perhaps it should go to this grand old man of Sligo who thought about it all for a moment before saying: 'The way to live is to be nice to people – if I didn't like someone I just avoided them but if people needed me then I would do as much as I possibly could to help them – what else can one do in this life?'

ACKNOWLEDGEMENTS

THERE ARE SO MANY PEOPLE WHO HAVE BEEN INSTRUMENTAL IN helping me on my journey. Some are still with us and regrettably, some are not, but I'm indebted to them all. It goes without saying that I am sure to miss out on a few here, for which I apologise in advance.

In terms of my playing career, I have to start in Donegal. A massive thanks to Manus McCole and the committees of Keadue Rovers FC and to my school team manager Colm 'Paddy' Murray and all my team mates who played in those sides – where would I be without all of you?

To Sean Fallon who took me to Celtic Park, Jock Stein who offered me the privilege of being his final signing and to Billy McNeill, who gave me my club debut. I devoted my club career to Celtic – seventeen years of titles, trophies and memories and there are so many great players and friends to thank for sharing those times with me. However, I could not look back without giving a special thanks to a man who would crawl over hot coals for the club and its supporters, not only was it a pleasure to be on the same pitch as him, he also nurtured me through the early days of my coaching career. He is, of course, my late colleague and friend Tommy Burns.

My association with the Republic of Ireland Jersey dated from the Youth team in 1977, through Johnny Giles invitation to join the senior side in 1979, right up until Brian Kerr left the job in

2005. A generous thank you to all those players and staff who shared and helped me achieve my ultimate dream. I don't like picking individuals out of what is, by definition, a team game, but I must make an exception with Gerry Peyton. Although a rival for the Republic of Ireland jersey, he was always an unselfish presence and huge help in my international career. The bulk of my eighty caps were achieved under the man whom I consider to be my best manager and that, of course, was Jack Charlton. Where would Irish football, let alone my career, be without him? Thank You, Jack.

I was privileged to be asked to take up the position of Technical Director in my country for eight years and to all those who gave wise counsel, assisted and became trusted friends in that period, thank you – you know who you are.

The supporters, of course – my eternal thanks to the supporters of the Republic of Ireland and Celtic Football Club. Your respective backing, passion and incredible enthusiasm was a massive factor in my achievements and the teams' successes. I will always be extremely grateful for your unrivalled support.

It was essential to me that *The Last Line* was an honest account of my life and career, yet told in the right spirit and for that, I would like to thank Gerard McDade, who frankly, pestered me for years to commit to the project as he believed that I had a story to tell. I'm glad that he did and also that we have had such a committed team at Ebury Press, under the guidance of Andrew Goodfellow, to bring that story to fruition. In addition, the legal advice of Donal Spring and Ailbhe Murphy has been indispensable to the book.

To the people of the Rosses and Burtonport, my eternal thanks for being there and the warmth and welcome I always receive when I return to Donegal.

Without family, we are nothing and so fond in my memory are Auntie Bridget Mary, Uncle John, Auntie Breedge and Uncle

Dan who looked after a young fella feeling lost and alone when he first arrived in Glasgow having signed for the Celtic. In that bracket, I will also include my extended family, Tommy and the late Jess Kerr who were a continuing source of support throughout my adult life as well as allowing me to marry their daughter! Connell Boyle is family and Sean Walsh is as good as, and together they are one half of the 'Four Amigos'.

To my late parents, Andrew and Grace – a simple 'thank you' is too little for what you gave me and words seem inadequate. The same sentiment to my sisters, Margaret, Mamie, Anne, Cathy and Bridget Mary. Denis, another 'amigo' and more than a brother, always.

My career and life would not amount to much if I didn't have the privilege of sharing it with the most important people of all and they are my wife Ann, son Andrew and daughter Melissa. Also, our grandson, Alan, who is a delightful addition and who keeps his grandad on his toes, reliving those football memories in the back garden!

Donegal has given me sanctuary but Glasgow has given me my own family and home.

Go raibh míle maith agaibh,
Packie Bonner, Glasgow 2015.

INDEX

(in subentries, AB = Andrew Bonner; PB = Packie Bonner)